THE ENVIRONMENTAL, SOCIAL AND GOVERNANCE (ESG) RATINGS ACTIVITIES REGULATION

ELGAR COMMENTARIES IN FINANCIAL LAW

Series Editor: Iris H.-Y. Chiu, *Professor of Corporate Law and Financial Regulation, University College London, UK*

Volumes in this series provide comprehensive commentary and analysis on major instruments across the spectrum of financial law, from both the European and international sphere. The series addresses a wide range of issues associated with financial law, from banking to capital markets, including topics dealing with wholesale and retail markets. With a clear and structured format that mirrors the logic of the instrument itself and facilitates pin-point searches, each *Commentary* examines the context, interpretation and implementation of key instruments governing the complex field of financial law. Featuring the original text of the respective articles, along with detailed lists of relevant cases and associated regulation, the *Commentaries* form valuable reference works for both scholars who want a platform for their research, and practitioners who need clear guidance on interpreting the rules.

For a full list of Edward Elgar published titles, including the titles in this series, visit our website at www.e-elgar.com.

THE ENVIRONMENTAL, SOCIAL AND GOVERNANCE (ESG) RATINGS ACTIVITIES REGULATION

A Commentary

Edited by

ANDREA MIGLIONICO

Associate Professor, School of Law, University of Reading, UK

ELGAR COMMENTARIES IN FINANCIAL LAW

Edward Elgar PUBLISHING

Cheltenham, UK · Northampton, MA, USA

Published by

Edward Elgar Publishing Limited
The Lypiatts
15 Lansdown Road
Cheltenham
Glos GL50 2JA
UK

Edward Elgar Publishing, Inc.
William Pratt House
9 Dewey Court
Northampton
Massachusetts 01060
USA

Authorised representative in the EU for GPSR queries only: Easy Access System Europe – Mustamäe tee 50, 10621 Tallinn, Estonia, gpsr.requests@easproject.com

A catalogue record for this book is available from the British Library

Library of Congress Control Number: 2025946990

This book is available electronically in the Elgaronline
Law subject collection
https://doi.org/10.4337/9781035338627

MIX
Paper | Supporting responsible forestry
FSC® C013604

ISBN 978 1 0353 3861 0 (cased)
ISBN 978 1 0353 3862 7 (eBook)
ISBN 978 1 0353 8165 4 (ePub)
Printed and bound by CPI Group (UK) Ltd, Croydon, CR0 4YY

CONTENTS

CHAPTER 2 TRANSPARENCY REQUIREMENTS

CHAPTER 3 INDEPENDENCE AND CONFLICTS OF INTEREST

CHAPTER 4 SUPERVISION BY ESMA

Section 1 General principles

TITLE IV DELEGATED AND IMPLEMENTING ACTS

TITLE V TRANSITIONAL AND FINAL PROVISIONS

EXTENDED CONTENTS

LIST OF CONTRIBUTORS

Iris H-Y Chiu is Professor of Corporate Law and Financial Regulation at the Faculty of Laws, University College London. She has published extensively in the areas of corporate governance and financial regulation, including *The Foundations and Anatomy of Shareholder Activism* (2010), *Investment Management and Corporate Governance* (2017), *The Legal Framework for Internal Control in Banks and Financial Institutions* (2015), *Banking Law and Regulation* (2019) and *Regulating the Crypto-economy* (2023). She has interests in financial regulation and governance, law and technology, corporate law and governance and the law and policy for business and finance generally. She is a Research Member of the European Corporate Governance Institute, and in 2020, a Senior Scholar at the European Central Bank's Legal Research Programme. She is also an academic member of the UCL Centre for Ethics and Law, of which she was Director between 2016 and 2024.

Francesco De Pascalis is a Senior Lecturer (Associate Professor) in Financial Law at Brunel Law School. Prior to joining Brunel Law School, he worked as a research fellow at the 'Rechtswissenschaftliches Institut' (Law Faculty) of the University of Zurich. At Brunel University of London, he is also member of the 'Research Centre on Law, Economics and Finance', the 'Research Centre for AI: Social and Digital Innovation' and the 'Research Centre for Entrepreneurship and Sustainability'. Dr. De Pascalis is an academic expert in the area of banking and finance law and regulation, sustainable finance and financial technology law. He has authored numerous publications in the areas of financial intermediation, FinTech and open banking regulation.

Irene-marié Esser is a Professor of Corporate Law and Governance in the School of Law at the University of Glasgow and Subject-Head of Commercial Law. She is also Dean of the Graduate School, College of Social Sciences. Since 2020 she is an Extraordinary Professor at Stellenbosch University, South Africa, and also a Visiting Professor at the National Law University Jodhpur, India. She was admitted as an Attorney of the High Court of South Africa in

2005. Her research spans doctrinal and empirical approaches, covering the UK, EU and South Africa in the field of corporate governance, company law and corporate social responsibility. Professor Esser acted as an External Consultant to the King IV Committee on Corporate Governance in South Africa. Reference has been made to her work in the King IV Report on Corporate Governance following her inclusive stakeholder protection approach. She was the Company Law Convener for the UK Society of Legal Scholars for three years, until 2021. Professor Esser has developed and presented a course at the University of Johannesburg on Board Governance since 2009, accredited by the IoDSA. She is on the editorial board of the European Business Law Review. https://www.gla.ac.uk/schools/law/staff/irene-marieesser/#

Iain MacNeil is Professor of Commercial Law at the University of Glasgow. He began his academic career after a decade working in investment banking in the City of London. He has undertaken research and collaborated with colleagues in Australia, Canada, China, Hong Kong and the United States. He is a Trustee of the British Institute of International and Comparative Law and Chair of the International Securities Regulation Committee of the International Law Association. He has acted as Senior Adviser on several projects examining national compliance with EU financial sector Directives.

Andrea Miglionico is an Associate Professor of Law at the University of Reading. He is Programme Director of Commercial LLM and Deputy Director of the Centre for Commercial Law and Financial Regulation (CCLFR). He was previously an Associate Lecturer and Research Fellow at the Centre for Commercial Law Studies, Queen Mary, University of London. He has taught undergraduate and postgraduate law courses in the United Kingdom and Europe. He holds an LLM Master of Laws from the London School of Economics and a PhD from the Queen Mary, University of London. Dr. Miglionico carries out research in the areas of financial markets regulation, digital banking and climate finance.

PREFACE

The rapid proliferation of environmental, social and governance (ESG) factors and sustainability movement on financial activities has raised concerns about the assessment of firms' performance with respect to sustainable investment strategies. The integration of ESG information into companies' decision-making process called into question the role of ESG ratings as data providers in the financial markets. Rating agencies began providing ESG metrics with the premise of predicting potential climate exposures and creating shareholder value. As intermediaries they gather information from various sources by monitoring companies in order to measure ESG performance and create a dataset for investors. They introduce a ratings scale aimed at ranking the sustainability of funds' portfolios with the objective of providing investors with a measure to evaluate how different funds target ESG standards.

ESG ratings contribute to determine investment decision-making as they focus on a company's strategy to internalize sustainability factors in board structures: their function is fundamental for the purpose of informing investors about material disclosures. However, the ESG raters have been under scrutiny because of the different metrics employed to assess a given firm's performance in relation to the same ESG activities. Rating scoring elaborates publicly available data and produces evaluations of firms' behaviour incorporating social and environmental values. A significant concern is to standardize ESG scoring by aligning ratings content with sustainability requirements. The variety of metrics developed in the ratings' proprietary methodologies can lead to risks of bias and 'greenwashing' when metrics of ESG data in ratings' models are elaborated to capture firms' behaviour with respect to sustainability. The practice of releasing ESG indexes is fraught with questions concerning the reliability and transparency of ratings' internal models, which makes for increased uncertainty about what sustainability needs to measure using non-financial indicators.

The absence of an accepted definition of ESG performance and the heterogeneity of the metrics complicate matters. The divergences across ESG ratings are likely to produce misleading reports owing to different interpretations of sustainable criteria. As a result, loopholes in interpreting the metrics can exacerbate the appetite for inflated ESG reports. The material risk for corporations would be the high costs of litigation and the reputational impact on markets arising from public scrutiny, which can lead to a downgrade from rating agencies. It is questionable whether raters do in fact elaborate an independent statement of ESG performance since the close relationship with the firms/users in the due diligence and definition of metrics affects the valuation of the company's ability to incorporate social and environmental factors in the financial report. The lack of consistency and accuracy in the disclosures but also the high degree of subjectivity as to what constitutes ESG performance can create incentives for opportunistic behaviours of rating agencies.

It is also observed that the practice of rating deviations seems incentivized at the individual firm level: these adjustments affect measures that relate to firm rankings, determining inflated ESG performance and flawed ESG ratings. Conflicts of interest and herding behaviour among ratings users inherently cast doubts on the credibility of ESG ratings. The lack of uniformity in the definitions of sustainable activities and the various ESG metrics makes for increased ambiguity in measuring companies' performance with regard to social and environmental values. Professional data providers have expanded in the climate sector in order to provide sustainability rankings and ratings, although the reliability of these certifications raises concerns about the lucrative 'user-pays' business model, which may result in doubtful outlooks.

The EU Regulation on ESG ratings providers came into force after long gestation and compromise texts before reaching a final agreement. The new legislation aims to improve the quality of metrics used in ratings models and to facilitate the comparability and granularity of the ESG taxonomy. The objective to enhance the transparency and reliability of rating scoring analysis is manifest: the regulatory framework introduced a strict regime of controls and a monitoring system to ensure quality of rating reports. The Regulation sheds light on the ESG rating industries and the 'infomediation' market, which seems to be elevating the rating providers as powerful gatekeepers of sustainable finance.

ACKNOWLEDGEMENTS

This edited volume is the result of joint reflections and comments shared with authors and practitioners on the recent regulatory developments of the ESG sector. Preliminary findings of the Commentary have been presented at the Roundtable on ESG Ratings Regulation organized by the Centre of Ethics and Law at UCL on 7 November 2024. The volume has benefitted from insightful thoughts and observations of the volume contributors and participants (Professor Celine Tan, Professor Catherine Malecki, Dr. Lin Lin, Dr. Cheng-Yun Tsang and Dr. Ebbe Rogge) of the event which discussed potential issues and areas for future research on the ratings providers' activities. The contributions of the roundtable have been instrumental for a critical view of the EU legislation on ESG ratings and global perspectives in the field.

The editor would particularly like to thank Professor Iris Chiu and Professor Iain MacNeil for their continuous support and collaboration provided throughout this work.

The editor also owes a debt of gratitude to and acknowledges the welcome assistance of Fiona Todd, the commissioning editor, of Edward Elgar Law, and Rachel Cook, the senior project manager, for their perceptive suggestions and advice on an early draft. Their constructive feedback and rigorous competence significantly enhanced the content of this work. Special thanks are due to Kaitlin Bennett the deputy managing editor (digital), the editorial assistant, the senior desk editor and the copy editor for reviewing the manuscript. The author would also wish to thank the series editor of the Elgar Commentaries in Financial Law for feedback and comments on the research project.

The editor is particularly grateful to the Centre for Commercial Law and Financial Regulation (CCLFR), University of Reading Law School for stimulating intellectual environment and institutional support. Sincere thanks are also due to the Law Research Division at Reading for mentoring guidance and scholarly approach.

LIST OF ABBREVIATIONS

Term	**Definition**
BIS	Bank for International Settlements
CAD	Capital Adequacy Directive
CFTC	Commodities and Futures Trading Commission
CJEU	Court of Justice of the European Union
CRAs	Credit Rating Agencies
CRAR	Credit Rating Agencies Regulation
CRD	Capital Requirements Directive
CSDDD	Corporate Sustainability Due Diligence Directive
CSRD	Corporate Sustainability Reporting Directive
EBA	European Banking Authority
EC	European Commission
ECB	European Central Bank
ECGI	European Corporate Governance Institute
ECMI	European Capital Markets Institute
EFRAG	European Financial Reporting Advisory Group
EFTA	European Free Trade Association Surveillance Authority
EIOPA	European Insurance and Occupational Pensions Authority
EMIR	European Markets Infrastructure Regulation
ESAs	European Supervisory Authorities
ESAP	European Single Access Point
ESC	European Securities Committee
ESFS	European System of Financial Supervision
ESG	Environmental, Social and Governance
ESMA	European Securities and Markets Authority
EU	European Union
EURIBOR	Euro Interbank Offered Rate
FCA	Financial Conduct Authority
FSB	Financial Stability Board
FSMA	Financial Services and Markets Act
HM	His Majesty's Treasury

IASB	International Accounting Standards Board
IASC	International Accounting Standards Committee
ICMA	International Capital Markets Association
IFRS	International Financial Reporting Standards
IIO	Independent Investigating Officer
IOSCO	International Organization of Securities Commissions
ISSB	International Sustainability Standards Board
KPIs	Key Performance Indicators
LIBOR	London Inter-Bank Offered Rate
LLP	Legal Professional Privilege
LSE	London Stock Exchange Group
LTCM	Long Term Capital Management
MAD	Market Abuse Directive
MAR	Market Abuse Regulation
MiFID	Markets in Financial Instruments Directive
MiFIR	Markets in Financial Instruments Regulation
MMoU	Memorandum of Understanding
NCAs	National Competent Authorities
NFRD	Non-financial Reporting Directive
OUP	Oxford University Press
PCAOB	Public Company Accounting Oversight Board
PRA	Prudential Regulation Authority
REFIT	Regulatory Fitness and Performance
RTS	Regulatory Technical Standards
SFDR	Sustainable Finance Disclosure Regulation
S&P	Standard and Poor's
TFEU	Treaty on the Functioning of the European Union
TNFD	Taskforce on Nature-related Financial Disclosures
UK	United Kingdom
UN	United Nations
US	United States
USSPs	Union-wide Strategic Supervisory Priorities
WB	World Bank

TABLE OF CASES

TABLE OF LEGISLATION

EUROPEAN UNION

UNITED KINGDOM

TITLE I

SUBJECT MATTER, SCOPE AND DEFINITIONS

ARTICLE 1

SUBJECT MATTER

Andrea Miglionico

This Regulation introduces a common regulatory approach to enhance the integrity, transparency, comparability where possible, responsibility, reliability, good governance and independence of ESG rating activities, thereby contributing to the transparency and quality of ESG ratings and to the sustainable finance agenda of the Union. It aims to contribute to the smooth functioning of the internal market, while achieving a high level of consumer and investor protection and preventing greenwashing and other types of misinformation, including social washing, by introducing transparency requirements related to ESG ratings and rules on the organisation and conduct of ESG rating providers.

A. INTRODUCTION

1.01 This article provides an overview of the aims and objectives of the legislation pointing on the business activities of the environmental, social and governance (ESG) ratings providers in the EU. It is an introductory provision which sets the scope and rationale for regulating ESG ratings providers in the internal market. The legislative framework is a crucial step towards the sustainable finance agenda of the Union and marks a cornerstone piece of the package of measures that contribute to the European Green Deal.[1] The Regulation also

1 The author is grateful to the speakers and participants at the Roundtable on ESG Ratings Regulation, 7 November 2024, Centre of Ethics and Law at UCL for their insightful comments on the developments of regulatory framework. See https://commission.europa.eu/strategy-and-policy/priorities-2019-2024/european-green-deal_en.

amends the Sustainable Finance Disclosure Regulation (SFDR),[2] in order to ensure that if financial undertakings develop and disclose their own ESG ratings they disclose the same information as specialized ESG rating providers.

The Regulation had a long gestation through various amendments to the original text[3] before being approved in its agreed final version.[4] Ratings on ESG factors provide information about the sustainability performance of a company or a financial instrument, by assessing its exposure to sustainability risks and/or its impact on people and the environment. The need to impose new rules on ESG rating industries comes after the increasing growth of ESG ratings which poses challenges for the validity of this new industry in particular for the use of methodologies to measure corporate responsibility and the sustainable performance of financial firms.[5] The credibility of ESG rating statements and their independence from companies have been questioned, since numerous ESG data providers proliferated on the account of their reputational capital among investors.[6] The ESG Ratings Regulation establishes a set of stringent provisions on disclosure of methodologies, models and key rating assumptions such as time-horizon, overview of sources and whether they correspond to EU sustainability reporting standards, and risks and impact and in the case of double materiality. The legislation affords more reliability, comparability and transparency to maintain confidence in the rating activity. This translates into a more granular view of methodology, data processes including the EU Taxonomy[7] and Sustainable Finance Disclosure Regulation, and information on engagement with rated entities (for example unsolicited ratings need to be identified).[8] The Regulation would hopefully increase investor confidence in ESG ratings which provide an assessment of companies, funds and financial instruments as part of the market for sustainable finance. Under the new rules, ESG rating providers are authorized and supervised by the European Securities and Markets Authority (ESMA) and comply with transparency 1.02

2 Regulation (EU) 2019/2088.

3 See https://data.consilium.europa.eu/doc/document/ST-6255-2024-INIT/en/pdf.

4 Regulation (EU) 2023/2859, 2023/0177(COD).

5 Ventura Charlin, Arturo Cifuentes and Jorge Alfaro, 'ESG ratings: an industry in need of a major overhaul' (2024) 14(4) *Journal of Sustainable Finance & Investment* 1037.

6 David F. Larcker, Lukasz Pomorski, Brian Tayan and Edward M. Watts, 'ESG Ratings: A Compass without Direction' (2022) Stanford Closer Look Series, https://www.gsb.stanford.edu/faculty-research/publications/esg-ratings-compass-without-direction.

7 Regulation (EU) 2020/852.

8 Catherine Malecki, 'The EU proposal for a Regulation on the transparency and integrity of ESG rating activities on 13 June 2023: the missing piece of sustainable finance regulation' (2023) 17(2) *Law and Financial Markets Review* 156, 162.

requirements, in particular with regard to their methodology and sources of information.

1.03 The role of rating agencies in the capital markets has evolved taking into account ESG metrics with the premise of assessing climate risk and boosting confidence of investors in sustainable finance products.[9] As information intermediaries, ESG ratings gather information from the public and issue evaluations of firms' behaviour incorporating social and environmental values.[10] However, the ESG raters have been under scrutiny because of the different metrics employed to assess a given firm's performance in relation to the same ESG activities.[11] Specifically, ESMA raised concerns about the lack of transparency of rating providers' operations, a low level of comparability between ESG ratings, and potential conflicts of interest.[12] The practice of releasing ESG indexes poses challenges with regard to the reliability and transparency of ratings' internal models, which increase uncertainty about what sustainability needs to measure using non-financial indicators.[13] ESG ratings and scores are classified in aggregated ratings of E, S and G factors, ratings of individual factors (e.g. environmental) or ratings of subfactors (e.g. climate risks); ratings using double materiality perspective (assessing risk and impacts) or single materiality perspective (assessing only risks, or only impacts) or using international frameworks/standards (e.g. SDGs); and ratings involving the rating analysts or scores based purely on data analysis.[14]

---

9 Daniel Cash, 'Sustainable rating agencies' in Magdalena Ziolo (ed.), *Finance and Sustainable Development: Designing Sustainable Financial Systems* (Oxon-New York: Routledge 2021) 142–143.

10 Morningstar introduced a ratings scale aimed at ranking the sustainability of funds' portfolios with the objective of providing investors with a measure to evaluate how different funds target ESG standards. See Nickolay Gantchev, Mariassunta Giannetti and Rachel Li, 'Sustainability or performance? Ratings and fund managers' incentives' (2024) 155 *Journal of Financial Economics*, https://doi.org/10.1016/j.jfineco.2024.103831.

11 Michael S. Pagano, Graham Sinclair and Tina Yang, 'Understanding ESG ratings and ESG indexes' in Sabri Boubaker, Douglas Cumming and Duc K. Nguyen (eds), *Research Handbook of Finance and Sustainability* (Cheltenham: Edward Elgar 2018) 339–340.

12 ESMA, 'Text mining ESG disclosures in rating agency press releases' (10 February 2022), ESMA 80-195-1352, https://www.esma.europa.eu/document/text-mining-esg-disclosures-in-rating-agency-press-releases; ESMA, 'Report on Trends, Risks and Vulnerabilities' (17 March 2021), 20–21, https://www.esma.europa.eu/sites/default/files/library/esma50-165-1524_trv_1_2021.pdf.

13 Samuel Drempetic, Christian Klein and Bernhard Zwergel, 'The Influence of Firm Size on the ESG Score: Corporate Sustainability Ratings Under Review' (2020) 167 *Journal of Business Ethics* 355.

14 David Ramos Muñoz and Agnieszka Smoleńska, 'The Governance of ESG Ratings and Benchmarks (Infomediaries) as Gatekeepers: Exit, Voice and Coercion' (2023) European Banking Institute Working Paper Series 2023 - no. 149, https://ssrn.com/abstract=4531520.

B. THE ESG RATING PROVIDERS

The integration of ESG information into companies' decision-making process calls into question the role of ESG ratings as data providers in the financial markets. Rating agencies began providing ESG metrics with the premise of predicting potential climate exposures and creating shareholder value.[15] As intermediaries they gather information from various sources by monitoring companies in order to measure ESG performance and create a dataset for investors.[16] For instance, they introduce a ratings scale aimed at ranking the sustainability of funds' portfolios with the objective of providing investors with a measure to evaluate how different funds target ESG standards. **1.04**

ESG ratings contribute to determine investment decision-making as they focus on a company's strategy to internalize sustainability factors in board structures: their function is fundamental for the purpose of informing investors about material disclosures.[17] However, the ESG raters have been under scrutiny because of the different metrics employed to assess a given firm's performance in relation to the same ESG activities.[18] Rating scoring elaborates publicly available data and produces evaluations of firms' behaviour incorporating social and environmental values. A significant concern is to standardize ESG scoring by aligning ratings content with sustainability requirements. The variety of metrics developed in the ratings' proprietary methodologies can lead to risks of bias and 'greenwashing' when metrics of ESG data in ratings' models are elaborated to capture firms' behaviour with respect to sustainability.[19] The practice of releasing ESG indexes is fraught with questions concerning the reliability and transparency of ratings' internal models, which makes for increased uncertainty about what sustainability needs to measure using non-financial indicators.[20] **1.05**

15 Luca Enriques, Alessandro Romano and Andrew F. Tuch, 'Green Gatekeepers' (September 2024) ECGI Law Working Paper N° 800/2024, http://ssrn.com/abstract_id=4948397.

16 Florian Berg, Florian Heeb and Julian Kölbel, 'The economic impact of ESG ratings' (2024) SAFE Working Paper No. 439, https://doi.org/10.2139/ssrn.4088545.

17 Jorge Cruz-Lopez, Jordan B. Neyland and Dasha Smirnow, 'It's Hard to Hit a Target that Doesn't Exist: A Novel Conceptual Framework for ESG Ratings' (2024) 8(1) *The Business, Entrepreneurship & Tax Law Review*, https://scholarship.law.missouri.edu/betr/vol8/iss1/5/.

18 George Serafeim and Aaron Yoon, 'Stock price reactions to ESG news: the role of ESG ratings and disagreement' (2022) 28 *Review of Accounting Studies* 1500, https://doi.org/10.1007/s11142-022-09675-3.

19 Kenza Bryan, 'ESG ratings: whose interests do they serve?' *Financial Times* (2 October 2023), https://www.ft.com/content/fbe10867-fea1-4887-b404-9f9e301e102e.

20 Julian Kölbel, Florian Berg and Roberto Rigobon, 'Rating the ESG rating agencies' *Financial Times* (4 July 2023), https://www.ft.com/content/e9eaa11a-31e0-4f60-9a65-b6883546e8da.

1.06 The absence of an accepted definition of ESG performance and the heterogeneity of the metrics complicate matters. The divergences across ESG ratings are likely to produce misleading reports owing to different interpretations of sustainable criteria.[21] As a result, loopholes in interpreting the metrics can exacerbate the appetite for inflated ESG reports. The material risk for corporations would be the high costs of litigation and the reputational impact on markets arising from public scrutiny, which can lead to a downgrade from rating agencies. It is questionable whether raters do in fact elaborate an independent statement of ESG performance since the close relationship with the firms/users in the due diligence and definition of metrics affects the valuation of the company's ability to incorporate social and environmental factors in the financial report.[22] The lack of consistency and accuracy in the disclosures but also the high degree of subjectivity as to what constitutes ESG performance can create incentives for opportunistic behaviours of rating agencies.[23]

1.07 The practice of rating deviations seems incentivized at the individual firm level: these adjustments affect measures that relate to firm rankings, determining inflated ESG performance and flawed ESG ratings.[24] Conflicts of interest and herding behaviour among ratings users inherently cast doubts on the credibility of ESG ratings.[25] The lack of uniformity in the definitions of sustainable activities and the various ESG metrics makes for increased ambiguity in measuring companies' performance with regard to social and environmental values. Professional data providers have expanded in the climate sector in order to provide sustainability rankings and ratings, although the reliability of these certifications raises concerns about the lucrative 'user-pays' business model, which may result in doubtful outlooks.[26] Further improvements in defining ESG standards ensue from the climate litigation risk, which is gaining much attention on account of its impact on the reputational capital of firms.

---

21 Ebbe Rogge and Lara Ohnesorge, 'The Role of ESG Rating Agencies and Market Efficiency in Europe's Climate Policy' (2022) 28(2) *Hastings Environmental Law Journal*, 137–138.

22 Marco Dell'Erba and Michele Doronzo, 'Sustainability Gatekeepers: ESG Ratings and Data Providers' (2023) 25(2) *University of Pennsylvania Journal of Business Law*, 360.

23 Joe Zammit-Lucia, 'Untangling ESG mess will need more than regulation' *Financial Times* (10 July 2023), https://www.ft.com/content/246010cd-5274-4f20-b63a-7eaaa6186251.

24 Dane M. Christensen, George Serafeim and Anywhere Sikochi, 'Why is Corporate Virtue in the Eye of The Beholder? The Case of ESG Ratings' (2022) 97(1) *The Accounting Review*, 147.

25 Florence Jones, 'Ratings Providers fail to include corporate lobbying in sustainability assessments' *SustainableViews* (15 January 2025), https://www.sustainableviews.com/ratings-providers-fail-to-include-corporate-lobbying-in-sustainability-assessments-22de2092/.

26 Andreas Engert, 'ESG ratings: Guiding a movement in search for itself' in Thilo Kuntz (ed), *Research Handbook on Environmental, Social and Corporate Governance* (Edward Elgar 2024) 316–317.

Individual investors rely on the ratings because of their perceived authority, while institutional investors rely on them because of their market authority. The fact that financial products need to be labelled for ensuring substantial revenues to companies implies a high demand for ESG ratings. Further, the fact that financial firms need to be rated for gaining reputation in the securities markets means not only a pushed involvement of rating activities but also a qualified reliance on flawed assessment.[27] In this view, the frenetic growth in structured finance brought about not only a biased relationship with issuers but also a lucrative use of rating agencies.[28] **1.08**

What is crucial for the operation of the protection for investors is the soundness of CRAs' actions in interpreting disclosed information and assessing the creditworthiness of companies, thereby increasing investor confidence. Investors should be ensured of the appropriate level of information on which to make decisions. It is evident that retail investors are unskilled and make poor decisions about risk even when they have obtained full information about the products. Essentially, adequacy of disclosure is a gauge to determine what an investor knew or should have known based on the information available to that investor.[29] Standardized disclosure of rating methodologies would certainly contribute to a better understanding of the value of credit ratings and create incentives to use the best available methodologies and to invest in better rating methodologies, since the outcome would be immediately copied by other rating agencies. **1.09**

C. ESG RATINGS AND SUSTAINABLE FINANCE

The absence of an accepted definition of ESG performance and the heterogeneity of the metrics complicate matters. Christensen et al. argue that ESG ratings can show a significant information intermediary function by helping investors and other stakeholders to choose companies that exhibit their preferred ESG outcomes, although greater ESG disclosure leads to greater ESG **1.10**

---

27 Giulia Mennillo and Timothy J. Sinclair, 'A hard nut to crack: Regulatory failure shows how rating really works' (2019) 23(3) *Competition & Change* 266, 273–274.

28 Gerard Caprio Jr., Aslı Demirgüç-Kunt and Edward J. Kane, 'The 2007 Meltdown in Structured Securitization: Searching for Lessons, not Scapegoats' (2010) 25(1) *The World Bank Research Observer*, 132–133.

29 Steven L. Schwarcz 'Information Asymmetry and Information Failure: Disclosure Problems in Complex Financial Markets' in William Sun, Jim Stewart and David Pollard (eds), *Corporate Governance and the Global Financial Crisis* (Cambridge: Cambridge University Press 2011) 95.

rating disagreement.[30] The question at stake is: how can the rating methodologies produce valuable information about modelling prudential risk and capital at risk for investors and regulators.[31] Valuation, while involving an inherent subjective element, can still be carried out using more standardized procedures; and the underlying data and risk factor simulations can be made available to external parties seeking to reach their own judgements on the valuation of assets and other exposures.[32]

1.11 The divergences across ESG ratings are likely to produce misleading reports owing to different interpretations of sustainable criteria, accelerating and prolonging the firm's exposure.[33] It is questionable whether raters elaborate an independent statement of ESG performance since the relationship with the firms/users in the due diligence and definition of metrics affects the valuation of the company's ability to incorporate social and environmental factors in the financial report. This can be attributed to the lack of consistency and accuracy in the disclosures but also to the high degree of subjectivity as to what constitutes ESG performance.[34] Berg et al. document a correlation between ESG scores and outcome variables, finding that ESG raters have an appetite for data rewriting after a methodology change without announcing it to the public.[35] This practice of rating deviations seems incentivized at the individual firm level: these adjustments affect measures that relate to firm rankings, determining inflated ESG performance and flawed ESG ratings.[36]

1.12 Conflicts of interest and herding behaviour among ratings users inherently cast doubts on the credibility of ESG ratings.[37] Rating agencies accumulated reputational capital and gained an influential role among ESG investors, but there is little evidence about rating criteria because of the 'subscriber-pay' business

30 Dane M. Christensen, George Serafeim and Anywhere (Siko) Sikochi, 'Why is Corporate Virtue in the Eye of The Beholder? The Case of ESG Ratings' (2022) 97(1) *The Accounting Review*, 147–148.

31 Javier El-Hage, 'Fixing ESG: Are Mandatory ESG Disclosures the Solution to Misleading Ratings?' (2021) 26(2) *Fordham Journal of Corporate & Financial Law* 359, 368–369.

32 IOSCO, 'Environmental, Social and Governance (ESG) Ratings and Data Products Providers. Consultation Report' (July 2021), CR02/21, p. 8.

33 Maryam Rostoum, 'The Environmental, Social, and Governance (ESG) Ratings Industry: How can publicly-traded companies improve their overall ESG scores?' (2021), https://doi.org/10.7916/d8-rs4p-a916.

34 Claude Lopez, Oscar F. Contreras and Joseph Bendix, 'ESG ratings: the road ahead' (2020) MPRA Paper No. 103259, p. 7–8, https://mpra.ub.uni-muenchen.de/103259/.

35 Florian Berg, Kornelia Fabisik and Zacharias Sautner, 'Rewriting History II: The (Un)Predictable Past of ESG Ratings' (2021) ECGI Finance Working Paper No 708/2020, p.23–24, https://corpgov.law.harvard.edu/2020/11/11/rewriting-history-ii-the-unpredictable-past-of-esg-ratings/.

36 Moritz Kraemer, 'The case for 'truly-long-term' debt ratings' *Financial Times* (8 July 2021), https://www.ft.com/content/d702f0e5-1a7e-4cd6-b47e-d97c9ff34887.

37 Ingo Walter, 'Sense and Nonsense in ESG Ratings' (2020) 5(2) *Journal of Law, Finance, and Accounting* 307.

model, which makes the rating industry far from sustainable.[38] The business activities of rating agencies incentivize users of ESG evaluations to engage in conditions where the rated entity is also a client of the rating provider for other ancillary services (e.g. investment advisory, credit risk assessment, securities disclosure).[39] ESG ratings determine investment decision-making as they focus on a company's strategy to internalize sustainability factors in board structures: their function is fundamental for the purpose of informing investors about material disclosures.[40] Therefore, a greater demand for sustainability reporting has determined the expansion of ESG ratings, which perform the role of data providers for corporate disclosure. As Gratcheva et al. have observed, 'the ESG ratings industry has emerged and grown considerably over the past decade in response to the market demand for sustainability-related data, evolving from specialized companies providing ESG-specific products to influencers of public debate on sustainable finance.'[41] The quality of data products raises concerns for the opaque consistency and comparability in sustainability-related information which affect the measure of a company's exposure to ESG risks.

---

38 IOSCO, 'Environmental, Social and Governance (ESG) Ratings and Data Products Providers. Final Report' (November 2021), FR09/21, p. 30, https://www.iosco.org/library/pubdocs/pdf/IOSCOPD690.pdf.

39 ESMA, 'Call for evidence on Market Characteristics for ESG Rating Providers in the EU' (3 February 2022), 6–7, https://www.esma.europa.eu/press-news/consultations/call-evidence-market-characteristics-esg-rating-providers-in-eu.

40 Robert G. Eccles and Timothy Youmans, 'Implied Materiality and Material Disclosures of Credit Ratings' (2015) Harvard Business School Working Paper No. 15-079, p. 2–3.

41 Ekaterina M. Gratcheva, Teal Emery and Dieter Wang, 'Demystifying Sovereign ESG' (2020), The World Bank, Equitable Growth, Finance and Institutions Insight, p. 15, http://hdl.handle.net/10986/35586.

ARTICLE 2

SCOPE

Andrea Miglionico

1. This Regulation applies to ESG ratings issued by ESG rating providers operating in the Union.

ESG rating providers are considered to be operating in the Union in the following cases:

(a) for ESG rating providers established in the Union:

(i) when they issue and publish their ESG ratings on their website or through other means; or

(ii) when they issue and distribute their ESG ratings by subscription or other contractual relationships to regulated financial undertakings in the Union, to undertakings that fall within the scope of Directive 2013/34/EU, to undertakings that fall within the scope of Directive 2004/109/EC, or to Union institutions, bodies, offices and agencies or Member State public authorities;

(b) for ESG rating providers established outside the Union, when they issue and distribute their ESG ratings by subscription or other contractual relationships to regulated financial undertakings in the Union, to undertakings that fall within the scope of Directive 2013/34/EU, to undertakings that fall within the scope of Directive 2004/109/EC, or to Union institutions, bodies, offices and agencies or Member State public authorities.

2. This Regulation does not apply to any of the following:

(a) private ESG ratings that are not intended for public disclosure or for distribution;

(b) ESG ratings issued by regulated financial undertakings in the Union that are used exclusively for internal purposes or for providing in-house or intragroup financial services or products;

(c) ESG ratings issued by regulated financial undertakings in the Union that:

(i) are incorporated in a product or a service, where such products or services are already regulated under Union law, including under Regulation (EC) No 883/2004 of the European Parliament and of

the Council,[1] Regulation (EU) 2019/2088, Directives 2013/36/EU,[2] 2014/65/EU, 2009/138/EC,[3] 2009/65/EC,[4] 2011/61/EU[5] and (EU) 2016/2341[6] of the European Parliament and of the Council and Regulations (EU) 2020/1503,[7] (EU) 2023/1114[8] and (EU) 2016/1011 of the European Parliament and of the Council; and

(ii) are disclosed to a third party.

In the situations covered by the first subparagraph of this point, where a regulated financial undertaking in the Union discloses an ESG rating to third parties as part of its marketing communications, it shall include on its website the same information as that required by point 1 of Annex III to this Regulation and it shall disclose in those marketing communications a link to those website disclosures, except where it is subject to Article 13(3) of Regulation (EU) 2019/2088.

Competent authorities designated in accordance with the sectoral legislative acts referred to in the first subparagraph of this point shall monitor compliance by regulated financial undertakings in the Union with the requirements of the first subparagraph of this point, in accordance with the powers granted by those sectoral legislative acts;

(d) ESG ratings issued by ESG rating providers established outside the Union that are not authorised or recognised under Title II and that meet the following conditions:

(i) the ESG rating is distributed at the own exclusive initiative of the user of the ESG rating established in the Union without any prior contact, solicitation, promotion, advertisement or any other initiative by the ESG rating provider, or by any third party on behalf of

---

1 Regulation (EC) No 883/2004 of the European Parliament and of the Council of 29 April 2004 on the coordination of social security systems (OJ L 166, 30.4.2004, p. 1).

2 Directive 2013/36/EU of the European Parliament and of the Council of 26 June 2013 on access to the activity of credit institutions and the prudential supervision of credit institutions, amending Directive 2002/87/EC and repealing Directives 2006/48/EC and 2006/49/EC (OJ L 176, 27.6.2013, p. 338).

3 Directive 2009/138/EC of the European Parliament and of the Council of 25 November 2009 on the taking-up and pursuit of the business of Insurance and Reinsurance (Solvency II) (OJ L 335, 17.12.2009, p. 1).

4 Directive 2009/65/EC of the European Parliament and of the Council of 13 July 2009 on the coordination of laws, regulations and administrative provisions relating to undertakings for collective investment in transferable securities (UCITS) (OJ L 302, 17.11.2009, p. 32).

5 Directive 2011/61/EU of the European Parliament and of the Council of 8 June 2011 on Alternative Investment Fund Managers and amending Directives 2003/41/EC and 2009/65/EC and Regulations (EC) No 1060/2009 and (EU) No 1095/2010 (OJ L 174, 1.7.2011, p. 1).

6 Directive (EU) 2016/2341 of the European Parliament and of the Council of 14 December 2016 on the activities and supervision of institutions for occupational retirement provision (IORPs) (OJ L 354, 23.12.2016, p. 37).

7 Regulation (EU) 2020/1503 of the European Parliament and of the Council of 7 October 2020 on European crowdfunding service providers for business, and amending Regulation (EU) 2017/1129 and Directive (EU) 2019/1937 (OJ L 347, 20.10.2020, p. 1).

8 Regulation (EU) 2023/1114 of the European Parliament and of the Council of 31 May 2023 on markets in crypto-assets, and amending Regulations (EU) No 1093/2010 and (EU) No 1095/2010 and Directives 2013/36/EU and (EU) 2019/1937 (OJ L 150, 9.6.2023, p. 40).

the provider; an ESG rating distributed in the Union by a provider established outside the Union whose market share in the Union for its ESG rating activities becomes substantial or that has a website in at least one of the official languages of the Union, which is a language that is not customary in the sphere of international finance, shall not be considered to be distributed at the own exclusive initiative of the user of ESG rating.

The own exclusive initiative of a user of ESG rating as referred to in the first subparagraph of this point shall not entitle an ESG rating provider established outside the Union to distribute ESG ratings to that user in a recurrent manner, nor to distribute ESG ratings to any other user of ESG ratings in the Union;

(ii) there is no substitute for the ratings offered by any ESG rating provider authorised under this Regulation;

(e) the publication or distribution of data on environmental, social and human rights, and governance factors;

(f) credit ratings issued pursuant to Regulation (EC) No 1060/2009, and any ESG-related scores or assessments that are produced or published as part of the methodologies for credit ratings or as an input or output of the creditworthiness assessment;

(g) products or services that incorporate an element of an ESG rating, including investment research as laid down in Directive 2014/65/EU;

(h) external reviews of European Green Bonds, as provided for in Regulation (EU) 2023/2631;

(i) external reviews or second-party opinions on bonds marketed as environmentally sustainable, sustainability-linked bonds, and bonds, loans and other types of debt instruments marketed as sustainable, to the extent that such external reviews and second-party opinions do not contain ESG ratings issued by the external reviewer or the second-party opinion provider;

(j) ESG ratings issued by Union institutions, bodies, offices and agencies or Member State public authorities where such ratings are not published or distributed for commercial purposes;

(k) ESG ratings issued by an authorised ESG rating provider where such ratings are published or distributed by a third party;

(l) ESG ratings issued by members of the European System of Central Banks where such ratings are not published or distributed for commercial purposes;

(m) mandatory disclosures pursuant to Articles 6, 8, 9, 10, 11 and 13 of Regulation (EU) 2019/2088;

(n) disclosures pursuant to Articles 5, 6 and 8 of Regulation (EU) 2020/852;

(o) ESG ratings developed exclusively for accreditation or certification processes, which do not target investment analysis, financial analysis, investment decision-making or financial decision-making;

(p) labelling activities provided that the labels granted to the relevant entities, financial instruments or financial products do not involve the disclosure of an ESG rating;
(q) ESG ratings published or distributed by non-profit organisations for non-commercial purposes.

3. By way of derogation from the first subparagraph, point (q), where non-profit organisations charge rated items or issuers of rated items to report data or to get rated through their platform, or where they charge users of ESG ratings to access any information on ESG ratings, they shall be subject to the requirements of this Regulation. ESMA, the European Supervisory Authority (European Banking Authority) (EBA) established by Regulation (EU) No 1093/2010 of the European Parliament and of the Council,[9] and the European Supervisory Authority (European Insurance and Occupational Pensions Authority) (EIOPA) established by Regulation (EU) No 1094/2010 of the European Parliament and of the Council[10] (known collectively as 'European Supervisory Authorities' or 'ESAs') shall, through the Joint Committee, develop draft regulatory technical standards to specify the details of the presentation and content of the information to be disclosed pursuant to paragraph 2, first subparagraph, point (c), second subparagraph, taking into account the various types of financial products, their characteristics and the differences between them, and the need to avoid duplication of information already published in accordance with applicable regulatory requirements.

ESMA shall submit the draft regulatory technical standards referred to in the first subparagraph to the Commission.

Power is delegated to the Commission to supplement this Regulation by adopting the regulatory technical standards referred to in the first subparagraph of this paragraph, in accordance with Articles 10 to 14 of Regulations (EU) No 1093/2010, (EU) No 1094/2010 and (EU) No 1095/2010.

9 Regulation (EU) No 1093/2010 of the European Parliament and of the Council of 24 November 2010 establishing a European Supervisory Authority (European Banking Authority), amending Decision No 716/2009/EC and repealing Commission Decision 2009/78/EC (OJ L 331, 15.12.2010, p. 12).

10 Regulation (EU) No 1094/2010 of the European Parliament and of the Council of 24 November 2010 establishing a European Supervisory Authority (European Insurance and Occupational Pensions Authority), amending Decision No 716/2009/EC and repealing Commission Decision 2009/79/EC (OJ L 331, 15.12.2010, p. 48).

A. INTRODUCTION

2.01 This article defines the applicability of the Regulation to rating providers operating in the European Union. It is a general provision which sets a catalogue of cases in which ESG rating providers issue, distribute and publish their ratings through various sources such as website, subscription or contractual relationships. The operation of ESG ratings providers highlights the user-pays and issuer-pays business model in which raters formulate their evaluations. ESG ratings are mostly subscriber-pays, which differ from the issuer-pays for credit ratings that are remunerated by firms rather than investors.[11] The article points to different modes of entry and regulatory control with respect to ratings of financial institutions, corporates subject to EU reporting, EU institutions or Member States authorities. Most interestingly, the provision identifies categories of ratings which are excluded from the framework of this Regulation. Specifically, the private use of ESG ratings and the own exclusive initiative of a user of ESG rating are not classified as providers and are outside the scope of the regulatory regime. Other forms of ESG ratings which do not target commercial matters (non-profit organizations for non-commercial purposes) and are developed for labelling activities which do not involve the disclosure of an ESG rating are not subject to the requirements of the Regulation. The article also designates the European Supervisory Authorities (ESMA, EBA and EIOPA) as a reference point for regulatory technical standards on the details of the presentation and content of the information to be disclosed in the ESG ratings. Specifically, the direct supervision on ESG ratings providers is assigned to ESMA with a limited role for Member State Competent Authorities supporting ESMA in supervision and enforcement. In terms of passporting regime, as per general EU approach, authorization extends across the Union. The article introduces disclosure rules on the governance of ESG ratings providers by prohibiting any forms of conflicts of interest that can

11 In the investor-pays business model, the rating agency earns revenues from investors who wish to learn the firm's non-financial performance. In the issuer-pays business model, the rating agency charges a fee to the firm then publicly discloses the firm's non-financial performance. In the credit ratings market, investors are interested in the informational content of ratings; the expected stock price reaction to the rating drives the willingness of the firm to pay for a publicly observable rating. See Stefano Lovo and Jacques Olivier, 'Who should pay for ESG ratings?' (2025), https://papers.ssrn.com/sol3/papers.cfm?abstract_id=5106010.

amount in the issuance, distribution and publication of ratings. The spirit of the provision is to enhance transparency in the methodologies, models and key rating assumptions.

The pressing need to address the sustainability risk in the firms' business activities as well as the problems associated with the regulatory reporting have become the key challenges for financial firms.[12] Further, the debate about the implications of environmental issues for the governance of companies and potential hazards that climate change can pose to financial stability has intensified even more.[13] The integration of the ESG factors into decision-making processes calls into question the controversial role of ESG ratings as data providers in the corporate sector.[14] The divergences across ESG criteria assessed in the ratings are likely to produce misleading reports owing to different interpretations of sustainable criteria.[15] As a result, the lack of uniformity in the definitions of sustainable activities and the various ESG metrics inflates climate risk litigation, and makes for increased ambiguity in measuring firms' performance with regard to social and environmental values.[16] **2.02**

The ESG ratings have become relevant benchmarks for measuring the suitability of climate and environmental factors in corporate internal models.[17] In this context, the rating agencies play a gatekeeper role in climate change, given the fact that firms have incentives to comply with ESG factors in order to avoid a negative impact on stock returns. The main challenge is to define valid methodologies for the metrics that raters use to design their assessments.[18] Another criticism stems from the usefulness of ratings, which is fraught with unclear methodologies and divergences in the elaboration of forecasts.[19] The **2.03**

---

12 Scatigna et al., 'Achievements and Challenges in ESG Markets' (2021) *BIS Quarterly Review* 83.

13 Michael S. Pagano, Graham Sinclair and Tina Yang, 'Understanding ESG ratings and ESG indexes' in Sabri Boubaker, Douglas Cumming and Duc K. Nguyen (eds), *Research Handbook of Finance and Sustainability* (Edward Elgar 2018) ch.18.

14 Gaia Balp and Giovanni Strampelli, 'Institutional Investor ESG Engagement: The European Experience' (2022) 23(4) *European Business Organization Law Review* 890–891.

15 Matteo Gargantini and Michele Siri, 'Information intermediaries and sustainability: the case of ESG ratings and benchmarks' (2024) in Kern Alexander, Matteo Gargantini and Michele Siri (eds), *The Cambridge Handbook of EU Sustainable Finance. Regulation, Supervision and Governance* (Cambridge: Cambridge University Press 2024) ch.11.

16 Maurice Dumrose, Sebastian Rink and Julia Eckert, 'Disaggregating confusion? The EU Taxonomy and its relation to ESG rating' (2022) 48 *Finance Research Letters*, https://doi.org/10.1016/j.frl.2022.102928.

17 Samuel Drempetic, Christian Klein and Bernhard Zwergel, 'The Influence of Firm Size on the ESG Score: Corporate Sustainability Ratings Under Review' (2020) 167 *Journal of Business Ethics* 333.

18 Marco Dell'Erba and Guido Ferrarini, 'ESG & Executive Remuneration in Europe' (2024) 25(3) *European Business Organization Law Review* 441–442.

19 Barbara Kurbus and Vasja Rant, 'A legal origins perspective on ESG rating disagreement' (2025) 74 *Research in International Business and Finance*, https://doi.org/10.1016/j.ribaf.2024.102702.

raters seem more incentivized to sell their products and act as vendors of the ESG brand in the market, rather than to bridge the gap between sustainable firms and investors.[20] According to the new legislation, the ratings should carefully weigh the E, S and G factors for aggregated ESG scores although the Regulation is silent on the methodologies for assessing firms' performance in these areas. On this view, the legislation intends to focus on time-horizon and sources of rating and whether they correspond to EU sustainability reporting standards.

B. THE APPLICATION OF THE REGULATORY FRAMEWORK

2.04 The new legislation recognizes the role of ESG ratings as information intermediaries of green assets and provides an equivalence, endorsement and recognition regime for raters outside the EU. The Regulation establishes a 'national treatment' equivalence regime enabling small ESG rating providers to access the EU market: while there is no requirement for an establishment in the EU, a legal representative is needed, which seems a less stringent information requirement for a recognition regime with respect to the authorization. ESG rating providers outside the EU that intend to operate within the Union will have to obtain approval of their ratings from an authorized provider in the EU, based on quantitative criteria, or be included in the register of EU ESG rating providers.

2.05 Notwithstanding the debated role of 'infomediaries,' ESG ratings represent a valuable source for investors and corporations given the significant influence of rating statements in the sustainability of firms. The implications of ratings for the instruments being rated have a direct impact on prices because these changes in assessment can affect investors' portfolios. Rating updates look like an advertising tool designed to attract ESG investors and, at the same time, a disincentive for investors to conduct their own assessment of green assets. Therefore, rating changes seem driven by economic targets, such as marketing the profitable 'opinion,' rather than by the motivation to inform. Despite the raters' claims of scrutiny, the changes in ratings do not seem to be related to changes in the sustainability of the rated firms.[21] ESG ratings exert a significant influence as gatekeepers by providing essential evaluations to sustainable

20 Veerle Colaert, 'The Changing Nature of Financial Regulation: Sustainable Finance as a New EU Policy Objective' (2022) 59(6) *Common Market Law Review* 1669, 1685–1686.

21 Paulo Viegas de Carvalho, Paul Anthony Laux and João Pedro Pereira, 'The stability and accuracy of credit ratings' (2014) 34–36, http://ssrn.com/abstract=2504972.

investments, and it is unlikely that regulators and investors will erode their position in the financial industry. Ratings providers as financial intermediaries are more attracted by high revenues than by providing up-to-date evaluations of the sustainability of assets. This creates similar anomalies with credit rating agencies which raise concerns on practices of 'shopping for raters' as issuers move from one rating agency to another until they get a favourable rating.[22] Rating shopping generally refers to a situation in which a firm arranges for several rating entities to assess its portfolio, but only discloses the most favourable rating.[23] Companies might shop for the highest ratings on their lucrative green issuance deals, including playing one rater against another when informally consulting them on structures to achieve high ratings.

A major function of ratings is to certify to relatively uninformed traders that **2.06** they do not face a significant informational disadvantage. However, asymmetries in the ESG market for information intermediaries hamper their ability to play this role.[24] The imbalanced relationship between issuers and investors is principally determined by lack of financial knowledge and causes a distortion of consumers' choices, particularly at the time when the investment operation is executed.[25] To ensure rating accuracy, the Regulation ensures that the ESG market achieved adequate disclosure protection in terms of improving the flow of price information.

Individual investors rely on the ratings because of their perceived authority, **2.07** while institutional investors rely on them because of their market authority. The fact that sustainable products need to be labelled for ensuring substantial revenues to companies implies a high demand for ESG ratings. Further, the fact that financial firms need to be rated for gaining reputation in the ESG market means not only a pushed involvement of rating activities but also a qualified reliance on flawed assessment.[26] The proliferation of ESG market brought about not only a biased relationship with issuers but also a lucrative use of ratings providers. What is crucial for the operation of the protection for investors is the soundness of ESG ratings' actions in assessing the

22 Vasiliki Skreta and Laura Veldkamp, 'Ratings Shopping and Asset Complexity: A Theory of Ratings Inflation' (2009), NBER Working Paper 14761, http://www.nber.org/papers/w14761.

23 Tinghua Duan, Frank Weikai Li and Roni Michaely, 'Consumers' Reaction to Corporate ESG Performance: Evidence from Store Visits' (2023), https://ink.library.smu.edu.sg/lkcsb_research/7359.

24 Daniel Cash, *ESG Rating Agencies and Financial Regulation* (Edward Elgar 2024) 125–126.

25 Sirio Aramonte and Frank Packer, 'Information Governance in Sustainable Finance' (2022), http://dx.doi.org/10.2139/ssrn.4309825.

26 Florian Kiesel and Felix Lücke, 'ESG in credit ratings and the impact on financial markets' (2019) 28(3) *Financial Markets, Institutions & Instruments* 263.

sustainability and sustainable strategies of companies, thereby increasing investor confidence.

C. THE REGIME OF EXEMPTIONS

2.08 The Regulation provides an articulated and long list of exclusions for ESG ratings activities which are outside the scope of legislation in case of missing authorization or recognition and private use of the ratings for non-financial purpose. The provision distinguishes the rating used in the creditworthiness of firms and subject to Regulation (EC) No 1060/2009 and ESG assessments of sustainable products. It also draws a line between external reviews or second-party opinions for green bonds introduced by Regulation (EU) 2023/2631 and ESG ratings providers. The regime of exemptions is completed with the exclusion of ratings issued, published or distributed for commercial purposes by members of the European System of Central Banks and the publication or distribution of data on environmental, social and human rights and governance factors. This regime suggests that the Regulation aims to avoid any overlaps with other categories of credit ratings and external reviews or opinions which are not intended to evaluate the sustainable financial performance of firms.

2.09 The implications of ratings for green assets have become central to the creditworthiness of the firms and their ability to access the ESG market.[27] In parallel, the effects of ratings on the instruments being rated have a direct impact on prices because these assessment changes can affect the pool of investors.[28] The anomalies are evident in the rating methodologies by the fact that in the business model conflicts of interest may induce biased ratings with the result of tainted information to investors.[29] It can be a problem of incomplete disclosure of information from the issuer since the market incentive for companies is to push ESG ratings for the highest assessed sustainable products.[30]

---

27 Masayasu Kanno, 'Does ESG performance improve firm creditworthiness?' (2023) 55 *Finance Research Letters*, https://doi.org/10.1016/j.frl.2023.103894.

28 Özlem Dursun-de Neef, Steven Ongena and Gergana Tsonkova, 'Green Versus Sustainable Loans: The Impact on Firms' ESG Performance' (2022) Swiss Finance Institute Research Paper Series No 22–42, https://ssrn.com/abstract=4115692.

29 George Serafeim and Aaron Yoon, 'Stock price reactions to ESG news: the role of ESG ratings and disagreement' (2022) 28 *Review of Accounting Studies* 1500.

30 Sung Eun Kim, 'The Duality of Variance among ESG Assessments' (2023) 88(2) *Missouri Law Review* 409.

D. THE ROLE OF EUROPEAN SUPERVISORY AUTHORITIES

The Regulation mandates the European Supervisory Authorities (ESAs) – ESMA, EBA and EIOPA – as responsible authorities to prepare regulatory technical standards on the content and methodologies of ESG ratings. The article intends to highlight the coordinated approach of ESAs and replicate the experience of Regulatory Technical Standards (RTS) on ESG disclosures which have been developed under the EU Regulation on sustainability-related disclosures in the financial services sector, which aims to strengthen protection for end-investors and improve the disclosures that they receive from a broad range of financial market participants and financial advisers, as well as regarding financial products.[31] In their technical role, the ESAs will need to consider further changes and potential reforms based on experiences shared by stakeholders through advices, opinions, recommendations and observations, both directly through desk-based research and feedback from the national competent authorities. The ESAs are empowered to propose technical adjustments after a comprehensive evaluation of the Regulation: the legislative mandates to develop the draft RTS, the impact assessment that analyzes the ESAs proposals and the final draft RTS. The final report will provide an overview of the feedback received from financial market participants to the consultation paper as well as ESAs' responses. The ESAs will welcome feedback to this consultation seeking input on proposed amendments to the Regulation. Following the close of the consultation the draft RTS will be finalized and submitted to the European Commission which has three months to decide whether to endorse the regulatory technical standards. The ESAs and the Commission will clarify controversial aspects of the applicability of the Regulation with respect to the scope of ESG ratings provided by regulated financial undertakings in the Union (e.g. disclosure obligations for asset managers).[32] **2.10**

31 See https://www.eba.europa.eu/activities/single-rulebook/regulatory-activities/transparency-and-pillar-3/joint-regulatory-technical-standards-esg-disclosure-standards-financial-market-participants.

32 ESMA is tasked with drafting supporting standards on the Regulation to support detailing the requirements.

ARTICLE 3

DEFINITIONS

Andrea Miglionico

For the purposes of this Regulation, the following definitions apply:

(1) 'ESG rating' means an opinion or a score, or a combination of both, regarding a rated item's profile or characteristics with regard to environmental, social and human rights, or governance factors, or regarding a rated item's exposure to risks or impact on environmental, social and human rights or governance factors, that is based on both an established methodology and a defined ranking system of rating categories, irrespective of whether such ESG rating is labelled as 'ESG rating,' 'ESG opinion' or 'ESG score';

(2) 'ESG opinion' means an ESG assessment that is based on a rule-based methodology and defined ranking system of rating categories, involving directly a rating analyst in the rating process;

(3) 'ESG score' means an ESG measure derived from data, using a rule-based methodology, and based only on a pre-established statistical or algorithmic system or model, without any additional substantial analytical input from a rating analyst;

(4) 'ESG rating provider' means a legal person whose activities include the issuance, and the publication or distribution, of ESG ratings on a professional basis;

(5) 'regulated financial undertaking in the Union' means an undertaking, regardless of its legal form, that is:

(a) a credit institution as defined in Article 4(1), point (1), of Regulation (EU) No 575/2013 of the European Parliament and of the Council;[1]

(b) an investment firm as defined in Article 4(1), point (1), of Directive 2014/65/EU;

(c) an AIFM as defined in Article 4(1), point (b), of Directive 2011/61/EU, including a manager of a qualifying venture capital fund as defined in Article 3, point (c), of Regulation (EU) No 345/2013 of the European

1 Regulation (EU) No 575/2013 of the European Parliament and of the Council of 26 June 2013 on prudential requirements for credit institutions and amending Regulation (EU) No 648/2012 (OJ L 176, 27.6.2013, p. 1).

Parliament and of the Council,[2] a manager of a qualifying social entrepreneurship fund as defined in Article 3, point (c), of Regulation (EU) No 346/2013 of the European Parliament and of the Council[3] and a manager of the ELTIF as defined in Article 2, point (12), of Regulation (EU) 2015/760 of the European Parliament and of the Council;[4]

(d) a management company as defined in Article 2(1), point (b), of Directive 2009/65/EC;

(e) an insurance undertaking as defined in Article 13, point (1), of Directive 2009/138/EC;

(f) a reinsurance undertaking as defined in Article 13, point (4), of Directive 2009/138/EC;

(g) an institution for occupational retirement provision as defined in Article 6, point (1), of Directive (EU) 2016/2341;

(h) a pension institution operating pension schemes, which are considered to be social security schemes covered by Regulations (EC) No 883/2004 and (EC) No 987/2009[5] of the European Parliament and of the Council, and any legal entity set up for the purpose of investment of such social security schemes;

(i) an alternative investment fund, as defined in Article 4(1), point (a), of Directive 2011/61/EU, supervised under the applicable national law;

(j) a UCITS as defined in Article 1(2) of Directive 2009/65/EC;

(k) a central counterparty as defined in Article 2, point (1), of Regulation (EU) No 648/2012 of the European Parliament and of the Council;[6]

(l) a central securities depository as defined in Article 2(1), point (1), of Regulation (EU) No 909/2014 of the European Parliament and of the Council;[7]

(m) an insurance or reinsurance special purpose vehicle authorised in accordance with Article 211 of Directive 2009/138/EC;

(n) a securitisation special purpose entity as defined in Article 2, point (2), of Regulation (EU) 2017/2402 of the European Parliament and of the Council;[8]

---

2 Regulation (EU) No 345/2013 of the European Parliament and of the Council of 17 April 2013 on European venture capital funds (OJ L 115, 25.4.2013, p. 1).

3 Regulation (EU) No 346/2013 of the European Parliament and of the Council of 17 April 2013 on European social entrepreneurship funds (OJ L 115, 25.4.2013, p. 18).

4 Regulation (EU) 2015/760 of the European Parliament and of the Council of 29 April 2015 on European long-term investment funds (OJ L 123, 19.5.2015, p. 98).

5 Regulation (EC) No 987/2009 of the European Parliament and of the Council of 16 September 2009 laying down the procedure for implementing Regulation (EC) No 883/2004 on the coordination of social security systems (OJ L 284, 30.10.2009, p. 1).

6 Regulation (EU) No 648/2012 of the European Parliament and of the Council of 4 July 2012 on OTC derivatives, central counterparties and trade repositories (OJ L 201, 27.7.2012, p. 1).

7 Regulation (EU) No 909/2014 of the European Parliament and of the Council of 23 July 2014 on improving securities settlement in the European Union and on central securities depositories and amending Directives 98/26/EC and 2014/65/EU and Regulation (EU) No 236/2012 (OJ L 257, 28.8.2014, p. 1).

8 Regulation (EU) 2017/2402 of the European Parliament and of the Council of 12 December 2017 laying down a general framework for securitization and creating a specific framework for simple, transparent and

(o) an insurance holding company as defined in Article 212(1), point (f), of Directive 2009/138/EC or a mixed financial holding company as defined in Article 212(1), point (h), of Directive 2009/138/EC, which is part of an insurance group that is subject to supervision at the level of the group pursuant to Article 213 of that Directive and which is not exempted from group supervision pursuant to Article 214(2) of that Directive;

(p) a financial holding company as defined in Article 4(1), point (20), of Regulation (EU) No 575/2013;

(q) a payment institution as defined in Article 4, point (4), of Directive (EU) 2015/2366 of the European Parliament and of the Council;[9]

(r) an electronic money institution as defined in Article 2, point (1), of Directive 2009/110/EC of the European Parliament and of the Council;[10]

(s) a crowdfunding service provider as defined in Article 2(1), point (e), of Regulation (EU) 2020/1503;

(t) a crypto-asset service provider as defined in Article 3(1), point (15), of Regulation (EU) 2023/1114 when performing one or more crypto-asset services as defined in Article 3(1), point (16), of Regulation (EU) 2023/1114;

(u) a trade repository as defined in Article 2, point (2), of Regulation (EU) No 648/2012;

(v) a securitisation repository as defined in Article 2, point (23), of Regulation (EU) 2017/2402;

(w) an administrator of benchmarks as defined in Article 3(1), point (6), of Regulation (EU) 2016/1011;

(x) a credit rating agency as defined in Article 3(1), point (b), of Regulation (EC) No 1060/2009;

(6) 'rating analyst' means a person who performs analytical functions for the purpose of issuing ESG ratings;

(7) 'rated item' means a legal person, a financial instrument, a financial product, a public authority or a body governed by public law which is explicitly or implicitly rated in the ESG rating, irrespective of whether such rating has been requested and irrespective of whether the legal person, public authority or body governed by public law has provided information for that ESG rating;

(8) 'financial instrument' means any of the instruments listed in Section C of Annex I to Directive 2014/65/EU;

---

standardized securitization, and amending Directives 2009/65/EC, 2009/138/EC and 2011/61/EU and Regulations (EC) No 1060/2009 and (EU) No 648/2012 (OJ L 347, 28.12.2017, p. 35).

9 Directive (EU) 2015/2366 of the European Parliament and of the Council of 25 November 2015 on payment services in the internal market, amending Directives 2002/65/EC, 2009/110/EC and 2013/36/EU and Regulation (EU) No 1093/2010, and repealing Directive 2007/64/EC (OJ L 337, 23.12.2015, p. 35).

10 Directive 2009/110/EC of the European Parliament and of the Council of 16 September 2009 on the taking up, pursuit and prudential supervision of the business of electronic money institutions amending Directives 2005/60/EC and 2006/48/EC and repealing Directive 2000/46/EC (OJ L 267, 10.10.2009, p. 7).

(9) 'user of ESG ratings' means a natural or legal person, a public authority, an agency or other body governed by public law, to which an ESG rating is distributed by subscription or other contractual relationships;

(10) 'competent authorities' means the authorities designated by each Member State in accordance with Article 30 of this Regulation;

(11) 'management body' means an ESG rating provider's body or bodies, which are appointed in accordance with national law, which are empowered to set the ESG rating provider's strategy, objectives and overall direction, which oversee and monitor management decision-making in the ESG rating provider, and which include the persons who effectively direct the business of the ESG rating provider;

(12) 'senior management' means the person or persons who effectively direct the business of the ESG rating provider and the member or members of the ESG rating provider's administrative or supervisory board;

(13) 'group of ESG rating providers' means a group of undertakings established in the Union consisting of a parent undertaking and its subsidiary undertakings within the meaning of Article 2 of Directive 2013/34/EU, and undertakings linked to each other by a relationship, whose activities include the provision of ESG ratings.

A. INTRODUCTION

3.01 This article provides a set of definitions on the ESG rating activities and operating models of rated entities. Particular attention is placed to the opinion or score formulated by ratings providers on ESG factors which are included in the composition of ratings but not underlying data. The assessment process is based on a rules-based methodology and defined ranking system of rating categories, involving directly a rating analyst in the rating or systems process. Specifically, the score is intended as an ESG measure derived from data, using a rule-based methodology, and based only on a pre-established statistical or algorithmic system or model, without any additional substantial analytical input from an analyst. The article also defines ESG rating provider as professional legal person directed to the issuance and publication or distribution of ESG ratings. From this definition, ratings providers resemble the operation of financial intermediaries of sustainable products which serve the objective to assess an entity, instrument and issuer exposure to ESG risks. The provision also identifies the function of rating analyst and qualifies user of ESG ratings as subscriber of rated items which increase transparency of the sustainable ratings industry. The gatekeeper role of ESG ratings is evident in the assessments of ESG factors which are used for investment decisions and influence capital allocation.[11]

3.02 The incorporation of climate information into companies' decision-making process calls into question the role of ESG ratings as third-party data providers in the financial markets. Professional ESG raters have started to elaborate climate figures that combine various sources of information and aggregate physical risk indices (e.g. climate model data for financial risk assessments).[12] Rating agencies began providing ESG metrics on firms' performance with the premise of predicting potential climate exposures and creating shareholder value. As intermediaries they gather information from various sources by monitoring companies in order to measure ESG risks and create a dataset for investors.[13] For instance, they introduce a ratings scale aimed at ranking the sustainability of funds' portfolios with the objective of providing investors with a measure to evaluate how different funds target ESG standards.

3.03 The ratings contain significant value assessments and contribute to determine climate exposure as they focus on a company's strategy to internalize sustainability factors in board structures: their function is fundamental for the purpose of informing investors about material disclosures. As Engert argued, 'ESG ratings articulate what ESG-minded investors demand of firms—they steer the juggernaut's course.'[14] Firms which are positively rated seem less exposed to litigation risk that means lower susceptibility to negative externalities and higher propensity to favourable disclosure report.[15] However, the ESG raters have been under scrutiny because of the different metrics employed to assess a given firm's performance in relation to the same ESG activities.

3.04 Rating scoring elaborates publicly available data and produces evaluations of firms' behaviour incorporating social and environmental values. A significant concern is to standardize ESG scoring by aligning ratings content with

---

11 Longjie Lu, 'Regulating ESG rating firms as the gatekeepers for sustainable finance' (2024) 19(2) *Capital Markets Law Journal* 184.

12 Fiedler et al., 'Business risk and the emergence of climate analytics' (2021) 11(2) *Nature Climate Change*, 91–92.

13 Matteo Gargantini and Michele Siri, 'Information Intermediaries and Sustainability. ESG ratings and benchmarks in the European Union' (2022) ECMI Working Paper Series No 15, https://ssrn.com/abstract=4327309.

14 Andreas Engert, 'ESG Ratings–Guiding a Movement in Search for Itself' (2023) ECGI Law Working Paper No. 727/2023, http://ssrn.com/abstract_id=4525932.

15 Florian Berg, Kornelia Fabisik and Zacharias Sautner, 'Is History Repeating Itself? The (Un)Predictable Past of ESG Ratings' (2021) ECGI Finance Working Paper No. 708/2020, http://ssrn.com/abstract_id=3722087.

sustainability requirements. The variety of metrics developed in the ratings' proprietary methodologies can lead to risks of bias and 'greenwashing' when metrics of ESG data in ratings' models are elaborated to capture firms' behaviour with respect to sustainability.[16] The practice of releasing ESG indexes is fraught with questions concerning the reliability and transparency of ratings' internal models, which makes for increased uncertainty about what sustainability needs to measure using non-financial indicators.[17]

The absence of an accepted definition of ESG performance and the heterogeneity of the metrics complicate matters. The divergences across ESG ratings are likely to produce misleading reports owing to different interpretations of sustainable criteria.[18] As a result, loopholes in interpreting the metrics can exacerbate the appetite for inflated ESG reports. The material risk for corporations would be the high costs of litigation and the reputational impact on markets arising from public scrutiny, which can lead to a downgrade from rating agencies.[19] It is questionable whether raters do in fact elaborate an independent statement of ESG performance since the close relationship with the firms/users in the due diligence and definition of metrics affects the valuation of the company's ability to incorporate social and environmental factors in the financial report. The lack of consistency and accuracy in the disclosures but also the high degree of subjectivity as to what constitutes ESG performance can create incentives for opportunistic behaviours of rating agencies.[20] **3.05**

The practice of rating deviations seems incentivized at the individual firm level: these adjustments affect measures that relate to firm rankings, determining inflated ESG performance and flawed ESG ratings.[21] Conflicts of interest and herding behaviour among ratings users inherently cast doubts on the credibility of ESG ratings.[22] Professional data providers have expanded in the **3.06**

---

16 Becky L. Jacobs and Brad Finney. 'Defining sustainable business beyond greenwashing' (2019) 37(2) *Virginia Environmental Law Journal*, 100–101.

17 HM Treasury. 'Future regulatory regime for Environmental, Social, and Governance (ESG) ratings providers' (2023) Consultation paper (pp. 10–11), https://www.gov.uk/government/consultations/future-regulatory-regime-for-environmental-social-and-governance-esg-ratings-providers.

18 Javier El-Hage, 'Fixing ESG: Are Mandatory ESG Disclosures the Solution to Misleading ESG Ratings?' (2021) 26(2) *Fordham Journal of Corporate and Financial Law*, 368–369.

19 Geetanjali Ganguly, Joana Setzer and Veerle Heyvaert, 'If at First You Don't Succeed: Suing Corporations for Climate Change' (2018) 38(4) *Oxford Journal of Legal Studies*, 865–866.

20 Florian Berg, Julian F. Kölbel and Roberto Rigobon, 'Aggregate Confusion: The Divergence of ESG Ratings' (2022) 26(6) *Review of Finance*, 1317–1318.

21 Suhas A. Sridharan, Yifan Yan and Teri Lombardi Yohn, 'ESG Rating Agency Incentives' (2023), https://ssrn.com/abstract=4476968.

22 David F. Larcker, Lukasz Pomorski, Brian Tayan and Edward M. Watts, 'ESG Ratings: A Compass without Direction' (2022) Rock Center for Corporate Governance at Stanford University Working Paper,

climate sector in order to provide sustainability rankings and ratings, although the reliability of these certifications raises concerns for the lucrative 'user-pays' business model that may result in doubtful outlooks.[23] The Regulation would improve the quality of metrics used in ratings models and to facilitate the comparability and granularity of the ESG taxonomy.

B. THE GATEKEEPERS OF SUSTAINABILITY

3.07 ESG profile of a firm and ESG performance are important indicators to sustainable investing although ESG uncertainty in portfolio decisions and asset pricing affect investors demand because they are more sensitive to ESG information. ESG rating uncertainty reduces investor demand, in particular for green stocks which rely on the assessments of raters. However, the lack of consistency across methodologies and data used by ESG rating agencies represent a barrier for investors when evaluating a firm's risk exposure.[24] Firms lack adequate methodologies and clear indicators for the assessment of environmental hazards. The ESG factors further developed the categories of socially responsible investing which emphasize the ethical and moral effects of investment decisions that should be assessed by ESG ratings. Information providers improve quality and availability although data continues to be one of the largest impediments to climate risk assessment. The content of the ESG requirements and its relevance to investment decision-making entail modelling approaches which should be informed by forward-looking predictions on the climate impact on corporate governance.[25] Integrating sustainability reporting in managerial decision-making entails the costs of gathering ESG information from professional data providers and the costs of changing organizational processes.

---

https://ssrn.com/abstract=4179647.

23 Robert G. Eccles, Jock Herron and George Serafeim, 'Reliable sustainability ratings. The influence of business models on information intermediaries' in Tessa Hebb, James Hawley, Andreas Hoepner, Agnes Neher, David Wood (eds), *The Routledge Handbook of Responsible Investment* (London: Routledge 2015) ch. 48.

24 Doron Avramov, Si Cheng, Abraham Lioui and Andrea Tarelli, 'Sustainable Investing with ESG Rating Uncertainty' (2022) 145(2) *Journal of Financial Economics* 642.

25 Dimitri Zenghelis and Nicholas Stern, 'The importance of looking forward to manage risks: submission to the Task Force on Climate-Related Financial Disclosures' (2016) Policy paper, The London School of Economics and Political Science, Grantham Research Institute on Climate Change and the Environment, London, https://www.lse.ac.uk/granthaminstitute/wp-content/uploads/2016/06/Zenghelis-and-Stern-policy-paper-June-2016.pdf.

Considerable attention to ESG claims has been paid in various quarters because of the financial benefits of mitigating climate-change effects, namely sustainable long-term value and higher risk-adjusted returns for shareholders.[26] Future return dynamics can also manifest themselves in the form of higher quality factors of production such as labour skills, and can be the result of companies' ESG behaviour in the market.[27] ESG investments that support social causes can generate better long-term financial returns and can lower the reputational risk of reporting information.[28] Lack of clarity about the social goals of corporations and ambiguity about sustainable objectives create obstacles to the achievement of a common understanding of ESG disclosures.[29] Integrating ESG factors into corporate and investor decision-making requires companies to change their business models and internal operational systems.[30] **3.08**

The key challenge is to improve the quality of metrics used in ratings models and to facilitate the comparability and granularity of the ESG taxonomy. The need to enhance the analysis of sustainability risk for firms aligns with the objective of this Regulation which addresses loopholes in the regulatory reporting of the ESG factors in the companies' business activities. The absence of adequate methodologies and clear indicators for the assessment of environmental issues as well as the divergences in the international arena on the definition of green investments creates information imbalances that limit the effectiveness of monitoring systems.[31] The broader challenge is standardization. Data is held in consistent formats, or at least translatable into consistent formats, across all institutions. Standardization will include a variety of granular data: agreement and support by regulators for standardized representations of contracts will support greater efficiencies in many aspects of regulatory reporting and oversight.[32] The absence of a common definition of sustainability and sustainable factors along with the various methodologies to assess the ESG performance **3.09**

26 Adam B. Badawi and Frank Partnoy, 'Social Good and Litigation Risk' (2022) 12(2) *Harvard Business Law Review*, 323–324.

27 Lauren Cohen, Umit G. Gurun and Quoc H. Nguyen, 'The ESG-Innovation Disconnect: Evidence from Green Patenting' (2021) ECGI Finance Working Paper No. 744/2021, https://ssrn.com/abstract=3718682.

28 Mark Fulton, Bruce Kahn and Camilla Sharples, 'Sustainable Investing: Establishing Long-Term Value and Performance' (2012), http://dx.doi.org/10.2139/ssrn.2222740.

29 Emirhan Ilhan, Philipp Krueger, Zacharias Sautner and Laura T. Starks, 'Climate Risk Disclosure and Institutional Investors' (2023) 36(7) *Review of Financial Studies* 2617.

30 Dorothy S. Lund and Elizabeth Pollman, 'The Corporate Governance Machine' (2021) 121(8) *Columbia Law Review* 2565.

31 Daniel C. Esty and Quentin Karpilow, 'Harnessing Investor Interest in Sustainability: The Next Frontier in Environmental Information Regulation' (2019) 36(2) *Yale Journal on Regulation* 625.

32 Florencio Lopez-de-Silanes, Joseph A. McCahery and Paul C. Pudschedl, 'ESG Performance and Disclosure' (2020) *Singapore Journal of Legal Studies* 217.

cast doubts on the incentive structure of firms. Considerable advancements in the transition to ESG taxonomy are found at the EU level where several pieces of legislation adopted a mandatory approach to foster green investments and disclosure obligations.[33] However, such a regulatory framework does not include enforcement mechanisms which create a sort of protection for companies that are basically shielded from the 'comply or explain' principle of the climate-policy monitoring system.[34] Further improvements in enforcing ESG standards ensue from the climate risk litigation, which is gaining much attention on the account of its impact on the reputational capital of firms.[35]

C. ESG RATINGS AND SUSTAINABILITY RISK

3.10 To enhance transparency, financial firms tend to rely on ESG data on their decision-making process, as their clients may not disclose information. However, there is a risk of collusive behaviour between other than firms and raters which derives from the high revenues that can be gained though providing lenient assessments.[36] Validating this data is challenging, let alone conducting due diligence: a lack of dialogue and consistency among different banks creates uncertainty surrounding the extent of their commitments. First, there is no comparability: the way these data are measured are not transparent and are difficult to compare among different jurisdictions. For example, it is unclear what benchmark is adopted by banks, as the most objective benchmarks are usually measured through global standard settings (e.g. Taskforce on Nature-related Financial Disclosures). Secondly, there are no binding effects; they are only for reference purposes. Thirdly, there is no real-time update of their practice whether these policies and regulations are complied with by the banks and their corporate clients. Customers rely on the information strategically disclosed by firms to form their perceptions about products' environmental attributes. The conventional method of interbank comparison becomes untenable when addressing sustainability initiatives. ESG ratings providers should address this opacity which exposes the firms' activities to the risk of incomplete and inaccurate data (e.g. greenwashing), methodological inconsistencies

33 Sebastian Steuer and Tobias H. Tröger, 'The Role of Disclosure in Green Finance' (2022) 8(1) *Journal of Financial Regulation* 13–14.

34 Catherine Malecki, 'Climate Finance: A Herculean Task for the Climate Transition' (2020) 25(6) *Environmental Liability* 296.

35 Javier Solana, 'Climate change litigation as financial risk' (2020) 2(4) *Green Finance* 344.

36 Xiang Xiao, Ge Ge and Ziqin Yu, 'Inhibition or inducement: ESG rating changes and earnings management – Based on the perspective of external supervision' (2024) 64 *Finance Research Letters*, https://doi.org/10.1016/j.frl.2024.105428.

and sustainability reporting issues. However, the lack of clarity in defining sustainable assets and ESG metrics (e.g. greenhouse gas emissions, diversity percentages and tax payments) has introduced ambiguity in assessing firms' performance regarding social and environmental values.[37]

Sustainable finance has gained significant emphasis on account of the large debate around the impact of climate change on companies' business models.[38] The ESG ratings reduce the scarcity of climate information and ensure consistency in reporting requirements. As Gordon observed, 'addressing climate change risk can improve risk-adjusted returns for investors holding a diversified portfolio of equity and other investments.'[39] The lack of standardization and comparability of data leaves room for discretionary evaluations of climate change risks, thereby allowing corporations to determine which items of information to include in the disclosures.[40] It is commonly considered that financial reporting reflects a backward-looking and judgement-based approach of information, which raises concerns as regards the achievement of long-term sustainability goals.[41] Integrating sustainability reporting in managerial decision-making entails the costs of gathering ESG information from professional data providers and the costs of changing organizational processes. **3.11**

Firms would not have particular incentives to disclose items of information which involve negative exposure to investors and shareholders. It is likely that they would avoid analyses on materiality parameters because of the high costs of accessing this information.[42] In the absence of mandatory disclosure obligations, firms have an appetite to limit the volume of reporting in order to reduce the burdensome procedures of internal control systems.[43] Further, firms find scant incentives to update their measurement methodologies, making the **3.12**

---

37 Elizabeth Pollman, 'The Making and Meaning of ESG' (2024) 14(2) *Harvard Business Law Review* 403.

38 Marcel Jeucken, *Sustainable Finance and Banking. The Financial Sector and the Future of the Planet* (London: Routledge 2001) 71–72. See also Peer C. Zumbansen and Javad Nasiry, 'Sustainable Transformation of Business and Finance. A democratic challenge in an age of climate change and artificial intelligence' (2023) McGill SGI Academy Impact Paper, https://ssrn.com/abstract=4473822.

39 Jeffrey N. Gordon, 'Unbundling Climate Change Risk from ESG' (2023), https://clsbluesky.law.columbia.edu/2023/07/26/unbundling-climate-change-risk-from-esg/.

40 Torsten Ehlers, Diwen (Nicole) Gao and Frank Packer, 'A taxonomy of sustainable finance taxonomies' (2021) BIS Papers No 118, https://www.bis.org/publ/bppdf/bispap118.pdf.

41 Greg Lusk, 'Looking Forward and Backward at Extreme Event Attribution in Climate Policy' (2022) 25(1) *Ethics, Policy & Environment* 38–39.

42 Aisha I. Saad and Diane Strauss, 'A New "Reasonable Investor" and Changing Frontiers of Materiality: Increasing Investor Reliance on ESG Disclosures and Implications for Securities Litigation' (2020) 17(2) *Berkeley Business Law Journal* 408–409.

43 Iris H-Y Chiu, 'Mandatory Disclosure in Corporate Social Responsibility – The Promises and Limitations' in Michael Nietsch (ed), *Compliance und soziale Verantwortung im Unternehmen* (Nomos, Baden-Baden 2019) 47.

assessment process particularly vulnerable when it comes to capturing climate risks.[44] The classification of material climate risk drivers and their concentration in financial activities depends on the availability of relevant data, which affects the management decision to disclose hazard events. Accurate estimation of climate exposures lowers the costs of tracking pollution emissions and contributes to the mitigation of endogenous financial shocks arising from environmental damages.[45] Although ESG criteria are being refined by industry and rating providers, firms are in need of integrating key and accepted parameters into their business strategies.[46] Sustainable finance and climate change have emerged as an area of renewed interest in the wake of the global financial crisis, when the assessment of firms' risk management was shown to be the key to the prevention of systemic disruption.[47] On this view, ESG ratings reduce the impact of sustainability risk on firms and the challenge of implementing disclosure obligations which raise major concerns regarding firms' behaviour in causing climate exposures.[48] Valuation, while involving an inherent subjective element, can still be carried out using more standardized procedures; and the underlying data and risk factor simulations can be made available to external parties seeking to reach their own judgements on the valuation of assets and other exposures.[49]

44 Daniel Attenborough, 'Corporate Disclosures on Climate Change: An Empirical Analysis of FTSE All-Share British Fossil Fuel Producers' (2022) 22(2) *European Business Organization Law Review*, 334–335.

45 Lee H. Seltzer, Laura Starks and Qifei Zhu, 'Climate Regulatory Risk and Corporate Bonds' (2022) NBER Working Paper 29994, http://www.nber.org/papers/w29994.

46 Georg Inderst, Christopher Kaminker and Fiona Stewart, 'Defining and measuring green investments: implications for institutional investors' asset allocations' (2012) OECD Working Papers on Finance, Insurance and Private Pensions No. 24, https://www.oecd.org/environment/WP_24_Defining_and_Measuring_Green_Investments.pdf.

47 Saloni P. Ramakrishna, *Climate Change Risk Management in Banks. The Next Paradigm* (Berlin: De Gruyter 2024) 42–43.

48 Claire Economidou et al., 'Is sustainability rating material to the market?' (2023) 52(1) *Financial Management* 127.

49 Malcolm Baker, Mark L. Egan and Suproteem K. Sarkar, 'Demand for ESG' (2024) NBER Working Paper 30708, http://www.nber.org/papers/w30708.

TITLE II

PROVISION OF ESG RATINGS IN THE UNION

ARTICLE 4

REQUIREMENTS TO OPERATE IN THE UNION

Iain MacNeil

Any legal person that wishes to operate as an ESG rating provider in the Union shall be subject to one of the following:

(a) an authorisation issued by ESMA as referred to in Article 6;
(b) an equivalence decision as referred to in Article 10 and fulfilment of the conditions referred to in that Article;
(c) an authorisation for endorsement as referred to in Article 11;
(d) a recognition as referred to in Article 12.

A. INTRODUCTION

4.01 Title II sets out the basic entry requirements for ESG rating providers who wish to operate in the EU. Article 4 sets out four options: the first is an authorization to engage in the regulated activity of providing ESG ratings; the second is an equivalence decision granted by ESMA under Article 10 to a third country firm; the third is that an ESG rating provider established in the Union and authorized in accordance with Article 8 may endorse ESG ratings provided by an ESG rating provider established outside the Union and belonging to the same group, subject to conditions; and the fourth is that pending an equivalence decision, a third country ESG rating provider that qualifies as a small company may be recognized by ESMA as eligible to provide ESG ratings in the EU. Each of these options is elaborated in the paragraphs below.

As in many other regulatory domains, authorization is the standard mode of entry for firms wishing to enter into the regulated activity of issuing ESG ratings in the EU. The EU regulatory regime for credit rating agencies, which entered into force in 2009 as a response to the global financial crisis,[1] refers to 'registration' rather than 'authorization', but the focus and substance of that regime is nevertheless very similar to this Regulation. **4.02**

The meaning of 'ESG ratings' is clarified by Article 3(1) to include an ESG opinion and an ESG score or a combination of both. The former refers to an ESG assessment that is based on a rules-based methodology and defined ranking system of rating categories, involving directly a rating analyst in the rating process or systems process. The latter refers to an ESG measure derived from data, using a rule-based methodology, and based only on a pre-established statistical or algorithmic system or model, without any additional substantial analytical input from an analyst. **4.03**

The scope of the Regulation applies to ESG ratings issued by ESG rating providers operating in the EU as defined by Article 2(1). Various exemptions from the Regulation (and by implication authorization) are provided by Article 2(2) including, inter alia, private ESG ratings that are not intended for public distribution and ESG ratings issued by financial undertakings that are used exclusively for internal purposes or for intra-group financial services or products. **4.04**

An implementing decision under Article 10 is a decision that an ESG rating provider established outside the EU (aka a 'third country provider') is authorized and supervised in the third country and that the Commission has adopted an equivalence decision stating that ESG providers in the third country comply with binding requirements that are equivalent to the requirements of this Regulation and that compliance is subject to effective supervision. The equivalence technique forms part of many EU legislative instruments in the financial sector, but it is not a uniform regime as there are differences in its mode of operation according to the financial markets, products and risks under consideration.[2] Further commentary on the equivalence regime for ESG ratings is provided under Article 10. **4.05**

---

1 See generally https://finance.ec.europa.eu/capital-markets-union-and-financial-markets/financial-markets/regulating-credit-rating-agencies_en#:~:text=The%20first%20set%20of%20rules,supervised%20by%20national%20competent%20authorities.

2 See generally Niamh Moloney, 'Third Countries and EU Financial Market Access: Technocracy, Politics, and the End of Deference?' in Jaeger, T, Lehmann, M, Somek, A, and Waibel, M (eds), *Consolidating*

4.06 Endorsement of ESG ratings under Article 11 bears some resemblance to an equivalence decision but it is more limited in the access granted to the EU market and more restrictive in terms of the conditions that are imposed. Article 11 permits an ESG rating provider established and authorized in the EU to endorse ESG ratings provided by an ESG rating provider established outside the EU and belonging to the same group, subject to conditions. An endorsed ESG rating shall be considered an ESG rating provided by the endorsing ESG rating provider, which remains fully responsible for such ratings and compliance with the Regulation. Further commentary on endorsement is provided under Article 11.

4.07 A recognition decision under Article 12 is available prior to the adoption of an equivalence decision under Article 10, or where adopted, in the event the equivalence decision is repealed. To be eligible for such a decision an ESG rating provider established outside the EU must fall with the net turnover limit (currently EUR 8,000,000) in Article 3(5) second subparagraph of the EU accounting directive[3] for the last three consecutive years. There are further conditions linked to a recognition decision which are the discussed in the commentary on Article 12.

Brexit (Verlag Publishing 2023), LSE Legal Studies Working Paper No. 16/2023, https://ssrn.com/abstract=4492090 or http://dx.doi.org/10.2139/ssrn.4492090

3 Directive 2013/34/EU L182/19.

ARTICLE 5

TEMPORARY REGIME FOR SMALL ESG RATING PROVIDERS

Iain MacNeil

1. **By way of derogation from Article 4, an ESG rating provider categorised as a small undertaking or as a small group within the meaning of Article 3(2), first subparagraph, or Article 3(5), first subparagraph, respectively, of Directive 2013/34/EU (the 'small ESG rating provider') that is established in the Union and wishes to operate in the Union shall only be subject to Article 15(1), (5) and (7), Articles 23 and 24 and Articles 32 to 37 of this Regulation, provided that it:**
   (a) **notifies ESMA of its intention to operate in the Union; and**
   (b) **has been registered by ESMA before it starts operating in the Union.**
2. **Within 90 working days of receipt of the notification referred to in paragraph 1, point (a), ESMA shall decide whether to register the notifier as a small ESG rating provider. ESMA shall inform the notifier of its decision within five working days thereof.**
3. **Where an ESG rating provider referred to in paragraph 1 of this Article ceases to be categorised as a small ESG rating provider, or three years after its registration in accordance with paragraph 1, point (b), of this Article, whichever occurs first, the ESG rating provider shall become subject to all provisions of this Regulation and shall within six months apply for authorisation to operate in the Union pursuant to Chapter 1 of this Title.**
4. **The ESG rating providers referred to in paragraph 1 of this Article may choose to opt in to this Regulation by applying to ESMA for authorisation pursuant to Article 6. Where ESG rating providers choose to opt in, this Regulation shall become applicable to them in its entirety.**

A. INTRODUCTION

5.01 Article 5 sets out a special regime for small ESG rating providers with exemptions from the standard requirements under the Regulation. Recital 48 recognizes the need to have measures supporting smaller ESG rating providers and while the global dominance of large US firms is not mentioned it is a well-established fact. The exemptions are subject to the provision of notification to ESMA and registration with ESMA prior to the start of operations in the EU. As well as setting aside the need for authorization, the special regime limits the application of general principles to: the principle of independence in Article 15(1); the principle of due diligence in Article 15(5); and the principle that rating methodologies are rigorous, systematic, independent and capable of justification and applied in a transparent manner in Article 15(7). These principles represent the core of the general obligations imposed on ESG ratings providers and they overlap to some extent with the other general principles that do not apply to small ESG rating providers. Thus, the precise scope of these exemptions remains unclear and may not amount to much if the applicable principles are interpreted broadly.

5.02 The reference to a small undertaking or group in Article 5(1) is to undertakings which on their balance sheet dates do not exceed the limits of at least two of the three following criteria:

(a) balance sheet total: EUR 5,000,000;
(b) net turnover: EUR 10,000,000;
(c) average number of employees during the financial year: 50.

5.03 Article 5 limits the application of other provisions of the Regulation to Articles 23 and 24 (transparency and disclosures) and the powers referred to in Articles 32 to 37 (powers of competent authorities, ESMA's supervisory powers, sanctions). This means in particular that a small ESG ratings provider is not subject to the requirement to separate its ratings business from other activities (Article 16) nor to the requirements as regards the expertise and conflicts of interest of ESG ratings analysts (Article 17).

The regime for small ESG rating providers is temporary in nature as it ends three years after registration with ESMA or earlier if the ESG rating provider ceases to qualify as a small undertaking as defined in Article 5(2). In that case, the ESG rating provider is required to apply for authorization within 6 months. 5.04

CHAPTER 1

AUTHORIZATION OF ESG RATING PROVIDERS ESTABLISHED IN THE UNION TO OPERATE IN THE UNION

ARTICLE 6

APPLICATION FOR AUTHORIZATION TO OPERATE IN THE UNION

Iain MacNeil

1. Legal persons established in the Union that wish to operate in the Union pursuant to Article 2(1), point (a), shall apply to ESMA for authorisation.

2. An application for authorisation as referred to in paragraph 1 shall contain all of the information listed in Annex I to this Regulation and shall be submitted in any of the official languages of the Union. Council Regulation No 1[1] shall apply *mutatis mutandis* to any other communication between ESMA and ESG rating providers and their staff.

3. ESMA shall develop draft regulatory technical standards to specify further the information listed in Annex I.

ESMA shall submit the draft regulatory technical standards referred to in the first subparagraph to the Commission by 2 October 2025.

Power is delegated to the Commission to supplement this Regulation by adopting the regulatory technical standards referred to in the first subparagraph of this paragraph in accordance with the procedure laid down in Articles 10 to 14 of Regulation (EU) No 1095/2010.

4. An authorised ESG rating provider shall comply at all times with the requirements under which the initial authorisation was granted.

5. ESG rating providers shall notify ESMA of any material changes to the circumstances under which the initial authorisation was granted, including any opening or closing of a branch within the Union, without undue delay.

---

1 Council Regulation No 1 determining the languages to be used by the European Economic Community (OJ 17, 6.10.1958, p. 385).

A. INTRODUCTION

6.01 Article 6 sets out the information required to be submitted to ESMA in connection with an application for authorization as an ESG rating provider. Annex 1 provides a list of the relevant information and ESMA is empowered to develop draft regulatory standards to specify further the information listed in Annex 1. Delegation of such powers to ESMA and other EU agencies has become common in recent years as a technique to separate technical aspects and implementation from the policy choices that are the main focus of legislative instruments.[2]

6.02 An authorized ESG ratings provider is required to comply with the conditions for initial authorization at all times and to notify ESMA of any material changes to the conditions for initial authorization without delay.

2 See Elizabeth Howell, 'EU agencification and the rise of ESMA: are its governance arrangements fit for purpose?' (2019) 78(2) *Cambridge Law Journal* 324–354.

ARTICLE 7

EXAMINATION BY ESMA OF THE APPLICATION FOR AUTHORIZATION TO OPERATE IN THE UNION AS AN ESG RATING PROVIDER

Iain MacNeil

1. Within 25 working days of receipt of an application as referred to in Article 6(2), ESMA shall assess whether the application is complete. Where the application is not complete, ESMA shall set a deadline by which the applicant is to provide any missing information.
2. Once it assesses that an application is complete, ESMA shall notify the applicant thereof.
3. Within 90 working days of the notification referred to in paragraph 2 of this Article, ESMA shall adopt a fully reasoned decision, as referred to in Article 8(1), to grant or refuse authorisation to operate as an ESG rating provider in the Union.
4. ESMA may extend the period referred to in paragraph 3 of this Article to 120 working days, in particular where the applicant:
   (a) envisages endorsing ESG ratings as referred to in Article 11;
   (b) envisages using outsourcing; or
   (c) requests exemption from compliance in accordance with Article 22.
5. The decision adopted by ESMA pursuant to paragraph 3 shall take effect on the fifth working day following its adoption.
6. If the applicant does not provide any requested missing information by the expiry of the deadline referred to in paragraph 1, ESMA shall reject the application.

If no decision is adopted by ESMA within the period referred to in paragraph 3 or 4, the application shall be deemed rejected.

A. INTRODUCTION

7.01 Article 7 sets out the process for examination of applications for authorization received by ESMA. The first step is for ESMA to determine that an application is complete and notify the applicant.

7.02 The second stage in the process is the adoption of a fully reasoned decision to authorize or refuse authorization. This is normally subject to a 90-day time-limit but that may be extended to 120 days in the circumstances identified in Article 7(4).

7.03 The third stage is the taking effect of an authorization decision, which is on the fifth day following its adoption.

7.04 Applications are deemed to be rejected in the circumstances falling within Article 7(6).

ARTICLE 8

DECISION TO GRANT OR REFUSE AUTHORIZATION TO OPERATE IN THE UNION AND NOTIFICATION OF THAT DECISION

Iain MacNeil

1. **ESMA shall adopt a fully reasoned decision authorising an applicant to operate in the Union as an ESG rating provider where it concludes from its examination of the application referred to in Article 7 that the applicant complies with the requirements for the provision of ESG ratings set out in this Regulation.**

   Where ESMA, after examining the application, concludes that the applicant does not meet the requirements for the provision of ESG ratings set out in this Regulation, it shall adopt a fully reasoned decision refusing that authorisation.
2. **ESMA shall inform the applicant within five working days of the decision referred to in paragraph 1.**
3. **ESMA shall inform the Commission, EBA and EIOPA of any decision taken pursuant to paragraph 1.**
4. **The authorisation shall be effective for the entire territory of the Union.**

A. INTRODUCTION

8.01 Article 8 sets out the circumstances in which ESMA shall authorize an applicant as an ESG rating provider. The reference to 'shall authorize' is more explicit in terms of the obligation of ESMA than the counterpart provisions relating to credit rating agencies[1] or investment firms[2] but it remains the case that ESMA must conclude that the applicant complies with the conditions for the provision of ratings set out in this Regulation. An authorization decision must be communicated to the applicant within five working days and the Commission, EBA and EIOPA must be informed of the decision.

8.02 An authorization is effective for the entire Union, with the result that ESG ratings can be issued across the entire EU.

1 See Article 17 of Regulation 1060/2009 on credit rating agencies, OJ [2009] L302/1 (as amended), aka the Consolidated Credit Rating Agency Regulation (CCRAR).

2 See Article 7 of Directive 2014/65/EU on Markets in Financial Instruments OJ L173/349 (as amended).

ARTICLE 9

SUSPENSION OR WITHDRAWAL OF AUTHORIZATION

Iain MacNeil

1. ESMA shall adopt a decision suspending or withdrawing the authorisation of an ESG rating provider referred to in Article 8(1), first subparagraph, where the ESG rating provider:
  (a) has expressly renounced the authorisation or has provided no ESG ratings for the preceding 12 months;
  (b) has obtained its authorisation by making false statements or by any other irregular means;
  (c) no longer meets the conditions under which it was authorised; or
  (d) has seriously or repeatedly infringed this Regulation.

2. ESMA shall inform the ESG rating provider without undue delay of any decision taken pursuant to paragraph 1. The decision on the withdrawal or suspension of authorisation shall take immediate effect throughout the Union.

3. ESMA shall also inform the competent authorities, the Commission, EBA and EIOPA of any decision taken pursuant to paragraph 1.

A. INTRODUCTION

9.01 Article 9 sets out the circumstances in which ESMA is required to withdraw or suspend the authorization of an ESG rating provider. The reference to inactivity as a basis for withdrawal or suspension of authorization follows the approach for investment services[1] and credit ratings[2] except that the period of time is extended in Article 9 to 12 months.

9.02 A decision on withdrawal or suspension takes immediate effect and must be communicated to the Commission, the EBA and EIOPA.

1 See Article 8 of MiFID II as amended.
2 See Article 20 of the CRA Regulation 1060/2009 as amended.

CHAPTER 2

EQUIVALENCE, ENDORSEMENT AND RECOGNITION OF ESG RATING PROVIDERS ESTABLISHED OUTSIDE THE UNION TO OPERATE IN THE UNION

ARTICLE 10

EQUIVALENCE REGIME

Iain MacNeil

1. An ESG rating provider established outside the Union that wishes to operate in the Union pursuant to Article 2(1), point (b), shall only be able to do so where it is included in the register referred to in Article 14 and provided that all of the following conditions are met:

(a) the ESG rating provider established outside the Union is authorised or registered as an ESG rating provider in the third country concerned and is subject to supervision in that third country;

(b) the ESG rating provider established outside the Union has notified ESMA that it wishes to operate in the Union and has submitted to ESMA proof of its authorisation or registration as an ESG rating provider, the documents required for such authorisation or registration in the third country concerned, as well as the name of the third-country competent authority responsible for its supervision, and has received confirmation from ESMA as regards the completeness of the information provided;

(c) the Commission has adopted an equivalence decision pursuant to paragraph 2;

(d) the cooperation arrangements referred to in paragraph 4 are operational.

2. The Commission may adopt an equivalence decision by means of an implementing act stating that the legal framework and supervisory practice of a third country ensure that:

(a) ESG rating providers authorised or registered in that third country comply with binding requirements which are equivalent to the requirements of this Regulation;

(b) compliance with the binding requirements referred to in point (a) is subject to effective supervision and enforcement on an ongoing basis in that third country.

Such an implementing act shall be adopted in accordance with the examination procedure referred to in Article 48.

3. The Commission may adopt a delegated act in accordance with Article 47 to specify the conditions referred to in paragraph 2, first subparagraph, of this Article. The Commission may subject the application of the implementing act referred to in paragraph 2 of this Article to:

(a) the effective fulfilment on an ongoing basis by the third country concerned of any condition set out in that implementing act that aims to ensure equivalent supervisory and regulatory standards;
(b) the ability of ESMA to effectively exercise the monitoring responsibilities referred to in Article 33 of Regulation (EU) No 1095/2010.

4. ESMA shall establish cooperation arrangements with the third-country competent authorities whose legal framework and supervisory practices have been recognised as equivalent in accordance with paragraph 2. Such arrangements shall specify at least the following:
(a) the mechanism for exchanging information on a regular and ad hoc basis between ESMA and the third-country competent authorities concerned, including access to all relevant information requested by ESMA regarding the ESG rating provider authorised or registered in that third country;
(b) the mechanism for prompt notification to ESMA where a third-country competent authority deems that the ESG rating provider authorised or registered in that third country and supervised by that third-country competent authority is breaching the conditions of its authorisation or registration, or other provisions of national law in that third country;
(c) the procedures concerning the coordination of supervisory activities, including on-site inspections;
(d) the mechanism for prompt notification to ESMA where a third-country competent authority takes any regulatory or supervisory actions in relation to the ESG rating provider authorised or registered in that third country, including any change that might have an impact on the ESG rating provider's continued compliance with applicable laws and regulations;
(e) the mechanism for prompt notification to the third-country competent authority where ESMA issues a public notice in accordance with Article 35 to the ESG rating provider authorised or registered in that third country.

For the purpose of the first subparagraph of this paragraph, where ESMA is informed that an ESG rating provider established outside the Union no longer meets the conditions to be authorised or registered in its country of authorisation or registration, ESMA shall remove it from the register referred to in Article 14.

5. For the purpose of paragraph 1, point (b), ESMA shall assess whether the information is complete within 20 working days of its receipt. If ESMA deems that the information is not complete, ESMA shall set a deadline by which the ESG rating provider is to provide any missing information. Once it assesses that a submission is complete, ESMA shall inform the ESG rating provider of the outcome of the process no later than 60 working days from the date of the initial notification.

A. INTRODUCTION

10.01 Article 10 sets out the process by which an ESG rating provider authorized or registered in a third country can access the EU market through an equivalence decision adopted by the Commission. Recital 29 provides some context for understanding the equivalence regime through its reference to the objectives of market integrity, investor protection and proper enforcement. Underlying that observation is the reality that many of the major ESG rating providers are based outside the EU and it is therefore necessary for the EU to integrate effectively with the operation of the global ESG rating market.

10.02 In principle, regulatory regimes can be divided into two main categories in terms of their treatment of third country firms. Those based on 'deference' allow third country firms to enter the host national market based on an evaluation that their home country regime is equivalent to the host regime. On the other hand, in 'national treatment' regimes, firms from third countries are required to conform to the host state regulatory regime. Hybrid variants can of course be developed with elements of each approach and dynamic development is evident as the policy on equivalence responds to political and regulatory priorities.[1]

10.03 For an equivalence decision to be adopted it is necessary that the Commission be satisfied that ESG rating providers in the third country are subject to equivalent regulation and that compliance is subject to effective supervision. The relevant implementing decision can include a forward-looking dimension in that it can be subject to effective fulfilment on an on-going basis of conditions that ensure equivalence and ensure that effective supervision is in place. ESMA has indicated in the context of CRAs that the overall evaluation of equivalence is holistic, which means that there remains some scope for divergence so long as the objectives of the EU regime are met.[2]

---

1 See generally Moloney (2023), commentary on Article 4.

2 See ESMA, Technical advice on regulatory equivalence – US, Canada and Australia (2012) p. 3 (available at https://www.esma.europa.eu/sites/default/files/library/2015/11/2012_-259_0.pdf) stating, in connection with CCRAR, that 'The equivalence assessment conducted by ESMA follows an objective-based approach, where the capability of the regime in the third country to meet the objectives of the EU Regulation is assessed from a holistic perspective.'

It remains to be seen how important the equivalence regime will become in practice in the context of ESG rating providers. Generally speaking, there has been a significant variation in the number of equivalence decisions made by the Commission (under advice from ESMA) in connection with other equivalence regimes, with relatively few in respect of CCRAR which is similar in its approach to the ESG Ratings Regulation.[3] That outcome can be explained to some extent by the different options open to third country firms to access the EU market – and in this connection Recital 29 notes that endorsement is likely to be attractive to third country ESG rating providers structured as a corporate group, while recognition is likely to be attractive to providers who qualify as 'small' under the Regulation. Endorsement is discussed further under Article 11 and recognition under Article 12. 10.04

It is also a condition for gaining EU market access through an equivalence decision that cooperation arrangements between ESMA and the competent authorities of the third country are operational. 10.05

3 See generally https://finance.ec.europa.eu/eu-and-world/equivalence-non-eu-financial-frameworks_en

ARTICLE 11

ENDORSEMENT OF ESG RATINGS PROVIDED BY ESG RATING PROVIDERS ESTABLISHED OUTSIDE THE UNION

Iain MacNeil

1. An ESG rating provider established in the Union and authorised in accordance with Article 8 may endorse ESG ratings provided by an ESG rating provider established outside the Union and belonging to the same group provided that all of the following conditions are met:

(a) the ESG rating provider established in the Union has applied to ESMA for authorisation of such endorsement;

(b) the ESG rating provider established in the Union fulfils the following indicators of minimum substance:

(i) it has its own premises or premises for its exclusive use in a Member State;

(ii) it has at least one active bank account of its own in the Union; and

(iii) it has an appropriate analytical and decision-making presence in the Union having regard to the nature, scale or complexity of its activities in the Union;

(c) the endorsement of the ESG rating does not impair the quality of the assessment of the rated item, or the issuer of a rated item, or the arrangement of on-site reviews or visits, where provided for in the ESG rating methodology used by the ESG rating provider established outside the Union;

(d) the ESG rating provider established in the Union has verified and is able to demonstrate on an ongoing basis to ESMA that the issuance and distribution of endorsed ESG ratings fulfils requirements which are at least as stringent as the requirements of this Regulation; the ESG rating provider established in the Union shall be permitted to demonstrate compliance with those requirements without being required to refer to the specific process followed for each individual rating;

(e) the ESG rating provider established in the Union has the necessary expertise to effectively monitor the ESG ratings provided by the ESG rating provider established outside the Union, in order to manage any associated risks;

(f) there is an objective reason why the ESG ratings need to be endorsed for their use in the Union, which can include factors such as the specificities of the ESG ratings, the need for proximity of the production of the ESG ratings to the issuer or to a specific economic reality, a particular industry, centres of excellence for sub-components of environmental, social and human rights, or governance factors, the availability of specific skills required for the production of the ESG ratings, the material availability of input data and the development of ESG ratings through the collaboration of global teams;
(g) the ESG rating provider established in the Union provides ESMA at its request with all information necessary to enable ESMA to supervise compliance by the ESG rating provider established outside the Union, where relevant to the endorsed rating, with this Regulation on an ongoing basis;
(h) where an ESG rating provider established outside the Union is subject to supervision, an appropriate cooperation arrangement is in place between ESMA and the competent authority of the third country where the ESG rating provider is established, to ensure an efficient exchange of information.

2. An ESG rating provider established in the Union that applies for authorisation of an endorsement as referred to in paragraph 1, point (a), shall provide ESMA with all information necessary to satisfy ESMA that, at the time of application, the conditions referred to in that paragraph are fulfilled.
3. Within 45 working days of receipt of a complete application for authorisation of an endorsement as referred to in paragraph 1, point (a), but no later than 85 working days after receipt of the initial application, ESMA shall examine the application and decide either to authorise the endorsement or to refuse it. ESMA shall notify the applicant of that decision within five working days.
4. An endorsed ESG rating shall be considered to be an ESG rating provided by the endorsing ESG rating provider. The endorsing ESG rating provider shall not use the endorsement to avoid or circumvent the requirements of this Regulation.
5. An endorsing ESG rating provider shall remain fully responsible for the endorsed ESG ratings and for compliance with the requirements of this Regulation.
6. Where ESMA has well-founded reasons to consider that the conditions laid down in this Article are no longer fulfilled, it shall have the power to require the endorsing ESG rating provider to cease the endorsement, without prejudice to the imposition of any applicable

supervisory measures, fines and periodic penalty payments in accordance with Articles 35, 36 and 37.

A. INTRODUCTION

11.01 The endorsement process in Article 11 can be considered as a modified version of the Article 10 equivalence regime that is applicable to instances where an ESG rating provider organized as a group has an establishment in the EU.[1] It is a hybrid model that adopts elements of both the deference and national treatment approaches mentioned in para 10.002. This is because Article 11(1)(d) requires that ESG ratings that are endorsed by a group's EU establishment must meet the requirement that they are issued and distributed under a home state regulatory regime that is at least as stringent as the requirements of this Regulation. There are further requirements relating to 'minimum substance' that aim to ensure that the EU establishment has a real and effective presence in the EU. Importantly, Article 11(5) provides that an ESG rating provider that has endorsed ESG ratings issued by an ESG rating provider established outside the Union shall remain fully responsible for such ESG ratings and for compliance with the obligations under this Regulation.

11.02 The requirement in Article 11(1)(5) is somewhat cryptic in its objective and effect. The requirement that 'there is an objective reason why the ESG ratings have to be endorsed for their use in the Union…' seems to some extent self-referential and circular as the requirement for endorsement arises as a result of previously unregulated ESG ratings now falling within the scope of this Regulation. The implication seems to be that endorsement should not be available as a substitute for an equivalence decision (which is a more stringent process) but the reference in recital 27 to '…an objective reason justifying why the endorsed ratings are issued by a provider established outside the Union' does

1 In this sense the endorsement procedure follows the model in the CRAR – see ESMA, 'Final Report, Technical advice on CRA regulatory equivalence – CRA 3 update' para 13 (available at https://www.esma.europa.eu/sites/default/files/library/esma33-9-207_technical_advice_on_cra_regulatory_equivalence_-_cra_3_update.pdf) where ESMA states that 'The endorsement MF [methodological framework] consists of a subset of the criteria considered in the equivalence MF. However, unlike the equivalence regime, the endorsement regime contains safeguards beyond the legal and supervisory framework of the third country to ensure the quality of the rating activities.'

not seem to align clearly with the requirement of Article 11(1)(f) that '...there is an objective reason why the ESG ratings have to be endorsed for their use in the Union.' While the two requirements may be intended as reciprocals, the former likely relates to the group structure and capabilities of the ESG rating provider and the latter to the normative effect of the Regulation. But even with this confusion the compliance burden and risk seem low as there are a wide range of factors that fall within the scope of objective reasons why the endorsement process is adopted.

The process for an EU authorized ESG rating provider to gain endorsement is set out in Article 11(2). Reference is also made to the power of ESMA to withdraw endorsement if there are well-founded reasons to consider that the conditions for the grant of endorsement are no longer fulfilled. **11.03**

ARTICLE 12

RECOGNITION OF ESG RATING PROVIDERS ESTABLISHED OUTSIDE THE UNION

Iain MacNeil

1. **Until such time as the Commission has adopted an equivalence decision as referred to in Article 10 or, where adopted, in the event that the equivalence decision is repealed, an ESG rating provider established outside the Union with an annual net turnover of all of its activities that is below the maximum amount set in Article 3(2), second subparagraph, of Directive 2013/34/EU, for each of the last three consecutive years may operate in the Union provided that ESMA has recognised that ESG rating provider in accordance with this Article. An ESG rating provider established outside the Union that belongs to a group as defined in Article 2, point (11), of Directive 2013/34/EU whose consolidated annual net turnover of all of the group's activities is below the maximum amount set in Article 3(5), second subparagraph, of Directive 2013/34/EU, for each of the last three consecutive years may operate in the Union provided that ESMA has recognised that ESG rating provider in accordance with this Article. To that end, ESMA may take into account either an assessment by an independent external auditor or a certification of the competent authority of the third country where the ESG rating provider is established.**
2. **ESG rating providers established outside the Union that wish to be recognised as referred to in paragraph 1 shall comply with the requirements laid down in this Regulation and submit an application for recognition to ESMA.**
3. **An ESG rating provider established outside the Union that wishes to be recognised as referred to in paragraph 1 shall have a legal representative. That legal representative shall be a legal person established in the Union and expressly appointed by the ESG rating provider to act on its behalf. The legal representative shall demonstrate to ESMA that the**

ESG rating provider meets the requirements of this Regulation on an ongoing basis and shall be accountable to ESMA in that respect. The legal representative shall, upon request, provide ESMA with all information necessary to satisfy ESMA that the ESG rating provider fulfils the requirements of this Regulation.

4. An ESG rating provider established outside the Union shall, when submitting an application for recognition as referred to in paragraph 2, provide ESMA with the following:
   (a) all information listed in Annex I;
   (b) all information necessary to demonstrate that the conditions laid down in paragraph 1 of this Article are met;
   (c) all information necessary to satisfy ESMA that the ESG rating provider established outside the Union has established the necessary arrangements to meet the requirements referred to in paragraphs 2 and 3 of this Article;
   (d) the list of its actual or prospective ESG ratings which are intended for distribution in the Union;
   (e) where applicable, the name and contact details of the third-country competent authority responsible for its supervision.

   Within 90 working days of receipt of the application for recognition referred to in paragraph 2, ESMA shall decide whether to grant recognition. ESMA shall inform the applicant of its decision within five working days of the decision.
5. ESMA shall recognise the ESG rating provider established outside the Union provided that all of the following conditions are met:
   (a) the ESG rating provider established outside the Union has complied with paragraphs 2, 3 and 4;
   (b) where the ESG rating provider established outside the Union is subject to supervision, ESMA shall seek to put in place an appropriate cooperation arrangement with the relevant competent authority of the third country where the ESG rating provider is established, in order to ensure an efficient exchange of information.
6. ESMA shall adopt a decision rejecting the application where ESMA is prevented from exercising effectively its supervisory functions under this Regulation by the laws, regulations or administrative provisions of the third country where the ESG rating provider is established, or, where applicable, by limitations in the supervisory and investigatory powers of that third country's competent authority.
7. ESMA shall impose fines in accordance with Article 36, or suspend or, where appropriate, withdraw the recognition referred to in paragraph 1 of this Article, in line with Article 9, where it has well-founded

reasons, based on documented evidence, to consider that the ESG rating provider:

(a) is acting, or has been acting, in a manner which is clearly prejudicial to the interests of users of ESG ratings or to the orderly functioning of markets;

(b) has seriously infringed this Regulation;

(c) has made false statements or used any other irregular means to obtain the recognition.

8. Where the ESG rating provider recognised under this Article by ESMA no longer meets the conditions laid down in paragraph 1, it shall notify ESMA thereof without undue delay.

The ESG rating provider shall notify ESMA within three months of the date when it no longer meets the conditions laid down in paragraph 1 if it wishes to continue offering its services in the Union and shall apply for authorisation within 12 months of that date. In the absence of such notification, the ESG rating provider shall cease to operate in the Union.

9. ESMA shall develop draft regulatory technical standards to determine the form and content of the application for recognition referred to in paragraph 2 and, in particular, the presentation of the information required in paragraph 4.

ESMA shall submit the draft regulatory technical standards referred to in the first subparagraph to the Commission by 2 October 2025.

Power is delegated to the Commission to supplement this Regulation by adopting the regulatory technical standards referred to in the first subparagraph of this paragraph in accordance with the procedure laid down in Articles 10 to 14 of Regulation (EU) No 1095/2010.

A. INTRODUCTION

12.01 Article 12 sets out a regime for small ESG rating providers established in third countries to access the EU market. The regime falls within the category of 'national treatment' as mentioned in para 10.002 as the provider is required to comply with this Regulation. There is no requirement for an establishment in the EU, but the provider is required to have a legal representative in the EU who is accountable to ESMA for the provider's compliance with this Regulation.

The Article 12 regime for small providers differs from the temporary regime in Article 5 in that it is in principle of unlimited duration. However, unlike the Article 5 regime, Article 12 offers no exemptions from compliance with this Regulation. Article 12(2) is explicit in requiring 'recognised' providers from third countries to comply with this Regulation. Furthermore, recognition is made conditional on there being no barriers in the home country to effective supervision by ESMA. But Article 12 falls short of requiring a cooperation agreement to be in place with any home state competent authority as ESMA is required only to 'seek' to put such an arrangement in place. **12.02**

The process for gaining recognition does not subject applicants to the more stringent information requirements associated with an application for authorization in Article 6. ESMA is empowered to draft RTS in connection with the content of applications for recognition. **12.03**

ARTICLE 13

COOPERATION ARRANGEMENTS

Iain MacNeil

1. Any cooperation arrangement as referred to in Article 10(4), Article 11(1), point (h), and Article 12(5), point (b), shall be subject to guarantees of professional secrecy which are at least equivalent to those set out in Article 46. The exchange of information performed under such cooperation arrangements shall be intended for the performance of the tasks of ESMA or the third-country competent authorities.

2. With regard to transfers of personal data to a third country, ESMA shall apply Regulation (EU) 2018/1725 of the European Parliament and of the Council.[1]

A. INTRODUCTION

13.01 Article 13 sets out requirements for cooperation arrangements with third country supervisors in connection with professional secrecy.

13.02 In the case of transfer of data to third countries, ESMA is bound by the requirements applicable to other EU institutions.

1 Regulation (EU) 2018/1725 of the European Parliament and of the Council of 23 October 2018 on the protection of natural persons with regard to the processing of personal data by the Union institutions, bodies, offices and agencies and on the free movement of such data, and repealing Regulation (EC) No 45/2001 and Decision No 1247/2002/EC (OJ L 295, 21.11.2018, p. 39).

CHAPTER 3

REGISTER AND ACCESSIBILITY OF INFORMATION

ARTICLE 14

REGISTER OF ESG RATING PROVIDERS AND ACCESSIBILITY OF INFORMATION ON THE EUROPEAN SINGLE ACCESS POINT

Andrea Miglionico

1. **ESMA shall establish and maintain a register that contains the following information:**
   - **(a) the identities of the ESG rating providers authorised pursuant to Article 8 or registered under the temporary regime for small ESG rating providers pursuant to Article 5(1);**
   - **(b) the identities of the ESG rating providers established outside the Union that comply with the conditions laid down in Article 10 and the third-country competent authorities responsible for the supervision of those ESG rating providers;**
   - **(c) the identities of the endorsing ESG rating providers and the endorsed ESG rating providers established outside the Union referred to in Article 11, and, where applicable, the third-country competent authorities responsible for the supervision of the endorsed ESG rating providers;**
   - **(d) the identities of the ESG rating providers established outside the Union that have been recognised in accordance with Article 12, the legal representatives established in the Union of those ESG rating providers and, where applicable, the third-country competent authorities responsible for the supervision of those ESG rating providers.**
2. **The register referred to in paragraph 1 shall be publicly accessible on the website of ESMA and shall be updated without delay, as necessary.**
3. **From 1 January 2028, when making public any information referred to in Article 19(1) and Article 23(1) of this Regulation, the ESG rating provider shall submit that information at the same time to the collection body referred to in paragraph 6 of this Article for the purpose of making it accessible on the European single access point (ESAP) established under Regulation (EU) 2023/2859.**

In order to verify whether a person is operating in the Union pursuant to Article 2(1), ESMA may use the powers conferred on it by Articles 32, 33 and 34 in respect of the person concerned or any third parties who enable the person concerned to carry out the ESG rating activity.

4. That information shall comply with the following requirements:

(a) be prepared in a data extractable format as defined in Article 2, point (3), of Regulation (EU) 2023/2859 or, where required under Union law, in a machine-readable format, as defined in Article 2, point (4), of Regulation (EU) 2023/2859;

(b) be accompanied by the following metadata;

(i) a full business name and, if applicable, the name used for marketing purposes and the abbreviation of the name of the ESG rating provider to which that information relates;

(ii) where available, the legal entity identifier of the ESG rating provider as specified pursuant to Article 7(4), point (b), of Regulation (EU) 2023/2859;

(iii) the type of information as classified pursuant to Article 7(4), point (c), of Regulation (EU) 2023/2859;

(iv) the size of the ESG rating provider as specified pursuant to Article 7(4), point (d), of Regulation (EU) 2023/2859;

(v) an indication of whether the information contains personal data.

(h) the level of cooperation of the ESG rating provider with ESMA, without prejudice to the need to ensure the disgorgement of profits gained or losses avoided by that ESG rating provider due to the infringement;

(i) any previous infringements by the ESG rating provider;

(j) measures taken after the infringement by the ESG rating provider to prevent its repetition.

5. For the purposes of paragraph 4, point (b)(ii), the ESG rating provider shall obtain a legal entity identifier.

6. For the purpose of making the information referred to in paragraph 1 of this Article accessible on ESAP, the collection body as defined in Article 2, point (2), of Regulation (EU) 2023/2859 shall be ESMA.

7. From 1 January 2028, the information referred to in paragraph 1 and in Article 11(3), Article 35(6) and Article 38(1) of this Regulation shall be made accessible on ESAP. For that purpose, the collection body as defined in Article 2, point (2), of Regulation (EU) 2023/2859 shall be ESMA.

That information shall:

(a) be prepared in a data extractable format as defined in Article 2, point (3), of Regulation (EU) 2023/2859;

(b) be accompanied by the following metadata:

(i) **all the names of the ESG rating providers to which the information relates;**
(ii) **where available, the legal entity identifier of the ESG rating provider as specified pursuant to Article 7(4), point (b), of Regulation (EU) 2023/2859;**
(iii) **the type of information as classified pursuant to Article 7(4), point (c), of Regulation (EU) 2023/2859;**
(iv) **an indication of whether the information contains personal data.**

8. **For the purpose of ensuring an efficient collection and management of information submitted in accordance with paragraph 3, ESMA shall develop draft implementing technical standards to specify:**
(a) **any other metadata to accompany the information;**
(b) **the structuring of data in the information;**
(c) **for which information a machine-readable format is required and which machine-readable format is to be used.**

For the purposes of the first subparagraph, point (c), ESMA shall assess the advantages and disadvantages of different machine-readable formats and conduct appropriate field tests, in consultation with relevant stakeholders.

ESMA shall submit the draft implementing technical standards referred to in the first subparagraph to the Commission.

Power is conferred on the Commission to adopt the implementing technical standards referred to in the first subparagraph of this paragraph in accordance with Article 15 of Regulation (EU) No 1095/2010.

9. **Where necessary, ESMA shall adopt guidelines for entities to ensure that the metadata submitted in accordance with paragraph 8, first subparagraph, point (a), are correct.**

A. INTRODUCTION

14.01 The article empowers ESMA to govern the registry of the authorized ESG rating providers under the conditions set in Articles 5 and 8 and Articles 10–12 of the Regulation. It is a provision which confers to ESMA the authority to monitor the registration process of ESG ratings, in particular the identities of providers operating outside the Union under the third-country supervisory regime. Paragraph 2 highlights the responsibility of authority to undertake the control over ESG ratings' activities which should be made publicly accessible on the website of ESMA and should be updated in a timely manner. The article reflects the regulatory requirements of maintaining complete disclosure on information and characteristics of ratings providers which need to comply with the European Single Access Point (ESAP) established under Regulation No 2859 of 2023.[1]

B. THE ESAP REGIME

The establishment of the ESAP, a centralized platform that provides clear and comprehensive information for investors and other users, constitutes a cornerstone section of the Capital Markets Union Action Plan.[2] The purpose of the ESAP is to facilitate access to publicly available information of relevance to financial services, capital markets and sustainability.[3] The ESAP is a fundamental enabler of the EU's Digital Strategy and the Digital Finance Strategy[4]: any in-scope information, document or report made public under EU law by an entity – including credit rating agencies – needs to be submitted to the collection body in a data extractable format or in a machine-readable format simultaneously with their publication. The ESAs have issued a consultation paper on draft technical standards (ITS) specifying certain tasks of collection bodies and certain functionalities of the European Single Access Point.[5] The draft implementing ITSs are designed to enable users to understand the financial and sustainability information centralized on the single access point. The ESAP is expected to operate in Level 1 legislation being a two-tier system where information is first submitted by entities to the collection bodies (Officially Appointed Mechanisms, offices and agencies of the EU, national authorities) and then made available by the collection bodies to the ESAP.[6] **14.02**

1 The ESAP Regulation is complemented with an Omnibus Regulation 2023/2869 and an Omnibus Directive 2023/2864.

2 See https://finance.ec.europa.eu/capital-markets-union-and-financial-markets/capital-markets-union/capital-markets-union-2020-action-plan_en; see also https://www.consilium.europa.eu/en/press/press-releases/2023/05/23/easy-access-to-corporate-information-for-investors-provisional-agreement-reached-on-the-european-single-access-point-esap/.

3 See https://www.european-financial-data-space.com/European_Single_Access_Point_(ESAP).html.

4 See also https://finance.ec.europa.eu/publications/digital-finance-package_en. See also https://commission.europa.eu/publications/european-commission-digital-strategy_en.

5 ESAs, 'Draft Implementing Technical Standards specifying certain tasks of collection bodies and certain functionalities of the European single access point under Regulation (EU) 2023/2859' (23 November 2023) Consultation paper, JC 2023 78, https://www.esma.europa.eu/document/consultation-paper-draft-its-specifying-certain-tasks-collection-bodies-and-certain.

6 ESAs, 'Final Report on draft Implementing Technical Standards specifying certain tasks of collection bodies and certain functionalities of the European single access point under Regulation (EU) 2023/2859'

The requirements would allow users to be able to access and use financial and sustainability information effectively in a centralized ESAP platform.[7] The ESAP would define how reporting entities should be categorized by industry and size, which identifier should be used, what types of information should be made available and the characteristics of the public application programming interface (API) available to data users.[8] One of the main tasks of collection bodies is the automated validations to be performed on the information submitted by entities and the application of open standard licenses. The API program responds to the need to protect investors in the sustainability- and ESG-related information, and to enhance the use of green fintech platforms for data collection.[9] The ESAP marks a step forward towards the transparency of information with the use of automated software to expedite decision-making process.[10] It would facilitate easy access to reliable and comparable data for rating agencies, financial analysts, research providers and asset managers, which need such data to make informed decisions.[11]

14.03 The provision mandates ESMA to monitor the transparency of that information through the enforcement mechanisms set under Articles 32–34. Paragraph 4 indicates a list of stringent requirements for information shared by ratings entities which should comply with the data extractable format and machine-readable format as defined in the ESAP. The size and volume of the business, and all metadata about the activities of ratings providers have to be disclosed to make accessible the information to investors. The ESMA has an obligation to develop and operate as collection body under the ESAP and monitors the legal entity identifier of rating provider.[12] All information regarding the

---

(29 October 2024) JC 2024 74, https://www.eiopa.europa.eu/esas-finalise-rules-facilitate-access-financial-and-sustainability-information-esap-2024-10-29_en.

7 Martina Macpherson, 'Meeting the EU's Sustainability Disclosure Rules – a mission (im)possible?' in Gunnar Rimmel, Güler Aras, Diogenis Baboukardos, Joanna Krasodomska, Christian Nielsen and Frank Schiemann (eds), *Research Handbook on Sustainability Reporting* (Edward Elgar 2024) ch. 13.

8 Jean-François Pons, 'The European Single Access Point: a game-changer for ESG data?' (February 2022), EUROFI Regulatory Update, p.30, https://www.eurofi.net/wp-content/uploads/2022/05/eurofi_the-european-single-access-point_a-game-changer-for-esg-data_paris_february-2022.pdf.

9 Eugenia Macchiavello and Michele Siri, 'Sustainable Finance and Fintech: Can Technology Contribute to Achieving Environmental Goals? A Preliminary Assessment of 'Green Fintech' and 'Sustainable Digital Finance'' (2022) 19(1) *European Company and Financial Law Review* 171–172.

10 Ross P. Buckley, Douglas W. Arner, Dirk A. Zetzsche, Rolf H. Weber and Mia Trzecinski, 'Technology, fintech and capital markets: the EU experience with digital transformation' in Iris Chiu and Iain MacNeil (eds), *Research Handbook on Global Capital Markets Law* (Edward Elgar 2023) ch. 2.

11 Giulia Schneider, 'ESG Data and EU Competition Enforcement: From 'Green' to 'Digital' Antitrust in Sustainable Markets' (2025), https://ssrn.com/abstract=4729388.

12 David Leung, Benedicte Nolens, Douglas W. Arner and Jon Frost, 'Corporate Digital Identity: No Silver Bullet, but a Silver Lining' (June 2022) BIS Papers No 126, https://www.bis.org/publ/bppdf/bispap126.pdf.

endorsement of ESG ratings provided by ESG rating providers established outside the Union should be made accessible on ESAP.

Paragraphs 8–9 of the article delegate ESMA to develop draft implementing technical standards and guidelines to monitor the collection and management of information on ratings providers.[13] Specifically, digital devices are used to codify and structure the data in a machine-readable format to ensure accessibility and ease of use for both investors and national competent authorities. The ESMA is also mandated to conduct appropriate field tests, in consultation with relevant stakeholders, to verify whether the metadata elaborated by machine-readable format are correct and reliable. The purpose is to assess the existing machine-readable formats that may be considered to effectively develop the technical standards. In this context, the ESMA has a delicate task to evaluate whether text-based disclosures (including those under other regulations, such as the CSRD and SFDR) should be processed in a machine-readable format and in which format.[14] The results of the implementation of technical standards are submitted to the European Commission for final approval. The Regulation sets a specific responsibility for ESMA to assess which information should be presented in a machine-readable format and to determine the most suitable machine-readable format for that purpose. **14.04**

C. THE USE OF DIGITAL TECHNOLOGIES ON ESG DATA COLLECTION

Technological systems such as artificial intelligence and machine learning applications can be deployed to improve the measurement of granular data and the provision of meaningful information.[15] The application of automated methods facilitate effective compliance processes, while ensuring standardization of data together with contractual certainty and predictability of enforcement actions in order to avoid misleading reports which generate greenwashing practices at the detriment of investors. ESG ratings assessments can be expedited through automated technologies, which, in turn, can enhance the transparency of reporting outcomes. Information providers continue to improve quality and availability although data continues to be one of the largest impediments to **14.05**

13 See https://www.esma.europa.eu/press-news/esma-news/esas-finalise-rules-facilitate-access-financial-and-sustainability-information

14 ESMA, 'Study on Data Formats for text-based disclosure' (24 May 2024), ESMA12-766636679-320, https://www.esma.europa.eu/sites/default/files/2024-07/ESMA12-766636679-320_Study_on_MiCA_Whitepaper_Data_Formats.pdf.

15 Simon Mundy, Patrick Temple-West and Kaori Yoshida, 'Inside the ESG software arms race' *Financial Times* (26 July 2023), https://www.ft.com/content/7a02a7ed-337f-4507-853a-0b230889d523.

ESG risk assessment. Further, digital technologies offer the possibility of the real-time calculation of future exposure based on data and simulation of risk factors which is relevant to detect environment-related events.[16] Technology can also improve information sharing and access to large volumes of climate data, which will allow firms to obtain a more insightful view of sustainable activities.[17] Data should be held in consistent formats, or at least should be translatable into consistent formats, across all institutions. The use of technology to gather data can help firms demonstrate that their activities are sustainable for the environment and society.[18] For instance, software applications (e.g. data-mining and machine-learning) can assist the management board to extract valuable information from ESG data and identify which section of the annual report needs to account for environmental risks.[19] Technological solutions such as automated predictive analysis could be employed to improve the quality of metrics used in ratings models and to facilitate the comparability and granularity of the ESG taxonomy. Specifically, cognitive computing software develops algorithms that decipher unstructured texts and generate rating scoring.[20] The potential of cognitive technologies to enhance the analysis of sustainability risk for firms is manifest: they extract information and translate it into knowledge in real time which, at the same time, expedite data sharing.[21]

14.06 The rapid advancement of digital technologies in environmental risk assessment offers opportunities to automate complex and manual investment analysis which is the key challenge of sustainable decision-making. For example, automated language systems such as Natural Language Processing (NLP) can be deployed to improve ESG ratings metrics and the evaluations of E, S and G factors in sustainability products.[22] NLP software can be used to improve

---

16 Klaus Rainer Kirchhoff, Sönke Niefünd and Julian von Pressentin, *ESG: Sustainability as a Strategic Success Factor* (Springer Nature 2024) 136–137.

17 Jun Dai and Qiumin Zhu, 'ESG performance and green innovation in a digital transformation perspective' (2024) 83(1) *American Journal of Economics and Sociology* 263–264.

18 Michael W. Peregrine and Alya Sulaiman, 'The Argument for Strong Board Oversight of Artificial Intelligence' (2023), https://clsbluesky.law.columbia.edu/2023/07/28/the-argument-for-strong-board-oversight-of-artificial-intelligence/.

19 Oliver Balch, 'Big data helps put numbers on sustainability' *Financial Times* (25 January 2021), https://www.ft.com/content/2a405cf6-9592-4de2-960b-4c3e5d0df030.

20 Marc Schmitt and Mark Cummins, 'Beyond Accuracy in Artificial Intelligence Based Credit Scoring Systems: Explainability and Sustainability in Decision Support' (2023), https://ssrn.com/abstract=4536400.

21 Jonathan Fluharty-Jaidee and Presha Neidermeyer, 'Artificial Intelligence and Environmental, Social and Governmental Issues: A Current Perspective' in Tarek Rana, Jan Svanberg, Peter Öhman, Alan Lowe (eds), *Handbook of Big Data and Analytics in Accounting and Auditing* (Singapore: Springer 2023) 90–91.

22 Aarav Patel and Peter A. Gloor, 'Creating a systematic ESG (Environmental Social Governance) scoring system using social network analysis and machine learning for more sustainable company practices'

accuracy and clarity in ESG reporting and methodologies; ratings providers should engage with technological applications which can expedite the standardization of data and the comparability of scores.[23] The use of technology holds out the promise of improving the assessment of ESG risk and the level of environmental exposures, and to enhance the transparency of monitoring processes.[24] However, the main downside is the risk that the application of sophisticated machine learning systems will exacerbate the possibility of technology malfunctioning and failing to achieve its stated purposes.[25] The question at stake is how the automated applications can adapt to ESG rating methodologies for producing information about modelling prudential risk and capital at risk for investors and regulators. The role of artificial intelligence (AI) systems in the ratings is likely to reduce the role of raters in assessing climate change data.[26] Achieving the full benefits of technology in ESG ratings therefore requires standardized access to institutions' operating systems and the data they contain. The opportunities provided by technology for the raters can be used in transformative ways which will yield far wider benefits than are sometimes envisaged. The potential benefits of technological innovation in ESG ratings should be weighed carefully against the risks. In the long term, there is scope for AI systems to be used as a service-provider for network interconnectedness and as a tool to monitor the ESG conduct of financial institutions.

Technological solutions can improve the elaboration of ratings' models: they **14.07**
reduce the risk of bias and greenwashing and can assist analyze 'structured' (reports) and 'unstructured' (statistical data) texts on ESG information.[27] These algorithmic applications aim to standardize ESG scoring by aligning ratings content with sustainability requirements. Specifically, the NLP can classify the variety of metrics elaborated in the ratings' proprietary methodologies: as has been observed, 'the natural language processing is used to generate

in Peter A. Gloor, Francesca Grippa, Andrea Fronzetti Colladon, and Aleksandra Przegalinska (eds), *Handbook of Social Computing* (Edward Elgar 2024) ch. 14.

23 Sean Stein Smith, *Blockchain, Artificial Intelligence, and Financial Services* (2nd edn, Springer 2024) 202–203.

24 Stavros Gadinis and Amelia Miazad, 'The ESG Information System' (2024) 47(2) *Seattle University Law Review*, 722–723.

25 Matthew U. Scherer, 'Regulating Artificial Intelligence Systems: Risks, Challenges, Competencies, and Strategies' (2016) 29(2) *Harvard Journal of Law & Technology*, 359.

26 Mardi Witzel and Niraj Bhargava, 'AI-related risk: The merits of an ESG-based approach to oversight' (2023) CIGI Papers, No. 279, https://hdl.handle.net/10419/299976.

27 Madelyn Antoncic, 'Uncovering hidden signals for sustainable investing using Big Data: Artificial intelligence, machine learning and natural language processing' (2020) 13 *Journal of Risk Management in Financial Institutions*, 109–110.

analytics scoring data points on performance and also inform the data users how many news articles that their score is based on.'[28] For example, Truvalue Labs is cognitive computing software which develops algorithms that decipher unstructured texts and generate rating scoring.[29] It is a provider of AI technology that elaborates metrics of ESG data to capture firms' behaviour with respect to sustainability. Truvalue Labs refines ESG information from various sources by monitoring companies in order to measure ESG performance and create a dataset for investors.[30] Another valuable NLP application is ClimateBert (Bidirectional Encoder Representations from Transformers), an algorithm which analyzes textual data of companies' annual reports.[31] Specifically, it is a language representation model that excerpts specific wording from company disclosures into accessible dataset in order to assess compliance with TCFD requirements.[32] These AI methods are particularly useful to identify loopholes in interpreting the metrics used in ratings models to predict potential ESG risk exposures: they can assist raters to formulate assessments while, at the same time, limiting the appetite for inflating the content of ESG reports. The use of automation of performance benchmarks to measure sustainable activities can reduce room for political opportunism and increase reliability on rating agencies outlooks.[33] This involves the application of AI, satellites and machine learning, which aim to enhance the quality of metrics.[34] Using technological advancement in the ESG ratings industry is likely to avoid the risk of providing doubtful evaluations and to favour reliance on an alternative set of information as a result of automated data providers.

---

28 George Serafeim and Aaron Yoon, 'Stock price reactions to ESG news: the role of ESG ratings and disagreement' (2023) 28(3) *Review of Accounting Studies* 1504–1505, https://doi.org/10.1007/s11142-022-09675-3.

29 See https://truvaluelabs.com/products/data. For a commentary, see Greg Bala, Hendrik Bartel, James P. Hawley and Yung-Jae Lee, 'Tracking "Real-time" Corporate Sustainability Signals Using Cognitive Computing' (2015) 27(2) *Journal of Applied Corporate Finance* 95–96.

30 George Serafeim, 'Public Sentiment and the Price of Corporate Sustainability' (2020) 76(2) *Financial Analysts Journal*, 31.

31 Julia Anna Bingler, Mathias Kraus, Markus Leippold and Nicolas Webersinke, 'Cheap talk and cherry-picking: What ClimateBert has to say on corporate climate risk disclosures' (2022) 47 *Finance Research Letters*, https://doi.org/10.1016/j.frl.2022.102776.

32 Jacob Devlin, Ming-Wei Chang, Kenton Lee, Kristina Toutanova, 'BERT: Pre-training of Deep Bidirectional Transformers for Language Understanding' (2019) Proceedings of the 2019 Conference of the North American Chapter of the Association for Computational Linguistics: Human Language Technologies, Volume 1, 4171.

33 Omar Selim, 'ESG and AI: The beauty and the beast of sustainable investing' in Herman Bril, Georg Kell and Andreas Rasche (eds), *Sustainable Investing Sustainable Investing. A Path to a New Horizon* (Oxon-New York Routledge 2020) ch. 12.

34 Soh Young In, Dane Rook and Ashby Monk, 'Integrating Alternative Data (Also Known as ESG Data) in Investment Decision Making' (2019) 48(3) *Global Economic Review* 247–248.

TITLE III

INTEGRITY AND RELIABILITY OF ESG RATING ACTIVITIES

CHAPTER 1

ORGANIZATIONAL REQUIREMENTS, PROCESSES AND DOCUMENTS CONCERNING GOVERNANCE

ARTICLE 15

GENERAL PRINCIPLES

Iris H-Y Chiu

1. ESG rating providers shall ensure the independence of their rating activities, including from all political and economic influences or constraints.

2. ESG rating providers shall have in place rules and procedures that ensure that their ESG ratings are issued, published and distributed in accordance with this Regulation.

3. ESG rating providers shall employ systems, resources and procedures that are adequate and effective to comply with their obligations under this Regulation.

4. ESG rating providers shall adopt and implement written policies and procedures that ensure that their ESG ratings are based on a thorough analysis of all information available to them that is relevant to their analysis in accordance with their rating methodologies.

5. ESG rating providers shall adopt and implement internal due diligence policies and procedures that ensure that their business interests do not impair the independence or accuracy of the ESG rating activities.

6. ESG rating providers shall adopt and implement sound administrative and accounting procedures, internal control mechanisms, and effective control and safeguard arrangements for information processing systems.

7. ESG rating providers shall use rating methodologies for the ESG ratings they provide that are rigorous, systematic, independent and capable of justification and shall apply those rating methodologies continuously and in a transparent manner.

8. ESG rating providers shall review the rating methodologies referred to in paragraph 7 on an ongoing basis and at least annually.

9. ESG rating providers shall monitor and evaluate the adequacy and effectiveness of the systems, resources and procedures referred to in paragraph 3 at least annually and take appropriate measures to address any deficiencies.

10. ESG rating providers shall establish and maintain a permanent, independent and effective oversight function to ensure oversight over all aspects of the provision of their ESG ratings. The oversight function shall have the necessary resources and expertise and have access to all information necessary to perform its duties. It shall have direct access to the management body of the ESG rating provider. ESG rating providers shall develop and maintain robust procedures regarding their oversight function.

11. ESG rating providers shall adopt all necessary measures to ensure that the information they use in issuing ESG ratings is of sufficient quality and from reliable sources. ESG rating providers shall clearly state that their ESG ratings are their own opinion.

12. ESG rating providers shall notify the rated item or the issuer of the rated item during its working hours and at least two full working days before the first issuance of the ESG rating in order to give the rated item or the issuer of the rated item an opportunity to inform the ESG rating providers of any factual errors. To that end, ESG rating providers shall make available, upon request by the rated item or by the issuer of the rated item, free of charge and on a non-commercial basis, the information referred to in point 1, points (b) and (c), and point 2, point (b)(ii), of Annex III, together with the date of the last update of data as well as, where relevant, any other data collected, estimated or computed that relates to the rated item or the issuer of a rated item.

13. ESG rating providers shall not be obliged to disclose information about their intellectual capital, intellectual property, know-how or the results of innovation that would qualify as trade secrets as defined in Article 2, point (1), of Directive (EU) 2016/943 of the European Parliament and of the Council.

14. ESG rating providers shall only make changes to their ESG ratings in accordance with their rating methodologies published pursuant to Article 23.

A. INTRODUCTION

15.01 This article addresses two regulatory matters. One relates to regulating rating methodologies, and the other relates to regulating the general organizational and governance soundness of the ESG rating provider. Both aspects collectively support the aim that ESG ratings should be independent and free from political and economic influences and constraints (Article 16(1)).

15.02 The independence of information signalling goods is of crucial importance for market reliance and trust, as skewed information signals can result in misallocation of financial resources, mispricing and market corrections, which can be time consuming for investors. This same quality is demanded of credit ratings,[1] financial benchmarks[2] as well investment research[3] that is not labelled as marketing information. Although concrete regulatory provisions for 'independence' are provided in the various forms of conflict of interest management (commented elsewhere in this volume) that ESG rating providers must undertake, the overarching expectation that rating providers meet the 'independence' quality reflects regulators' objectives for regulation and avoids the perspective that regulation merely descends into a form of proceduralization.[4] The ultimate aim of regulating firms to institute systems, procedures, policies and structures is to protect the quality of independence in information signalling goods.

B. REGULATING ORGANIZATIONAL SYSTEMS, PROCEDURES, POLICIES ETC.

This article contains several provisions that require ESG rating providers to put in place appropriate and sound organizational and governance structures within the firm in order to comply with the requirements of the Regulation. Regulating organizational and governance structures has become a norm in EU financial regulation. The intellectual foundation for this lies in 'new governance'[5] which seeks to recalibrate modern regulation to move away from top-down command-and-control designs to more varied regulatory designs that co-opt the capacity of the regulated firms, industry and stakeholders, to contribute to governing themselves, in order to meet regulatory objectives. **15.03**

New governance has been at the vanguard of financial regulation since the 1990s.[6] 'New governance' regulatory designs refer to an umbrella of regulatory approaches including principles-based regulation,[7] process-based regulation[8] **15.04**

---

1 The author thanks Professor Iain MacNeil and participants at the Roundtable on ESG Ratings Regulation, 7 November 2024, Centre of Ethics and Law, UCL for their comments and input, especially Dr Cheng-Yun Tsang, Monash University and Dr Ebbe Rogge, Leiden University. All errors and omissions are mine. Arts 1, 6, EU Regulation of Credit Rating Agencies 1060/2009.

2 Art 4(6), EU Benchmarks Regulation 2016/1011.

3 Art 36, Commission Delegated Regulation to Markets in Financial Instruments Directive 2017/565.

4 See notes 18 and 19, infra.

5 Orly Lobel, 'New Governance as Regulatory Governance' in David Levi-Faur (ed), *The Oxford Handbook on Governance* (Oxford: OUP 2012), ch 5; Julia Black, 'Mapping the Contours of Contemporary Financial Services Regulation' (2002) 2 *Journal of Corporate Law Studies* 253.

6 Julia Black, *Rules and Regulators* (Oxford: Clarendon Press, 1998); 'Mapping the Contours of Contemporary Financial Services Regulation' (2002) 2 *Journal of Corporate Law Studies* 253.

7 Such as found in FCA Handbook PRIN 2.

8 Cary Coglianese and David Lazer, 'Management-Based Regulation: Prescribing Private Management to Achieve Public Goals' (2003) 37 *Law and Society Review* 691.

and meta-regulation[9] which have been deployed in financial regulation in the UK (and also in other jurisdictions). Principles-based regulation refers to having in place broadly framed and open-ended principles to govern regulated entities,[10] co-opting the regulated industry to shape and co-develop interpretive jurisprudence for expected conduct. Procedural-based regulation[11] co-opts firms to design the appropriate procedures and systems for regulatory implementation, as would suit each firm's structures and capacity to meet regulatory outcomes. As regulators cannot micro-manage firms' implementation, procedural regulation often sets out broad contours leaving flexibility for firms to carry out the necessary implementation. This also ensures that firms and their managers take responsibility in the running of the firm to embed such compliance.[12] In sum, these new governance approaches are often referred to as meta-level or 'meta-regulation,' which is based on objective rather than narrowly-framed rules that may be one size fits all. This umbrella term not only encapsulates modernized regulatory techniques but, for the financial sector, it supports new forms of institutionalization, structural and strategic aspects for regulatory agencies and new approaches for financial regulation.

15.05 New governance also accommodates governance instruments of various types from prescriptive regulation to softer instruments such as guidelines and codes.[13] From the 1990s, it would not be an exaggeration to claim that new governance has 'remade' financial regulation for modern times.

15.06 New governance is seen as an efficient and effective form of regulation, moving away from traditional command-and-control designs as regulators are nested within a polycentric[14] governance landscape where they, firms and their stakeholders are networked together and exert different levers of influence, shaping regulatory norms and behaviour. The polycentric landscape for governance actors also means that it is not always the most productive for regulators to engage in comprehensive command-and-control forms of standard-setting. Some degree of open-endedness or flexibility in regulatory design

9 Sharon Gilad, 'It Runs in the Family: Meta-regulation and its Siblings' (2010) 4 Regulation and Governance 485; Christine Parker, *The Open Corporation* (Cambridge: Cambridge University Press 2000).

10 E.g. the UK FCA Handbook, PRIN module, and see Financial Services Authority, *Principles-based Regulation: Focussing on the Outcomes that Matter* (April 2007).

11 Note 8.

12 Orly Lobel, 'Setting the Agenda for New Governance Research' (2004) *Minnesota Law Review* 665.

13 Lobel (2012).

14 Chris Tollefson, Anthony R. Zito and Fred Gale, 'Symposium Overview: Conceptualizing New Governance Arrangements' (2012) 90 Public Administration 3; Cristie Ford and Mary Condon, 'Introduction to "New Governance and the Business Organization" Special Issue of Law and Policy' (2011) 33 Law and Policy 449.

would allow regulated firms to more efficiently and precisely design regulatory implementation appropriate for its structures and resources.

In this manner, financial regulators would engage in regulatory designs aimed at the 'publicisation of private accountability,'[15] which involves regulators leaving it open-ended as to how firms would implement internal procedures and systems to achieve certain compliance goals. Ideally, firms would internalize regulatory objectives and implement the most effective procedures 'from within' to achieve public accountability.[16] New governance framing for regulatory designs helps regulators achieve efficient risk-based approaches to prioritizing and using their regulatory resources,[17] while cultivating in firms a greater sense of ownership and responsibility towards delivering on regulatory objectives.[18] This also promotes quality regulator-regulated relationships not defined by antagonism but by increased cooperation and trust. **15.07**

However, regulation focusing on compelling firms to have various procedures, systems and other proxy 'channels' for desirable behaviour can be criticized as ultimately directing regulated entities' minds only to the procedures, losing sight of the ultimate goals of regulation. This is the risk of proceduralization[19] on the part of regulated firms, myopically carrying out activities while losing sight of the regulatory objectives that are to be met. Proceduralization refers to the generation of work processes and lists for box-ticking that may **15.08**

15 Parker, *The Open Corporation* (2000), at 246; Jody Freeman, 'Extending Public Law Norms Through Privatization' (2003) 116 *Harvard Law Review* 1285, see critique in Fenner L. Stewart, 'The Corporation, New Governance and the Power of the Publicisation Narrative' (2015) 21 *Indiana Journal of Global Legal Studies* 513.

16 Kimberley D Krawiec, 'Let's Talk: What FinReg Can Learn from New Governance (and Vice Versa)' (2019) 44 Law and Social Inquiry 1241; Stewart (2015), *ibid*, Ford and Condon (2011).

17 Julia Black, 'Regulatory Styles and Supervisory Strategies' in Niamh Moloney et al (ed), *The Oxford Handbook of Financial Regulation* (Oxford: Oxford University Press 2015), ch 8.

18 Parker and Nielsen's empirical survey found that the institution of procedures and systems signal senior management commitment to manage compliance risk, and can result in the practical effect of constraining and monitoring behaviour, hence procedural regulation can entail substantive culture changes at firms. The existence of systems and procedures facilitate information collection, and more systematic preparation of reports for senior management to carry out monitoring. Parker and Nielsen also found that staff training systems and systems for handling consumer complaints are examples of procedures and systems established to manage compliance risk that have a positive impact upon changes in behaviour in the organization, Christine Parker and Vibeke Lehmann Nielsen, 'Corporate Compliance Systems: Could They Make Any Difference?' (2009) 41 *Administration and Society* 3.

19 Michael Power, *Organised Uncertainty: Designing a World of Risk Management* (Oxford: Oxford University Press, 2008) on how the existence of excessive procedures in firms may give an appearance of compliance and make it difficult for regulators to tell if the compliance is genuine or cosmetic, shielding underlying problems.

demonstrate a form of compliance but not necessarily with substantive meaning.[20] Regulators may also be susceptible to the same myopic mindset when supervising regulated entities.

15.09 The 'modernisation' of financial regulation suffered a spectacular setback with the onset of the global financial crisis 2008. It was called into question why 'new governance' techniques, deployed in prudential regulation of banks[21] and principles-based regulation for investment services, would continue to create hazards for their customers and stakeholders.[22] Many commentators reflected on the over-optimism on the part of regulators deploying new governance techniques, and urged that new governance should not be rendered obsolete but should be made more robust.[23]

15.10 This author has elsewhere commented on the continuity of new governance in financial regulation after the global financial crisis.[24] Such continuity can be based on the industry and structural conditions that financial regulators find themselves in the regulatory landscape, that are no different from pre-2008. Regulated firms remain powerful and able to provide capacity in their compliance, and regulators remain in need of working with firms in terms of information, being aware of innovations and dynamic supervision. Replacing the new governance approach with arms-length command-and-control supervision would not work, as regulators may not be able to stipulate precisely and

---

20 Kimberly Krawiec, 'Cosmetic Compliance and the Failure of Negotiated Governance' (2003) 81 *Washington University Law Quarterly* 487.

21 Cristie Ford, 'New Governance in the Teeth of Human Frailty: Lessons from Financial Regulation' (2010) *Wisconsin Law Review* 441.

22 The era of principles-based regulation for investment services in the UK since the 1990s also coincides with scandal after scandal of mis-selling, such as pensions, endowment mortgages and personal protection insurance, e.g. see Pension Justice, 'Understanding pension mis-selling 1990s: Causes and consequences' (2023), https://pensionjustice.co.uk/pension-mis-selling-1990s/#:~:text=Mis%2Dsold%20pensions%20in%20the%201990s&text=As%20many%20as%20two%20million,identify%20and%20compensate%20affected%20savers; Tim Edmonds, 'Endowment Mortgages' (House of Commons Library, 2015), https://commonslibrary.parliament.uk/research-briefings/sn00570/; Eilís Ferran, 'Regulatory Lessons from the Payment Protection Insurance Mis-selling Scandal in the UK' (2012) 13 *European Business Organisation Law Review* 247.

23 Misaligned incentives that regulators were blithely unaware of should be addressed, see Cristie Ford, 'New Governance in the Teeth of Human Frailty: Lessons from Financial Regulation' (2010) Wisconsin Law Review 441; 'Macro- and Micro-Level Effects on Responsive Financial Regulation' (2011) 44 UBC Law Review 589; Julia Black, 'Paradoxes and Failures: New Governance Techniques and the Financial Crisis' (2012) 75 Mod L Rev 1037. Also, on behavioural tendencies on the part of firms that are calculating and insufficiently concerned for the wider or 'systemic' consequences, discussed in Emilios Avgouleas, 'The Global Financial Crisis, Behavioural Finance and Financial Regulation: In Search of a New Orthodoxy' (2009) 9 *Journal of Corporate Law Studies* 23.

24 Iris H-Y Chiu, *Regulating (from) the Inside: The Legal Framework for Internal Control at Banks and Financial Institutions* (Oxford: Hart 2015); 'Regulating Financial Institutions for Micro-stability – What Can New Governance Offer?' (2024) 40(3) *Banking and Finance Law Review*, 453.

exactly for the myriad situations for regulated entities' 'correct' conduct. It would therefore be more optimal to learn from the lessons regarding weaknesses in new governance implementation of financial regulation, and to address these in post-crisis reforms.

New governance regulatory techniques remain important in post-crisis financial regulation reforms. The new era of post-crisis financial regulation is characterized, in some commentators' words, as the end of '[m]arket-based approaches emphasising liberalisation, deregulation and fiscal responsibility'[25] or an era of 'iron law.'[26] These perceptions reflect a changed character of new governance in financial regulation outworking, which no longer merely delegates to firms' self-implementation or relies excessively on market discipline. Financial regulation has now forayed into, inter alia: regulating aspects of corporate governance in order to boost prudent and compliant behaviour at firms;[27] more precisely providing standardized best practices in procedure-based regulation in order to minimize deviation from regulatory purposes;[28] requiring remedial behaviour on the part of firms based on pre-emptive forms of supervisory monitoring, such as stress-testing;[29] and also experimenting with personal liability regimes for individuals in order to support better internalization of responsibility, especially for managerial personnel.[30] **15.11**

25 Mohamed El Erian, 'Inverted Pyramid of Investments Need Shoring Up' (Financial Times, 8 April 2024), https://www.ft.com/content/cbbfec27-7b94-4404-ae0d-20a45d613d4a.

26 Roberta Romano, The Iron Law of Financial Regulation, 2021 Wallenberg Lecture of 28 October 2021, European Corporate Governance Institute, https://ecgi.global/content/2021-wallenberg-lecture#:~:text=Romano%20terms%20the%20%E2%80%9Ciron%20law,costs%20that%20can%20have%20adverse.

27 Discussed in Danny Busch, Guido Ferrarini, Gerard van Solinge (eds), *Governance of Financial Institutions* (Oxford: Oxford University Press 2019); also Iris H-Y Chiu, 'Financial Corporations and Corporate Governance' in T. Baums and Helmut Anheir (eds), *Advances in Corporate Governance* (Oxford: Oxford University Press 2020), ch. 4.

28 ESG discussed in relation to micro-prudential regulation, Chiu (2024).

29 https://www.bankofengland.co.uk/stress-testing. An episode of pre-emptive restructuring took place for the UK Co-operative Bank after failing a stress test, 'Bank stress tests: Co-op fails as Lloyds and RBS scrape through' (The Guardian, 16 December 2015).

30 Chiu (2015) on the roles of internal control, also the UK senior managers and certified persons regime which pin personal responsibility on managers for regulatory breaches in the area of their oversight, where negligence has occurred, Financial Services and Markets Act 2000 (as amended) s66A, 66B; FCA Handbook SYSC 23–27, also the Codes of Conduct for senior managers and certified persons which can attract personal liability COCON 2. See Alan Brener, 'Developing the senior managers regime' in Costanza A. Russo, Rosa M. Lastra and William Blair (eds), *Research Handbook on Law and Ethics in Banking and Finance* (Cheltenham: Edward Elgar 2019), ch 12. However there is critique that the design of the senior managers regime may need tweaking due to its minimal enforceability and potential for superficial demonstration of compliance, see Anat Keller and Andreas Kokkinis, 'The Senior Managers and Certification Regime in Financial Firms: An Organisational Culture Analysis' (2022) *22 Journal of Corporate Law Studies*; also Eleanore Hickman, 'Is the Senior Managers and Certification Regime Changing Banking for Good?' (2022) 85 *Modern Law Review* 1540.

15.12 Further, 'new and improved' governance in the form of organizational, systems, and procedural governance can give rise to regulatory enforcement actions on the basis of failings or weaknesses in these systems, procedures and structures themselves, without necessarily demonstrating that these failings or weaknesses have caused precise customer or social harm.[31] Such enforcement would be deterrent in nature, seeking to change behaviour in terms of 'taking and implementing seriously' the required organizational, systems, and procedural governance. The point is not necessarily that such governance is an end in itself. Rather, such governance is usually a proxy for the 'compliance compass' of the firm, its attitudes and culture towards respecting its regulatory contract. In this manner, supervisory enforcement of this nature could play a part towards culture change[32] on the part of firms in an industry whose culture is very much criticized.[33]

15.13 In this light, we first examine Parts 2, 3, 9 and 10 of this article in terms of the nature and effectiveness of general organizational and procedural governance for ESG rating providers. We then turn to Parts 5 and 6 that relate specifically to certain functions in ESG rating providers and how these are to be governed.

15.14 Parts 2 and 3 deal with ESG rating providers having rules, procedures or systems that enable them to comply with the Regulation and to ensure that their ratings are distributed in compliance with the Regulation. These are broadly framed 'catch-all' provisions that relate to the organizational 'compass' of the firm. They intend to embed a compliance culture within such compass so that 'things are carried out' within the firm in accordance with rules, systems or procedures that are consistently designed according to such a compliance-based compass. The main advantage of such broadly framed provisions for regulators is that they allow regulators to take enforcement action against firms where there is failure of the 'compliance compass' as manifest in certain shortcomings or weaknesses, without the need for each and every desirable organizational practice to be prescribed.

---

31 E.g. the 'PRA censures Wyelands Bank Plc for breaching Large Exposure limits and failings in its governance, controls and risk management' (4 April 2023), such supervisory action intending to deter and remedy the bank's internal control and management, before any real harm such as the nearing of insolvency risk. Also see Allen & Overy, 'FCA and PRA enforcement themes and trends (UK)' (2023) which looks at the subject matter for enforcement, many of which are procedural and organizational failings, such as in anti money laundering compliance, investor protection compliance etc.

32 Looking at the positive results in Parker and Nielsen (2009) for example.

33 Emily Shepherd, 'From Zeroes to Heroes: How culture in financial services can change for everyone's benefit' (Speech, City and Financial Global's 8th Annual Culture and Conduct Forum for the Financial Services Industry, 29 November 2022), https://www.fca.org.uk/news/speeches/zeroes-heroes-how-culture-financial-services-can-change-everyones-benefit.

The responsibility for ensuring that firm-wide compliant rules, systems and procedures are instituted would be a matter for internal governance within the firm. The EU does not provide for an equivalent of the UK's senior managers and certified persons regime where regulators prescribe certain functional roles and their responsibilities that firms need to allocate to individuals,[34] from which firms cannot deviate. These individuals would bear personal responsibility for the relevant organizational, internal control or governance area that has been so allocated.[35] Often, the individuals responsible for the overall organizational governance of the firm adhering to a compliance culture would be certain members of senior management and leaders of internal control functions such as compliance and internal audit functions.[36] **15.15**

Part 9 requires that ESG rating providers review the adequacy of their rules, systems and procedures at least annually in order to determine if they need to be adjusted or enhanced. This ongoing provision underpins the continuation of the 'compliance compass' of the firm. It is also likely that such review would be undertaken by the Oversight function, to which we now turn. **15.16**

C. OVERSIGHT FUNCTION

Part 10 provides that ESG rating providers must establish a permanent, independent and effective oversight function, which should oversee the compliant aspects of ratings generation and distribution, and should have all the relevant power, information and resources, including direct reporting to the management body. The oversight function is to be supported by robust rules and procedures regarding its operations. **15.17**

The requirements for the oversight function in the regulation are not dissimilar to those applicable to benchmark administrators, and bear strong resemblance to the provisions for internal control functions regulated in various pieces of EU financial regulation applicable to banks,[37] investment firms[38] and credit **15.18**

34 FCA Handbook SYSC 23, 24.

35 S66A, 66B, UK Financial Services and Markets Act.

36 Internal control is discussed below.

37 Art 74(1), 76(5) of the Capital Requirements Directive 2013 to be amended by the compromise text published on 4 December 2023, https://data.consilium.europa.eu/doc/document/ST-15882-2023-INIT/en/pdf.

38 Arts 21–24, Commission delegated regulation 2017/565 to the Markets in Financial Instruments Directive 2015.

rating agencies[39] for example. In this way, the oversight function is likely to be a pared-down version of 'internal control' functions, which are usually defined as having three lines of defences, i.e. compliance, risk management and internal audit.[40] The expectations of its set-up and how it is empowered and accountable are very similar to those applicable to internal control functions.

15.19 This commentator has elsewhere discussed[41] that the three lines of defence constituting the overall 'internal control' in financial firms have evolved as internal firm departments that serve firms' needs. Compliance functions manage the regulatory risks for firms, and may be combined with the in-house legal department of firms. Internal audit functions support firms' financial information collation and external reporting. Risk management functions are of more recent vintage but have developed to help manage and oversee financial firms' risk positions, usually in quantitative terms in relation to hedging, insurance and other risk mitigation operations. Being internal departments of financial firms and not centres of revenue generation, they serve the firm's protective purposes. However, in the wake of the global financial crisis where revelations were made of financial firms' recklessness and lack of internal control,[42] policy-makers in the EU and UK have opted to strengthen the gatekeeping roles of firms' internal control functions so that they can internally monitor and act as brakes against firms' regulatory risks.[43]

15.20 In order to refashion internal control functions as internal gatekeepers, EU financial regulation has introduced certain organizational safeguards for them, such as requiring them to be made permanent, as well as independent of business lines, so that their remuneration and other performance incentives are tied to business interests. There is also expectation that internal control functions should be led by sufficiently senior appointments in order to lend the functions authority and enhance effectiveness. In this manner, internal control functions are expected to perform their gatekeeping roles with sufficient independence of judgement and are not to be interfered with. Their capacities are protected by mandatory regulation that compels firms to make internal control

39 Arts 3, 9 in relation to conflict of interest management and outsourcing. Also Sect B, Annex I has a mirror provision to the Regulation of ESG rating providers.

40 Art 3(9c), Capital Requirements Directive 2013 to be amended by the compromise text published on 4 December 2023, above.

41 Chiu (2015).

42 E.g. see House of Lords and House of Commons Parliamentary Commission on Banking Standards, 'An accident waiting to happen': The failure of HBOS' (2013), https://publications.parliament.uk/pa/jt201213/jtselect/jtpcbs/154/154.pdf.

43 This gatekeeping framing is discussed in Chiu (2015).

functions sufficiently empowered, resourced and able to access any information within the firm. Finally, internal control functions should have a direct reporting line to the Board so that they may not be undermined by senior managers or executives.

The oversight function for ESG rating providers is a pared-down version of the fully fledged set-up of internal control for banks and investment firms, but is supported by many of the same crucial features, such as being permanent, independently instituted, sufficiently empowered and resourced and having a level of reporting and accountability that may not be undermined by senior managers and executives. In this manner, the oversight function would be the 'line of defence' that addresses ESG rating providers' compliance risks in terms of internal set-ups and management, the production and distribution of ratings, as well as external relations. **15.21**

As this commentator has earlier warned in relation to critical discussions relating to internal control functions, the 'internal gatekeeping' role of such functions would place personnel serving in these roles in a sometimes difficult position. They are part of the firm and are hired to serve the firm's needs, yet they have to maintain objectivity and independence and must be prepared to raise unpopular criticisms or warnings, sometimes in the face of senior managers and executives. Such a role is not straightforward from an organizational behaviour/psychology point of view.[44] It is argued that enhancing professionalism for internal control functions, and having the support of powerful professional bodies may help such personnel to assert independent expertise and voice within an organization.[45] **15.22**

Further, regulators' direct enforcement against weak individuals in internal control functions may serve as deterrent lessons[46] for internal control personnel not to compromise their objectivity and professionalism. However, the effectiveness of internal control functions cannot simply be assumed. The intersections between regulation, organizational behaviour and professionalization need to be interrogated if the internal gatekeeping role of these functions is truly to be enhanced. **15.23**

---

44 Jan Pfister, *Managing Organizational Culture for Effective Internal Control* (Berlin & Heidelberg: Physica-Verlag, 2009).

45 Chiu (2015).

46 See ESG discussed in ch. 11, Iris H-Y Chiu and Joanna Wilson, *Banking Law and Regulation* (Oxford: Oxford University Press 2019).

15.24 In this light, the oversight function of the ESG rating provider is likely to assume the roles of ensuring regulatory compliance, as well as ex post monitoring or 'internal auditing' of the firm's internal rules, systems and procedures. The responsibilities of such a function can be significant. It may be tasked to be involved in setting up the firm's rules, systems and procedures for conflict of interest management, compliant rating methodologies, external relations etc. It may also be tasked to educate other staff in the firm on these rules, systems and procedures. Further, it may have to be responsible for checking the levels of internal adherence, as well as carrying out periodic review. The oversight function may sometimes also be tasked with dealing with the deviations or 'wrongs' uncovered by the firm in relation to staff, the ex post consequences and remedial actions.

D. INTERNAL DUE DILIGENCE

15.25 Part 5 of the article requires ESG rating providers to implement internal due diligence policies and procedures in order to protect the independence and accuracy of their ratings. It is not explicitly stated what the due diligence relates to in this rather broad framing. It can relate to taking stock of all possible conflicts of interest situations that may taint the independence or accuracy of ratings. This is a reasonable expectation as, although the Regulation provides for specific conflict of interest management at the organizational and personnel levels in articles (commented elsewhere in this volume), these precise provisions may leave gaps, which this commentator has explored in relation to a potentially wide-ranging web of relations ESG rating providers may have with information sources, stakeholders etc.[47]

15.26 However it is also possible to interpret the due diligence as to be required of all potentially relevant sources of input for ESG ratings. This would support the requirement for ESG rating providers to carry out thorough analysis of all relevant information (see below). Such due diligence may be important, as ESG rating providers are encouraged to work on the basis of measuring double materiality[48] (Preamble 20), which means that they may have to work with a different and wider range of information that addresses the impact of

47 Iris H-Y Chiu, 'Regulating ESG Rating and Data Product Providers: Critically Examining EU Regulation through the Lens of Functional Regulatory Consistency' (2024) *European Journal of Risk Regulation*, DOI: https://doi.org/10.1017/err.2024.53.

48 'The Challenge of Double Materiality' (Deloitte, undated), https://www2.deloitte.com/cn/en/pages/hot-topics/topics/climate-and-sustainability/dcca/thought-leadership/the-challenge-of-double-materiality.html.

economic activities upon the environment, society and good governance, compared to the narrower framework for financially material risks, which can be based on market information or financial modelling.

In light of the current ambiguity, firms may have to treat the due diligence procedures as pertaining to both possibilities above, as both 'independence' and 'accuracy' of ratings are the qualities to be safeguarded. 15.27

The wider trend of regulators introducing mandatory due diligence procedures for regulated entities is also observed. These are part of the continuing importance of 'new governance' regulatory designs, where procedural proxies are seen as important for firms to ultimately 'do the right thing.' Due diligence procedures can improve a firm's information awareness and this forms the basis for any change in the strategies or policies of the firm. One of the most significant new trends in corporate regulation is mandatory due diligence in order to account for social harms and cost, such as in relation to human rights,[49] modern slavery in supply chains[50] and conflict minerals[51] for example. Being aware can be important for changing economic behaviour,[52] although excessive proceduralization without internalized responsibility can also result. Commentators have discussed the lack of guidance and selectivity with which firms implement due diligence procedures,[53] and some consolidation of best practices may be desirable.[54] 15.28

It can be queried how an ESG rating provider should implement such due diligence procedures and policies. Should this be undertaken by the Oversight function, or should this be embedded within other staff functions, such as rating analysts themselves working within a due diligence framework to ensure that they have all the information inputs they need? Firms need to consider 15.29

49 Pursuant to implementation of the UN Guiding Principles for Business and Human Rights, see discussion in Antoine Duval, 'Ruggie's Double Movement: Assembling the Private and the Public Through Human Rights Due Diligence' (2023) 41 *Nordic Journal of Human Rights* 273.

50 S54, UK Modern Slavery Act.

51 EU Conflict Minerals Regulation 2017/821, see critical discussion, which largely relates to scope in order to alleviate the compliance burdens of many corporates, Elif Härkönen, 'Conflict Minerals in the Corporate Supply Chain: Is Transparency the Solution to Human Rights Violations in the Tantalum, Tin, Tungsten and Gold Supply Chains?' (2018) 29 *European Business Law Review* 691.

52 Michael Bloomfield and Genevieve LeBaron, 'The UK Modern Slavery Act: Transparency through Disclosure in Global Governance' (undated), https://www.e-ir.info/2018/09/21/the-uk-modern-slavery-act-transparency-through-disclosure-in-global-governance/.

53 Alvise Favotto and Kelly Kollman, 'When Rights Enter the CSR Field: British Firms' Engagement with Human Rights and the UN Guiding Principles' (2022) 23 Human Rights Review 21.

54 Sarianna M. Lundan and Peter Muchlinski, 'Human Rights Due Diligence in Global Value Chains' in New Policy Challenges for European Multinationals (Emerald, 2012), https://www.emerald.com/insight/content/doi/10.1108/S1745-8862.

the potentially demanding nature of comprehensive due diligence policies in light of this Part's ambiguity, and determine how to allocate resources to such compliance.

E. INFORMATION PROCESSING SYSTEMS

15.30 Part 6 of this article requires that ESG rating providers implement sound administrative and accounting procedures, internal control mechanisms and effective control and safeguard arrangements for information processing systems. This Part focuses on information processing systems and their importance, so that the procedures, arrangements and mechanisms for them need to be sound and effectively controlled. It is uncertain what information processing systems mean, and this could refer to the body of frameworks involving both humans and machines in terms of collecting, filtering/selecting, analyzing and making findings regarding information inputs. In that case, information processing systems would be the key framework through which rating products are generated. This Part seems targeted at ensuring that firms protect the integrity and effective working this framework, although it can be questioned what regulatory value this Part adds since Part 2 already provides a broad, catch-all provision requiring firms to ensure that their ratings are generated and distributed within regulatory compliance. This discussion will also include commentary on Parts 4 and 11 as they relate to procedures and measures relating to the quality of information to be used. Part 4 relates to the obligation for ESG rating providers to implement written policies and procedures to ensure that they are able to engage in a thorough analysis of relevant information. These policies and procedures seem to be part of the overall information processing system, relating to how information should be used. Part 11 relates to 'all necessary measures' to ensure that the ESG rating provider uses information of sufficient quality from reliable sources. This Part also requires ESG rating providers to expressly label their products as 'opinions,' a point to be discussed later under the 'regulation of rating methodologies.'

15.31 There seem three elements to protecting information processing systems. First, 'sound administrative and accounting procedures' are required. These may include how quantitative computations are made for single materiality, or the quantitative representations of double materiality risks. ESG factors are not always susceptible to quantitative evaluations, and even what can be quantitatively evaluated, such as toxic releases, or GHG emissions, need to be further translated into what their single or double materiality impact may be.

Environmental[55] and social accounting[56] continue to be evolving phenomena, and it is queried how ESG rating providers can demonstrate the adoption of 'sound' standards and accounting procedures. On the one hand, open-textured requirements such as 'sound standards' import legal risk as rating providers have the burden to demonstrate this to supervisors. On the other hand, they can be best-placed to justify their policies and practices and the Regulation does not suggest intolerance of variances in such practices and policies in the industry.

Further, sound administrative and accounting procedures may also relate to qualitative frameworks of evaluations for ESG factors in single and double materiality assessments. These are quite varied in the market and not highly standardized. ESG rating providers should mind the burden upon them to show 'soundness' although this does not necessarily inhibit differences in techniques and practices. **15.32**

Next, this Part envisages that there are internal control mechanisms safeguarding these information processing systems. It is queried what these refer to, as overall, ESG rating providers are only asked to institute a general Oversight function and not a fully-fledged internal control framework with three lines of defences. Since there is a specific requirement for ensuring that information processing systems be subject to internal control, would this mean that the Oversight function should pay attention to how information processing systems are embedded within the firm's 'compliance compass,' and to ensure that such embedment is effective? **15.33**

Finally, information processing systems should be subject to 'effective control and safeguard arrangements.' It is uncertain if the duplication of control or internal control is necessary. In the alternative, 'control' could mean a form of supervisory management, that the operations of the system are subject to senior-level supervision and/or approvals, hence the use of the term 'control.' **15.34**

'Safeguard arrangement' could refer to the integrity of the information processing system, that it should be designed and used for the purposes of integrity in generating rating outputs and products, and should be protected from being tampered with, misused or abused. **15.35**

55 Carlos Mata, Ana Fialho, Teresa Eugénio, 'A Decade of Environmental Accounting: What We Know' (2018) 198 *Journal of Cleaner Production* 1198.

56 Rob Gray, Andrew Brennan & Jeff Malpas, 'New Accounts: Towards a Reframing of Social Accounting' (2015) 38 *Accounting Forum* 258.

15.36 Arguably, it is overall not sufficiently clear what the risks to information processing systems are, that need the relevant administrative, accounting, internal control, control and safeguard procedures under this Part. The risks for these procedural forms of regulation can be more clearly stated so that the quality of procedures can be evaluated by ESMA against the effective management of those risks. It can be argued that as Part 4 stipulates a duty for ESG rating providers to have written policies and procedures so that they can engage in a 'thorough analysis' of relevant information, one risk to information processing relates to omission. As Part 11 refers to information of sufficient quality from reliable sources, another risk could be poor information quality or defective/ flawed information of any kind.

15.37 Part 4 provides for written policies and procedures for 'thorough analysis' of relevant information to be in place, and it is queried what 'written policies' mean. Would the need for 'written' provide an air of importance or permanence to these policies and procedures distinguished from the other forms of meta or procedural regulation discussed? It would seem unlikely that there is a compliance hierarchy in respect of all the new governance regulatory techniques discussed in this article, and clarity is needed for ascertaining if a special regulatory expectation is attached to the 'written' nature of policies and procedures.

15.38 The need to implement policies to facilitate thorough analysis of information by analysts is not only found in this Regulation but also in the Regulation for credit rating agencies.[57] It is noted that there is no direct duty to engage in thorough analysis, meaning that a failure of thorough analysis is not itself actionable, but the failure of adequate policies and procedures. The inadequacy of those policies and procedures can nevertheless give rise to enforcement or supervisory action whether or not the analysis is itself impeached. This procedural regulation arguably addresses the risk to rating inaccuracy caused by errors, such as erroneous inclusions or omissions.

15.39 The risk of omission for ESG ratings may arguably be significant as there may be a wide variety of factors, discussed in different sources of information that can potentially be relevant to single or double materiality. Hence, policies and procedures may need to be clear and specific about the extensive range of sources analysts must consult or train machines with. Policies and procedures also need to be clear why sources are selected, for example, due to their

57 Art 8(2).

authoritative, peer-reviewed or expert nature, in order to justify any apparent omissions. In order to facilitate 'thorough analysis,' it is likely that policies and procedures themselves would need to be 'thorough' in terms of their coverage.

The quality of 'thoroughness' required above may be moderated by the need for these to be relevant to ESG rating analyses. In this respect firms have considerable discretion in terms of what they consider relevant, according to the values or perspectives they champion in respect of their rating products. The requirement of 'thoroughness' also relates to the 'life cycle' of ESG information in terms of their contextual, corporate-specific and ex post nature, such as relating to impact. As policy-makers have no desire to interfere with content of rating methodologies and prefer to promote diversity and competition (Preamble 36), it is argued that ESG rating providers' scope for considering what may be 'relevant' can go some way to justify their extent of 'thoroughness.' In order to mitigate regulatory risks, considerations of relevance should perhaps be very clearly set out in the policies and procedures for 'thorough analysis.' **15.40**

Part 11 is also a form of procedural regulation as it compels ESG rating providers to engage in 'all necessary measures' to ensure that information of sufficient quality from reliable sources are used. These measures relate likely to procedures for researching information sources and their nature, and also to checking for verifiability or veracity of sources. **15.41**

It is queried whether ESG rating providers would be funnelled down accepted channels of information sources such as subscription-based research and analytics, government and authoritative sources, international organizations' outputs for example. Would independent researchers' opinions count, or think tanks', or non-governmental organizations' reports and sources? Would academic research, which can essentially be debatable, count? It is uncertain how much scope firms have to justify their view of 'sufficient' quality and reliability, but this is perhaps something that firms at least need to make explicit in their policies. **15.42**

It is arguable that the information risks for information processing systems are not confined to omissions and information reliability and quality discussed in relation to Parts 4 and 11. There may be other information risks such as information misuse or even externally generated information problems, such as 'deep fake' attacks and cybersecurity risks. The open-endedness of Part 6, regarding what information risks are being addressed by meta or procedural regulation, may be due to policy-makers' envisaging that information **15.43** processing systems can combine both human and machine operations. Hence, it may be difficult to stipulate the full range of human as well as machine risks involved. Machine processing risks are in particular highlighted below.

15.44 ESG rating providers may use machine learning systems or generative artificial intelligence as part of their information processing or analyses. As the range of information for double materiality in particular would be rather extensive, ESG rating providers may need to have big data capabilities to collate, monitor and track extensive sources of public, third-party, expert and stakeholder input sources. Some ESG rating providers, such as Clarity.AI already openly acknowledge that they involve artificial intelligence systems in information processing and analysis. The risks emanating from machine learning and generative artificial intelligence systems are emerging in nature, and it is uncertain if they have all been mapped.[58] Well-discussed areas of risks include undue discrimination,[59] violations of privacy,[60] or fake or corrupt data.[61] The nature of control or safeguard mechanisms for such systems would be specially-tailored for these risks, and the general nature of Part 6 may not be able to precisely address them.

15.45 As the EU is also bringing into force a Regulation for the responsible design and use of artificial intelligence systems,[62] ESG rating providers should mind the compliance obligations in that Regulation. Perhaps the general nature of Part 6 should be read as integrated with these other cross-sectoral obligations

58 Xiaoge Zhang, Felix T. S. Chan, Chao Yan, Indranil Bose, 'Towards Risk-Aware Artificial Intelligence and Machine Learning Systems: An Overview' (2022) 159 Decision Support Systems 113800. Op-eds see 'Getting to Know and Map Your Biggest AI Risks' (McKinsey, 3 May 2021), https://www.mckinsey.com/capabilities/quantumblack/our-insights/getting-to-know-and-manage-your-biggest-ai-risks; Peter Smulovics, 'Navigating AI Risks: Strategies for Effective Control and Mitigation' (11 July 2023), https://www.linkedin.com/pulse/navigating-ai-risks-strategies-effective-control-peter-smulovics/.

59 F. Zuiderveen Borgesius, *Discrimination, Artificial Intelligence, and Algorithmic Decision-Making* (Council of Europe, Directorate General of Democracy, 2018), https://rm.coe.int/discrimination-artificial-intelligence-and-algorithmic-decisionmaking/1680925d73, https://pure.uva.nl/ws/files/42473478/32226549.pdf.

60 Karl Manheim and Lyric Kaplan, 'Artificial Intelligence Risks to Privacy and Democracy' (2019) 21 Yale *Journal of Law and Technology* 106.

61 E.g. see Bo Zhao, Shaozeng Zhang, Chunxue Xu, and Chengbin Deng, 'Deep Fake Geography? When Geospatial Data Encounter Artificial Intelligence' (2021) 48 Cartography and Geographic Information Science 338; Fiametta Marulli, Stefano Marone and Laura Verde, 'Sensitivity of Machine Learning Approaches to Fake and Untrusted Data in Healthcare Domain' (2022) 11 *Journal of Sensor and Actuator Networks* 21.

62 The EU AI Act is imminently expected to be approved, with its final draft finalized in early 2024, see https://digital-strategy.ec.europa.eu/en/policies/regulatory-framework-ai.

where applicable. In general, entities subject to financial regulation must not neglect other general or cross-sectoral compliance that is expected of them.[63]

F. REGULATING RATING METHODOLOGIES

This Article also addresses ESG rating providers' methodologies and provides a form of regulatory governance to ensure that methodologies are of expected quality, while not being standardized or interfered with to affect their innovation and diversity (Preamble 36). The regulatory expectations are that rating methodologies should be 'rigorous, systematic, independent and capable of justification and shall apply those rating methodologies continuously and in a transparent manner.' **15.46**

A number of these qualitative standards for rating methodologies have also been found in the regulation of credit rating agencies,[64] as well as the regulation of benchmarks.[65] This can give rise to an impression that these qualitative standards are cross-cutting and at a 'gold standard' level. This commentary argues that such consistency may be desired by EU policy-makers in having the comfort of perceiving the internal coherence of the voluminous body of EU financial regulation. However, the sense of real applicable consistency is mistaken. This commentary addresses each of the qualitative standards and where relevant, compares them to their regulatory counterparts elsewhere. It argues that there is no greater clarity achieved for ESG rating providers as to what may be required, and superficial consistency in the use of regulatory terms does not achieve much. The analysis here is kept succinct but the full critical work is found elsewhere.[66] **15.47**

Further, Part 8 provides for the ongoing, at least annual review of rating methodologies, and Part 14 stipulates that where methodological changes occur, these should be published according to the public transparency requirements under Article 23 (commented elsewhere in this volume). Presumably, the review and adjustment of rating methodologies would also have to meet the qualitative standards stipulated above. **15.48**

63 Iris H-Y Chiu, 'Technological Transformations in the Financial Sector: Principles for Lex Specialis, Lex Generalis and their Interrelationship' (2023) 40(1) *Banking and Finance Law Review*.

64 Art 8.

65 Art 12.

66 Chiu, 'Regulating ESG Rating and Data Product Providers,' above.

15.49 The first qualitative standard refers to rigour. This likely means that rating methodologies promote rigorous analysis. In relation to regulation of credit rating agencies, the meaning of 'rigour' is unpacked in the Commission delegated regulation,[67] as applied to the measurement of 'credit worthiness,'[68] which is the probability of borrower default concerning a debt financial instrument. For example, rigour includes comprehensiveness in considering all 'driving factors' of credit worthiness; using reliable and relevant models for analyzing these driving factors; ensuring the use of such models is sensitive to relevant risk factors; explainability in relation to each qualitative and quantitative factor considered and that the analytical framework is robustly controlled and approved within the credit rating agency.[69] The elements of 'rigour' are specific to the needs of measuring credit worthiness. We also find 'rigour' to be required for financial benchmarks' development.[70] However, in contrast, the meaning of 'rigour' is not further unpacked in Commission delegated legislation, which means that the substantive application to CRAs may not appropriately be extended to benchmark administrators.

15.50 In this manner, there is no real standardized understanding of 'rigour' as a general qualitative standard for the different methodologies in information mediation. This can create significant legal risk for ESG rating providers as measuring single and double materiality are developing areas where there may not be agreed ways of carrying out the selection of indicators, evaluations, weightings and aggregations. Indeed the ESG ratings landscape is replete with variances in output and low correlations, reflecting deep differences in methodologies.[71] Even if policy-makers are committed to preserving diversity and innovation in rating providers' methodologies, holding them to certain qualitative standards can create misleading expectations in relation to what is normatively acceptable.

15.51 Next, rating methodologies are to be 'systematic.' As unpacked by the Commission delegated regulation[72] for credit rating agencies, being systematic refers to applying analytical models, key assumptions and criteria evenly across

---

67 Commission delegated regulation 447/2012.

68 Art 3, *ibid.*

69 Art 4, *ibid.*

70 Art 12, Regulation of Benchmarks 2016/1011.

71 Sung Eun (Summer) Kim, 'The Duality of Variance Among ESG Assessments' (2023) 88(2) *Missouri Law Review*, https://scholarship.law.missouri.edu/mlr/vol88/iss2/7; Matteo Gargantini and Michele Siri, 'Information Intermediaries and Sustainability: ESG Ratings and Benchmarks in the European Union' (ECMI Working Paper 2022).

72 Art 5, Commission delegated regulation 447/2012.

the same asset class and not diverging unless there is a good reason. Being 'systematic' also includes being able to promptly incorporate findings from review. As the quality of being systematic is in relation to debt instruments of the same class, it is queried whether this quality can be appropriately required of rating corporate issuers more broadly. Issuers of the same sector may be conveniently classed together but even in different sectors, issuers exposed to similar E, S or G risks could arguably be classed together. In other words, categorising issuers together for a 'systematic' approach is not straightforward for ESG ratings, and there may different rationales for different groupings.

As argued by this commentator elsewhere, there may not be a need to, and indeed policy-makers seem to agree that, there are good reasons to keep the ESG rating provider market diverse. One consequence of this is that market participants should see the variances between ESG ratings, even for the same issuer by different rating providers, in a positive light, as long as these differences provide meaningful market choice. The main complaint users have, in relation to ESG infomediaries' products for issuers, including different ESG-themed stock market benchmarks, is variance and low correlations.[73] Kim,[74] however, argues that there is 'good' and 'bad' variance amongst ESG infomediaries' output. Good variance relates to deliberate differences made in the infomediary's methodological choices, which offer particular perspectives for certain market participants. These need not be standardized to be comparable, and are part of a market offering a menu of choices for investment analysis and research. These deliberate differences are quite justifiable and can cater for different investors' objectives. As ESG infomediaries may give different weights to different factors and indicators, and also balance and reconcile them in different ways, based on their values and conceptualizations, they offer investors different perspectives of corporate issuers. Investors can benefit from such good variances in a market for choice as long as differences are made clear and how these serve investors' objectives. **15.52**

In light of the need for the ESG ratings market to preserve good variances that are meaningful for market choice, it is queried whether requiring rating providers to ensure their methodologies are 'systematic' would cause concern as to the meaning of this legal risk. Would rating providers start looking for safety in some form of convergence? Would such an outworking meet investors' **15.53**

---

73 Lucy Pérez, Vivian Hunt, Hamid Samandari, Robin Nuttall and Krysta Biniek, 'Does ESG Really Matter and Why' (McKinsey Quarterly, 10 August 2022), https://www.mckinsey.com/business-functions/sustainability/our-insights/does-esgreally-matter-and-why.

74 Kim (2023).

demands or indeed be contradictory to the offerings of good variances as discussed above?

15.54 Next, ESG rating methodologies adopted should be 'independent and capable of justification.' Independence of judgement in producing ESG ratings is the overarching outcome that regulation aims to achieve, and relates to the proper management of conflicts of interest, elsewhere commented in this volume. 'Capable of justification' may be separate from the independence quality, interpreted as requiring ESG rating methodologies to be explainable in terms of how it achieves its result. However, a narrow reading would link the two qualitative factors together and suggest that 'capable of justification' refers only to explaining how the rating methodology allows independent judgement to be made. This standard is not found in the regulation for credit rating agencies or benchmarks and is unique to this Regulation.

15.55 This commentator has argued[75] that this qualitative standard is a relevant regulatory standard for ESG rating methodologies but other qualitative terms in Part 7 risk being inappropriately borrowed from other regulations or inappropriate in terms of the lack of clarity in their substantive meaning. However, in supporting a healthy ESG ratings market that offers variances in a meaningful way, regulation can usefully require ESG rating providers' methodologies to be explainable in terms of what makes them stand out and why they are adopted. Such a qualitative standard is more consistent with promoting choice. It is also arguable that this qualitative standard is potentially contradictory to the other qualitative terms borrowed from credit ratings and benchmark regulations, i.e. rigour and being systematic. Those terms lean towards aligning with convergent and acceptable 'ways of doing things.' It may be counterproductive to retain the borrowed terms as they lack substantive meaning applied to the ESG ratings market and are likely to cause unnecessary legal risk or unintended behavioural responses on the part of ESG rating providers.

15.56 Part 7 also requires rating methodologies to be capable of 'continuous application.' This term is similar to the one applied to credit rating methodologies and as unpacked by the Commission delegated regulation, being 'continuous' means capable of being applied without discontinuation, capable of incorporating findings from review and able to assist in comparing across different asset classes. It is submitted that this quality as defined for credit rating methodologies is uniquely applicable to credit ratings. It seems to import notions

75 Chiu, 'Regulating ESG Rating and Data Product Providers,' above.

of 'higher level' consistency that allows rating methodologies to be used across different classes of debt instruments.

This commentator is sceptical of the value-added to regulatory governance in applying the 'continuous' standard to ESG rating methodologies. Although users of ESG ratings would like comparability between rankings, and methodological consistency arguably underpins credible comparisons, it is likely more important to require ESG rating providers to explain clearly what is being measured across a selected cohort, the purpose and criteria for their selection and the application of analyses and evaluations. In this manner investors can decide if those selections/groupings for comparison are meaningful for their portfolio or allocation decisions. The qualitative standards regarding being systematic and continuous assume that the categories of subjects to be evaluated are relatively clear and established, and this may be the case for credit ratings. But where such an assumption cannot be made in the case of ESG ratings, what is important to investors is the initial rationalized and explained selection of a category or grouping of comparable issuers. The methodologies adopted must then be appropriate to the grouping so selected. Such methodologies may also be innovative, developing and subject to adjustment, so their responsiveness to change must not be curtailed by the fears of legal risk regarding what 'systematic' or 'continuous' may mean for ESG rating providers. On balance, these terms may be more counterproductive than effective in regulating ESG rating providers' methodological quality. 15.57

Finally Part 7 requires that ESG rating methodologies be capable of transparent application. This arguably supports the explainability of rating methodologies discussed earlier and is beneficial for informed market choice. 15.58

In sum, this commentator is wary of the appearance of regulatory consistency and turning into gold standards certain qualitative standards that are more particularly applicable to credit rating methodologies. The more meaningful requirements in this Part relate to being 'capable of justification' and 'transparent application.' These would more likely foster market discipline in scrutinising the variances that ESG rating providers have on offer. 15.59

The position argued for by this commentator is also aligned with Part 13, which deals with the protection of ESG rating providers' trade secrets. Policy-makers seem to acknowledge the importance of proprietary methodologies and rating providers' innovations and how they distinguish themselves in the market for ESG ratings. Hence, ESG rating providers need not disclose information 15.60

about their intellectual capital, intellectual property, know-how or the results of innovation that would qualify as trade secrets.

15.61 The protection of ESG rating providers from having to disclose their trade secrets is important in incentivizing innovation while striking a balance with facilitating a market for informed choice. It clarifies that the expectations of explainability and transparent application would not involve disclosing trade secrets, but should do enough to inform users and regulators as to what the ESG rating provider's offering is.

15.62 As the users of ESG ratings are predominantly a sophisticated market, the quality of explainability and transparent application can be calibrated to be appropriate to that and need not be at the level of the retail investor. The requirements of public transparency are commented elsewhere in this volume.

15.63 ESG rating providers supply their information products mainly to financial product providers. They may supply analysis, data and ratings for active managers and also to stock market benchmark developers. Some ESG rating providers also supply stock market benchmarks for passive managers. Hence, the user base is sophisticated. Active managers often apply or integrate relevant information products into their in-house frameworks and strategic decisions relevant to financial product design and marketing.[76] In this manner, ESG rating providers contribute to an upstream stage of financial product generation, and users transform their input into their product designs and marketing agendas at the mid-stream before ultimate investment products are offered downstream to investors, whether professional or retail. Often, active managers subscribe to more than one ESG rating provider's products[77] in order to gain scope or benefit from different perspectives or approaches in infomediaries' methodologies.

15.64 Stock market benchmark providers are influential in the passive investing market, which has grown exponentially as a global phenomenon.[78] Passively tracking a diversified portfolio of stocks that adhere to certain performance track records or upfront themes, is a popular and less expensive form of collective investing. This means that stock market benchmark developers wield

76 Quinn Curtis, Jill E. Fisch and Adriana Z. Robertson, 'Do ESG Mutual Funds Deliver on Their Promises?' (2021) 120 *Michigan law Review* 393.

77 Kim (2023).

78 'Global passive equity funds' assets eclipsed active in 2023 for first time' (Reuters, 1 February 2024), https://www.reuters.com/markets/us/global-markets-funds-passive-2024-02-01/#:~:text=The%20SPDR%20S%26P%20500%20ETF,billion%20and%20%2424.79%20billion%2C%20respectively.

immense influence in directing capital flows to issuers included in their benchmarks.[79] This area is however regarded as regulated under the EU Benchmarks Regulation 2016, and not under this Regulation. A topic for another time is the need to reconcile the regulatory governance of ESG rating providers and ESG benchmark administrators, as the Benchmarks regulation, which was responding more to the scandal of interest rate benchmark manipulation, does not arguably cater specifically for the issues relating to stock market benchmarks.[80]

Given ESG rating providers' sophisticated user base, it is reiterated that the regulatory governance for methodologies should centre upon fostering an informed market for choice. Where the qualitative standards for methodologies may result in unintended legal risks that are unclear in application to ESG rating providers, these should be considered for removal rather than inclusion. **15.65**

G. ESG RATINGS AS OPINIONS

Part 11 requires ESG rating providers to clearly state that ESG ratings are opinions. It is queried why this would be necessary given that Art 3 already defines ESG ratings as opinions, consistent with the approach taken in defining credit ratings as opinions too regarding creditworthiness. The legal effect of stating ESG ratings as opinions would that that ESG rating providers should be shielded from actions in civil liability for misrepresentation[81] if their evaluations become challenged or any predictive element in their ratings was not borne out, such as if an issuer rated well for S were to suffer a social scandal.[82] **15.66**

However, if an opinion is made without honest belief at all, or where an opinion could not reasonably be held based on the facts that exist,[83] then an action for misrepresentation can still lie under the common law. **15.67**

A related matter for discussion is that other than misrepresentation or actions relating to deceit, the Regulation does not provide for civil litigation in relation **15.68**

79 Tom Nangle, 'The hidden power of index providers' (Financial Times, 9 April 2024), https://www.ft.com/content/badb4ac9-eafe-4963-8406-4ede5cfa878d.

80 Chiu, 'Regulating ESG Rating and Data Product Providers,' above.

81 *Bisset v Wilkinson* [1927] AC 177.

82 Sebastian Utz, 'Corporate Scandals and the Reliability of ESG Assessments: Evidence from an International Sample' (2019) 13 *Review of Managerial Science* 483 finds that most ESG rating providers respond to scandals and adjust their ratings but ratings often cannot predict scandals.

83 *Smith v Land and House Property Corporation* (1884) 28 Ch D 7.

to breaches of regulatory law.[84] This is different from the Regulation of credit rating agencies, even if commentators regard the hurdles to successful civil litigation to be significant,[85] or doubt the effectiveness of civil litigation as a form of discipline.[86] Users' private law rights against ESG rating providers, in contract as well as in civil obligations, would likely be subject to fragmentation in relation to their prospects of proceeding in Member States' national private law regimes.

H. RELATIONS WITH ISSUERS

15.69 Part 12 deals with the least that is expected of ESG rating providers' relations with issuers. This Part provides issuers with the opportunity to review an ESG rating ahead of time before its first issue, and to inform the rating provider of any factual errors.

15.70 ESG rating providers' relations with issuers are a tricky issue. Closeness with the issuer may allow the rating provider to gain useful information input, but may compromise the objectivity and independence of the rating provider. Distance from the issuer, such as relying only on publicly available reporting, alongside other non-issuer information inputs, may provide an ESG rating provider with a more rounded selection of information sources, but the rating provider may not be aware of certain information only in the issuer's possession. The international recommendations made by IOSCO encourage rating providers to gain access to issuers and to foster constructive relations.[87] The position taken in the EU regulation seems more wary of such closeness and is concerned for undue influence. This provision can be seen as the provision of a minimum right for the issuer to be engaged with, while ESG rating providers' preferred practices are left for them to determine as long as compliance with the regulation can be achieved.

---

84 Art 35a.

85 Aron Verstandig, 'The Civil Liability Regime of the CRA-Regulation and the Requirement of Causation' in Gudula Deipenbrock and Mads Andenas (eds), Special Issue of International and Comparative Corporate Law Journal on Civil Liability of Credit Rating Agencies in the European Union – Selected Legal and Economic Aspects (2015) *ICLQ*; Andrea Miglionico, 'The European Union' in *The Governance of Credit Rating Agencies* (Cheltenham: Edward Elgar 2019, ch 9); Brigitte Haar, 'Civil Liability of Credit Rating Agencies after CRA 3 – Regulatory All-or-Nothing Approaches between Immunity and Over-Deterrence' (2013), https://papers.ssrn.com/sol3/papers.cfm?abstract_id=2198293.

86 Thomas MJ Möllers and Charis Niedorf, 'Regulation and Liability of Credit Rating Agencies – A More Efficient European Law?' (2015) 11 *European Company and Financial Law Review* 333.

87 Recommendations 8, 9, IOSCO (2021).

Issuers are given a minimum right to review an ESG rating before its first issue within 48 hours starting on a working day. This is a short turnaround for the issuer but it may address any fears of prolonged issuer engagement and undue influence upon the rating. Further, as the purpose of the short engagement is limited to informing of factual errors, the short turnaround does not afford the issuer an opportunity to engage in challenging the rating on the basis of opinion disagreement. It is noted that the international recommendations made by IOSCO do not stipulate a timeline for such review. **15.71**

In order to support issuers' minimum right as above, issuers are able to request certain limited pieces of information used by the ESG rating provider. It is surmised that these pieces of information are limited in order to protect ESG rating providers from being pressured into justifying their trade secrets protected under Part 13. However, it may not be the case that factual errors must only emanate from these limited pieces of information. **15.72**

Upon request by the issuer, the ESG rating provider must provide the information in Annex III (1)(aa), (1)(b) and 2(b)(2). These relate to (a) 'industry classification used'; 'an overview of data sources including whether data is sourced from the mandatory Corporate Sustainability Reporting Directive disclosures, from information disclosed under the Sustainable Financial Disclosure Regulation in relation to investment products, and whether sources are public or non-public and an overview of data processes, estimation of input data in case of unavailability and frequency of data updates'; and 'where applicable, the use of estimation and industry average and explanation of the underlying methodology.' **15.73**

In relation to the information in Annex III (1)(aa), which is 'industry classification used,' it is uncertain if this compels ESG rating providers to adopt certain industry-based groupings for comparing issuers, and to what extent these are standardized. Standardization is not necessarily a bad thing and can promote ease of use for investors, as long as they do not prematurely make assumptions that stifle diversity of perspectives. **15.74**

The information referred to in Annex III (1)(b) has been empirically shown to be desirable for users[88] as they are able to weigh up the diversity of input sources and what is being offered in methodological variances amongst rating providers. As the requirement is to provide an overview, this should prevent **15.75**

88 'ESMA identifies shortcomings in "immature" ESG ratings market' (Global Investor, Euromoney, 27 June 2022).

rating providers from being asked to disclose trade secrets in terms of proprietary and analytical methodologies.

15.76 Allowing issuers to ask rating providers to disclose if any estimated input or data has been used, such as industry average, would be helpful for issuers if their ESG rating is affected by such input and they have unique information or circumstances that would deviate from such an industry average. This is also in the spirit of allowing factual errors to be corrected so that ESG ratings are made more accurate and not just contested.

ARTICLE 16

SEPARATION OF BUSINESS AND ACTIVITIES

Iris H-Y Chiu

1. **ESG rating providers shall not provide any of the following activities:**
   (a) **consulting activities to investors or undertakings;**
   (b) **the issuance and distribution of credit ratings as defined in Article 3(1), point (a), of Regulation (EC) No 1060/2009;**
   (c) **the provision of benchmarks as defined in Article 3(1), point (5), of Regulation (EU) 2016/1011;**
   (d) **investment services and activities as defined in Article 4(1), point (2), of Directive 2014/65/EU;**
   (e) **statutory auditing on financial statements and assurance engagements on sustainability reporting within the meaning of Directive 2013/34/EU;**
   (f) **activities of credit institutions within the meaning of the Regulation (EU) No 575/2013, and insurance or reinsurance activities within the meaning of Directive 2009/138/EC.**
2. **By way of derogation from paragraph 1, an ESG rating provider may provide the activities referred to in paragraph 1, point (d) or (f), provided that it puts in place, in addition to the measures referred to in Articles 25 and 26, specific measures:**
   (a) **to ensure that each activity is exercised autonomously;**
   (b) **to avoid the creation of potential risks of conflicts of interest in decision-making within its ESG rating activities;**
   (c) **to ensure that its employees who are directly involved in the assessment process of a rated item do not provide any of the activities referred to in paragraph 1, point (d) or (f).**

   In implementing such measures, the ESG rating provider shall also take into account the activities of the group to which it belongs, if applicable.
3. **By way of derogation from paragraph 1, point (c), an ESG rating provider may lodge a request with ESMA to be authorised to provide benchmarks provided that it puts in place specific measures, including those referred to in paragraph 2. ESMA shall decide whether the**

measures proposed by the ESG rating provider are appropriate and sufficient regarding the potential risks of conflicts of interest. If ESMA considers that the measures are not appropriate or sufficient regarding the potential risks of conflicts of interest, paragraph 1, point (c), shall apply.

Any substantial change in the measures taken by the ESG rating provider or in their implementation shall be notified to ESMA by the ESG rating provider before such change is implemented. ESMA shall decide whether the measures remain appropriate and sufficient regarding the potential risks of conflicts of interest. If ESMA considers that the measures are no longer appropriate or sufficient regarding the potential risks of conflicts of interest, paragraph 1, point (c), shall apply.

ESMA shall take a decision as referred to in the first and second subparagraphs of this paragraph within 30 working days of receipt of complete information about the measures proposed by the ESG rating provider or any substantial changes thereto, or within the deadlines laid down in Article 7 where ESMA's assessment forms part of its evaluation of the ESG rating provider's application for authorisation.

4. **An ESG rating provider shall ensure that its employees who are directly involved in the assessment process of a rated item do not provide any of the activities referred to in paragraph 1, points (a), (b) and (e).**
5. **ESMA shall develop draft regulatory technical standards to specify the details of the measures and safeguards to be implemented pursuant to paragraphs 2, 3 and 4.**

   ESMA shall submit the draft regulatory technical standards referred to in the first subparagraph to the Commission by 2 October 2025.

   Power is delegated to the Commission to supplement this Regulation by adopting the regulatory technical standards referred to in the first subparagraph of this paragraph in accordance with Articles 10 to 14 of Regulations (EU) No 1095/2010.
6. **ESG rating providers shall ensure that the provision of services other than those referred to in paragraph 1 does not create risks of conflicts of interest within its ESG rating activities. Where there are risks of conflicts of interest, ESG rating providers shall refrain from offering such other services.**

A. INTRODUCTION

16.01 The separation of business activities required under this article is a structural separation in nature, meaning that the company that is in the business of providing ESG ratings cannot be involved in the other business lines prescribed. Preamble 39 clarifies that separation means having separate legal entities. Other companies within the same corporate group could be involved in these other business lines but in this manner, they are structurally separate from the ESG ratings business. Structural separation creates frictions for the sharing of information and resources, and is meant to address the conflicts of interest that arise if an ESG rating provider were able to engage in multiple lines of businesses.

16.02 Structural separation by regulatory fiat enjoyed a rejuvenation since the global financial crisis of 2008. Credit rating agencies in particular are now prohibited from offering rating business alongside business advisory or consulting services[1] as their closeness to issuers has been highlighted to be crucial for inflated ratings of structured products that were overvalued and tanked during the global financial crisis.[2] Conflicts of interest emanating from different business lines within the same entity pose risks for protecting the integrity and accuracy of information signalling goods provided by the entity. These goods are perceived to embed independent and are poised to be trusted by financial markets. Hence, the 'corruption' of judgement underlying information signalling goods would be an abuse of market trust, since market participants are not able to discern corrupted quality on the face of it.

16.03 It can be argued that where an information signalling good has suffered such corruption and eventually comes to light, market discipline would be sufficient to ensure that reliance becomes disengaged and other competitive market goods can rise to fill the gap. However, self-regulation and market discipline would not be able to prevent investment losses that occur due to misplaced

1 Regulation of credit rating agencies 1060/2009, Annex I, Sect B(1)(4).

2 Andrew Johnston, 'Corporate Governance is the Problem, not the Solution: A Critical Appraisal of the European Regulation on Credit Rating Agencies' (2011) 11 *Journal of Corporate Law Studies* 395; Lynn Bai, 'On Regulating Conflicts of Interests in the Credit Rating Industry' (2010) 13 *New York University Journal of Legislation and Public Policy* 253; Chester Spatt, 'Ratings Shopping and Asset Complexity: A Theory of Ratings Inflation' (2009) 56 *Journal of Monetary Economics* 696.

reliance. Hence, ex ante regulation to prevent the corruption of information signalling goods has a place for the purposes of preventing misallocation and serving investor protection.

16.04 This requirement has become a norm in EU financial regulation where mismanagement of conflicts of interest has either been the subject of a scandal or looms large as a governance risk. In the EU regulation of benchmarks for example, separation of business for benchmark administrators is also required unless the administrator is not 'significant.' This provision is pre-emptive in nature rather than responding specifically to a market failure or scandal. The regulation of benchmarks followed from the revelations of the manipulation of interest rate benchmark submissions, i.e. LIBOR and EURIBOR,[3] made by banks to self-regulatory benchmark administrators. Although the manipulation was carried out due to poorly managed conflicts of interest at the banks' end (due to their multiple business lines), and not at the end of the benchmark administrators, regulation introduced a pre-emptive requirement for separation of business in order to prevent benchmark administrators from succumbing to any future conflicts of interest.

16.05 However, regulatory fiat has not been able to reach certain businesses where conflicts of interest remain rife and may taint much-needed independent judgement, such as in the area of financial auditing, which supports the market for investor trust in issuers' publicly reported financial statements. The auditing industry engages in multiple lines of business advisory and consulting roles and yet auditors are expected to deliver an independent opinion on issuers' financial statements. Flawed and compromised audits have obscured investors' scrutiny from profoundly troubled firms such as Enron in the US in 2000[4] and Carillion in the UK in 2018.[5] Indeed Coffee has argued that auditors' conflicted roles corrupted their 'gatekeeping' role for financial markets.[6] Despite

---

3 'LIBOR Manipulation: Done for you, Big Boy', Financial Times (27 June 2012); Martin Wheatley, The Wheatley Review of LIBOR (Sep 2012); 'Interest rate "rigging" evidence "covered up" by banks' (BBC News, 22 May 2023), https://www.bbc.co.uk/news/business-65635243; R. Herrera, F. Climent, A. Momparler & P. Carmona, 'Can Euribor be Fixed?' 34 Economic Research-Ekonomska Istraživanja 2833–2852 (2021), https://doi.org/10.1080/1331677X.2020.1844029.

4 'Arthur Andersen's Legacy, 20 Years After Its Demise, Is Complicated' (WSJ, 31 August 2022), https://www.wsj.com/articles/arthur-andersens-legacy-20-years-after-its-demise-is-complicated-11661938200.

5 DWP and BEIS, *Public Inquiry into the Collapse of Carillion* (2018), paras 116–124, https://publications.parliament.uk/pa/cm201719/cmselect/cmworpen/769/76902.htm.

6 John C. Coffee Jr., 'Understanding Enron: "It's about Gatekeepers, Stupid"' (2002) 57 *Business Lawyer* 1403.

increased professional regulation of auditors that followed,[7] the industry has a powerful lobbying clout and has managed to resist any top-down suggestion of separation of business.[8] Even the voluntary efforts made by Ernst & Young to separate its auditing business have been internally torpedoed.[9]

Policy-makers recognize that structural separation, which affects legal organizational form, may not be sufficient to protect rating analysts' independence. If the corporate group expects the sharing and transferring of personnel within its different business lines, a soft form of influence over judgement can still occur despite structural separation. Hence, the article includes in Part 4 the prohibition on employees working directly on ESG ratings to be involved in consulting activities, credit rating, or statutory audit activities. These may be perceived as activities that 'get too close' to issuers and may affect rating analysts' judgement of an issuers' ESG ratings. **16.06**

B. SEPARATION OF BUSINESS ACTIVITIES

The activities that ESG rating providers are not supposed to engage in alongside ESG ratings businesses are as follows: consulting services to investors or issuers; issuing and distributing credit ratings; providing stock market benchmarks; providing services of statutory auditing for the financial statements of issuers; providing assurance services in relation to issuers' sustainability reporting; whether mandatory or voluntary reporting; regulated investment services activities; regulated banking activities; and regulated insurance or reinsurance activities. The discussion below teases out in turn what nature of conflicts of interest is sought to be prevented in relation to each of those business lines. **16.07**

First, ESG rating providers are not to engage in consulting services to investors or issuers. ESG rating providers mostly work on issuing ratings for corporate issuers, in order to inform investors of how well issuers manage material ESG risks to their financial performance.[10] This business model is usually on **16.08**

7 Such as the establishment of the PCAOB in the US considered acceptance of various independent reviews for reform in financial reporting, audit and the auditing industry in the UK, BEIS, 'Restoring Trust In Audit and Corporate Governance' (May 2022). These reforms have however been delayed under the Conservative government, 'UK government set to omit audit reform from legislative plans' (Financial Times, 30 August 2023), https://www.ft.com/content/57d2dfd5-92d1-4cb4-ac1e-9e0cd3c2aff4.

8 Competition and Markets Authority, *Statutory Audit Market Study* (9 October 2018), https://www.gov.uk/government/news/cma-recommends-shake-up-of-uk-audit-market.

9 'EY calls off plan to split audit, consulting units' (Reuters, 12 April 2023), https://www.reuters.com/business/ey-scraps-break-up-plan-ft-2023-04-11/#:~:text=April%2011%20(Reuters)%20%2D%20Accounting,over%20potential%20conflicts%20of%20interest.

10 Such as the business models of leading providers like Sustainalytics, MSCI.

a user-pays basis. If ESG rating providers engage in consulting services for certain investors, their preferences and influences may unduly shape rating providers' perspectives and methodologies, and in this manner, independence of judgement may be affected.

16.09 If ESG rating providers foray into consulting services for issuers, the issuer-pays revenue streams will entail conflicts of interest with the user-pays rating services. It would become uncertain if rating providers may be influenced by their corporate clients in issuing their ESG ratings. Further, corporate clients can be coached into meeting certain rating standards, whether or not there is genuine change of work processes or behaviour.

16.10 The EU[11] has recently introduced the policy of double materiality, so that corporations should also report on their impact on wider environmental, social and governance issues,[12] and investors and stakeholders can evaluate their impact and non-financial performance.[13] In this emerging area of ESG evaluation, which differs significantly from single materiality approaches,[14] ESG rating providers need to find their feet, develop their perspectives and methodologies and offer these as products of independence and expertise in a competitive market. The nature of this emerging area is that there would be plenty of debates and disagreements about what impact to measure or accord weight, and how to do so. Investors and issuers would have their preferences and perspectives too. ESG rating providers engaged too closely with investors or issuers may be influenced by these preferences, affecting the process of independent development of double materiality evaluations.

16.11 Next, ESG rating providers are not to provide credit rating services. Arguably these two areas require different types of expertise altogether, and it is queried why the provision of credit ratings would jeopardize the independent quality of ESG ratings. It is possible that work involving credit ratings would necessarily result in close working relationships between issuers and ESG rating providers, and such proximity may produce undue influence upon analysts working on ESG ratings.

---

11 European Green Deal, https://commission.europa.eu/strategy-and-policy/priorities-2019-2024/european-green-deal_en.

12 Corporate Sustainability Disclosure Directive 2022/2464.

13 This is the point of finance labelled with sustainability or ESG objectives under Arts 8, 9, Sustainability Financial Disclosure Regulation 2019/2088.

14 Andreas Engbert, 'ESG Ratings: Guiding a Movement in Search of Itself' (2023), https://www.ecgi.global/sites/default/files/working_papers/documents/esg.pdf.

Third, ESG rating providers are not to develop benchmarks, and this includes interest-rate or price benchmarks for debt-based financial instruments, as well as stock market benchmarks. The Regulation of benchmarks referred to in Part 1 (c) covers both types of benchmarks although they are functionally very different. Placing both types of benchmarks within the same regulatory category was an afterthought in the development of the Regulation, in order to capture products which have a reference function for financial transactions. However, this categorization results in stock market benchmark administrators being subject to a different regulatory regime from the regulation for ESG rating providers, resulting in certain regulatory gaps and unnecessary inconsistencies.[15] This is despite ESG benchmark administrators and ESG rating providers essentially perform similar functions in analyzing corporate issuers' management of single materiality risks. In this manner, the business lines are complementary, as ESG ratings provide the underlying analytics needed for benchmark development. Further, the ratings products and benchmark products can appeal to the same asset managers who have active and passive investment management business lines. For example, many ESG rating providers are also benchmark developers, such as MSCI.[16] The acquisition of ESG rating providers by benchmark providers such as S&P (in relation to the Dow Jones benchmarks) and the London Stock Exchange Group (in relation to its FTSE benchmarks), also reflect the industry's perception of complementarity. **16.12**

It is envisaged that with the advent of the double materiality policy, ESG ratings based on double materiality would be able to feed into benchmark development too. Preamble 39 seems to support the possibility that ESG rating and benchmark provision services can be complementary and need not strictly be separated, subject to adequate conflicts of interest management, as will be discussed in relation to the derogations below. **16.13**

Fourth, ESG rating providers are not to engage in the provision of investment services falling within the scope of the Markets in Financial Instruments Directive 2014 which covers a broad scope of investment intermediation services including asset and portfolio management, investment advice, trading and brokerage. It can be envisaged that where ESG ratings and investment services are co-provided by the same firm, conflicts of interest can arise in relation to how the ratings business line may influence portfolio management **16.14**

15 Iris H-Y Chiu, 'Regulating ESG Rating and Data Product Providers: Critically Examining EU Regulation through the Lens of Functional Regulatory Consistency' (2024) *European Journal of Risk Regulation*, doi:10.1017/err.2024.53.

16 https://www.msci.com/our-solutions/esg-investing/esg-ratings.

or investment advice to clients. But at the same time, such businesses are also complementary, as an investor looking for sustainable finance investments can benefit from an investment advisor that has in-house access to ESG ratings research. Again derogations are envisaged to be possible in relation to the stipulated separation, as discussed below.

16.15 Next, ESG rating providers are not to engage in statutory auditing of issuers' financial statements or providing assurance for issuers' sustainability reporting. Preamble 39 regards this area of work as generating more hazardous conflicts of interest so that derogations may not apply. In terms of statutory auditing of issuers' financial statements, the concern may lie in the close relationships that can be built up with issuers, which may unduly influence the independence of ratings provision.

16.16 In relation to providing assurance for issuers' sustainability reporting, the requirement that such business be strictly separate from ESG ratings provision is a sound one. Assurance for issuers' sustainability reports can involve working closely with issuers and becoming influenced by their perspectives. As sustainability assurance is not well standardized to date[17] and various quantitative and qualitative methods may be used, empirical research has found that such variances can obscure issuer domination over the assurance process[18] as well as generate cosmetic signalling purposes only.[19] Further, it is not certain that the assurance process would not shade into coaching issuers in terms of how material ESG risks should be reported. The lack of standardization and transparency in assurance processes as well as the closeness of issuer relations are significant factors that could create significant conflicts of interest for ESG rating providers and affect the independence of their outputs.

16.17 ESG rating providers also should not be engaged in the business lines of regulated banks or insurers/reinsurers. For regulated banks, it can be argued that as banks work closely with their borrowers, many of which are corporations, being able to access ESG ratings information may help with banks' assessment of borrowers' management of non-financial risks as part of overall

---

17 Anil Gürtürk, Rüdiger Hahn, 'An Empirical Assessment of Assurance Statements in Sustainability Reports: Smoke Screens or Enlightening Information?' (2016) 136 Journal of Cleaner Production 30. Variances are also highlighted in Amanda Sonnerfeldt, 'Regulating Third Party Assurance Engagements on Sustainability Reports: Insights from the Swedish Case' (2014) 11 *European Company Law* 137.

18 Alberto Fonseca, 'How Credible are Mining Corporations' Sustainability Reports? A Critical Analysis of External Assurance under the Requirements of the International Council on Mining and Metals' (2010) 17 *Corporate Social Responsibility and Environmental Management* 355.

19 Paolo Perego and Ans Kolk, 'Multinationals' Accountability on Sustainability: The Evolution of Third-party Assurance of Sustainability Reports' (2012) 110 *Journal of Business Ethics* 173.

creditworthiness.[20] In this manner, a banking group having an ESG ratings arm can be complementary to core banking business. However there is the hazard that banks' borrower-relations may unduly influence the ESG ratings business and affect the independence of output. A bank may give inflated ratings to its borrower and hence mislead the investment community on the borrower's ESG risks. On the other hand, borrowers could perceive that it would be inappropriate or unfair to use information regarding them for ESG ratings to feed into lending decisions, as poor ESG scores may result in higher cost of borrowing. Hence, the ESG ratings business could generate conflicts of interest or hazards to both business lines.

As insurers and reinsurers engage in risk underwriting business, it would be thought that having an ESG ratings business alongside could be complementary,[21] as the ESG research and analysis arm could provide insight as to non-financial risks that affect the core financial risks that are underwritten, such as in relation to disaster insurance, business insurance and asset-based insurance such as project and infrastructure insurance. However, similar to banks, insurers or reinsurers could have close relationships with corporate clients that affect their rating independence. On the other hand, corporate clients may perceive their insurer's use of ESG information to assess the insured risks to be unfair, if higher premiums result. In general, as ESG ratings measure non-financial risk, and often, how these affect financial risks, other businesses in financial risk intermediation, such as banking, investment and insurance businesses can all benefit from some incorporation of such insight. However, potential conflicts of interest can arise. **16.18**

C. DEROGATIONS FROM SEPARATION

Parts 2 and 3 provide for the derogations from separation of business activities as long as certain safeguards are met. This reflects policy-makers' acknowledgement that there may be useful synergies or economies of scale in cross-provision of financial activities and ESG rating activities. However, conflicts of interest need to be managed. **16.19**

20 Marina Brogi, Valentina Lagasio, Pasqualina Porretta, 'Be Good To Be Wise: Environmental, Social, and Governance Awareness as a Potential Credit Risk Mitigation Factor' (2022) 33 *Journal of International Financial Management and Accounting* 522.

21 Matthew Shea and James W Hutchin, 'The Importance of Environmental, Social, and Governance Risks to Surety Underwriters' (2018) 12 *Asia-Pacific Journal of Risk and Insurance* pp. 20170016, https://doi.org/10.1616/apjri-2017-0016.

16.20 First, ESG rating provision can exist alongside investment services or credit or insurance activities if certain conditions for conflicts of interest management are met. One condition relates to protecting the autonomy of the ESG rating activities, and reference is made to the requirements in Articles 25 and 26. Next, employees involved in ESG rating should not be involved in the financial allocation activities for investment services, credit or insurance underwriting. In this manner, the Regulation relies primarily on organizational governance and structures in order to manage conflicts of interest.

16.21 The second derogation from mandatory separation of activities is possible for benchmark development. The above has discussed how similar and complementary the activities covered within the scope of ESG rating provision and stock market benchmark development are. The Regulation requires that specific authorization needs to be obtained from ESMA for an ESG rating provider to carry out benchmark development, and ESMA would decide this within 30 days of application as long as application information is complete. This means that ESMA can scrutinize the conflicts of interest management systems and procedures, as well as policies maintained by the ESG rating provider in order to decide whether to allow the derogation and upon what conditions. Further, ESMA must be notified of any substantial changes in the rating provider's conditions without delay as the permission for derogation may then be affected.

16.22 ESMA's discretionary power can create some uncertainty, but as ESMA's decisions can be subject to appeal and Appeal Board decisions are publicly published, some manner of interpretive sense-making can develop in due course. It is also queried whether ESMA's authorization and supervision role would be able to check for private sector dominance or influence in terms of whether some ESG rating cum benchmark providers may become very powerful in the market. There is a developing overlap between the interests and objectives of financial regulation, such as financial stability and customer protection and the objectives and interests in competition regulation.[22] For example, where ESG rating providers cum benchmark providers become important or dominant, there are competition concerns. There are also concerns regarding their systemic influence in affecting financial allocations and flows, and systemic errors in these information goods can cause huge disruptions to market

22 Preliminarily explored in Iris H-Y Chiu and Despoina Mantzari, 'Regulating Fintech and BigTech: Reconciling the Objectives of Financial Regulation and Promoting Competition' in Konstantinos Stylianou (ed), *Fintech Competition: Law, Policy and Market Organisation* (Oxford: Hart Publishing, 2023), ch10.

confidence in the sustainable investment market, and create an adverse impact for financial stability. It would be curious as to whether ESMA's approval oversight role would monitor for conflict of interest management, financial stability and also anti-competitive effects. This under-explored area is likely to emerge in many areas of financial regulation where there are concerns about domination and significant influence, such as certain IT providers to financial institutions,[23] financial and digital platforms,[24] and where there may be consolidation of financial businesses.

It is clear that where no derogations are permitted, ESG rating providers must carry out their activities separately from these other activities, namely consulting activities for issuers or investors, credit rating provision and statutory auditing for financial statements or sustainability assurance for such reporting. Preamble 22b clarifies this is the position although it is not further unpacked why policy-makers regard these conflicts of interest to be more menacing than the others in the list. **16.23**

It is envisaged that ESMA will develop further technical standards and Commission legislation will flesh out the conditions for derogations to be permitted. In this way, ESMA may further clarify what factors would persuade its discretion to approve ESG rating providers being involved in benchmark development or otherwise. Further detail and conditions for ESMA's approval of investment services firms, credit or insurance institutions carrying on ESG rating activities may also be fleshed out in due course. **16.24**

23 See the Digital Operational Resilience Act 2022/2554, https://www.digital-operational-resilience-act.com/.

24 Lindsay Sain Jones and Tim R. Sample, 'On the Systemic Importance of Digital Platforms' (2023) 25 *University of Pennsylvania Journal of Business Law*, 141.

ARTICLE 17

RATING ANALYSTS, EMPLOYEES AND OTHER PERSONS INVOLVED IN THE PROVISION OF ESG RATINGS

Irene-marié Esser

1. ESG rating providers shall ensure that rating analysts, employees and any other natural person under their control or whose services are placed at their disposal, for example by way of a contractual arrangement, and who are directly involved in the provision of ESG ratings, including rating analysts directly involved in the rating process and persons involved in the provision of ESG scores, are appropriately trained and have the knowledge and experience necessary for the performance of the duties and tasks assigned, including, where appropriate, a sufficient understanding of any potential material financial risk to the rated item and any potential material impact of the rated item on the environment and on society in general.

2. ESG rating providers shall ensure that the persons referred to in paragraph 1 are not allowed to initiate or participate in negotiations regarding fees or payments with any rated item or issuer of a rated item, or with any person directly or indirectly linked to the rated item or the issuer of a rated item by control.

3. With the exception of holdings in diversified collective investment schemes, including managed funds, and of investments made under discretionary portfolio management:

(a) the persons referred to in paragraph 1 who are directly involved in the determination of an individual rating of a rated item shall not buy or sell any financial instrument issued, guaranteed, or otherwise supported by any entity that is rated within their area of analytical responsibility or by any entity within the group of that entity, nor engage in any transaction in such financial instruments;

(b) persons occupying a senior management position in the ESG rating provider shall not buy or sell any financial instrument issued, guaranteed or otherwise supported by any entity rated by the ESG rating provider, or

by any entity within the group of that entity, nor engage in any transaction in such financial instruments.

4. **The persons referred to in paragraph 1 shall not be directly involved in or otherwise influence the determination of an ESG rating of the relevant rated item where those persons:**
   (a) **own financial instruments of the rated item, other than holdings in diversified collective investment schemes, including managed funds, and investments made under discretionary portfolio management;**
   (b) **own financial instruments of any entity related to a rated item, the ownership of which might cause or might be generally perceived as causing a conflict of interest, other than holdings in diversified collective investment schemes, including managed funds, and investments made under discretionary portfolio management;**
   (c) **have had in the last year an employment, business or other relationship with the entity rated by the ESG rating provider or any entity within the group of that entity that might cause or might be generally perceived as causing a conflict of interest.**
5. **ESG rating providers shall ensure that the persons referred to in paragraph 1 and persons occupying a senior management position in the ESG rating provider:**
   (a) **take all reasonable measures to protect property and records in the possession of the ESG rating provider from fraud, theft or misuse, taking into account the nature, scale and complexity of the ESG rating provider's business and the nature and range of its ESG rating activities;**
   (b) **do not share confidential information that has been entrusted to the ESG rating provider with anyone who is not directly involved in the provision of ESG rating activities, including rating analysts and employees of any person directly or indirectly linked to the ESG rating provider by control, and any other natural person whose services are or have been placed at the disposal of, or are under the control of, any person directly or indirectly linked to the ESG rating provider by control;**
   (c) **do not use or share confidential information for any other purpose than the provision of ESG rating activities, including for the trading of financial instruments; and**
   (d) **do not solicit or accept money, gifts or favours from anyone with whom the ESG rating provider does business.**
6. **Where the persons referred to in paragraph 1 consider that any other person referred to in that paragraph has engaged in conduct that they consider to be illegal, they shall immediately report that to the oversight function. The ESG rating provider shall ensure that such reporting does not have any negative consequences for the person reporting.**
7. **Where a rating analyst terminates his or her employment with the ESG rating provider and, within one year of that termination, joins a rated item or an issuer of a rated item the determination of an individual**

rating of which he or she has been directly involved in, the ESG rating provider shall review the relevant work of the rating analyst over the one-year period preceding his or her departure in order to verify whether there has been any conflict of interest.

8. The persons referred to in paragraph 1, and persons occupying a senior management position in the ESG rating provider, shall not take up a senior management position within a rated item or an issuer of a rated item the determination of an individual rating of which they have been involved in for a period of nine months after the date of such rating.

A. INTRODUCTION

17.01 Article 17(1) requires ESG rating analysts to be appropriately trained and to have the capability to integrate double materiality into their evaluation. An 'ESG rating analyst' is defined in Article 3(6) as 'a person who performs analytical functions for the purpose of issuing ESG ratings.'

17.02 This article also deals with potential conflicts of interest on the part of rating analysts: they cannot engage in fee negotiations linked to a rated item or issuer; they cannot deal in the securities of the issuer; they cannot be involved in the determination of an ESG rating where they own securities of the issuer or had an employment or other relationship in the past year that can comprise their independence.

17.03 Rating analysts are subject to a duty of confidentiality in respect of information received in connection with the evaluation of issuers and rated items.

17.04 Rating analysts and senior management cannot take up a senior management position with an issuer for nine months. Where a ratings analyst takes up such a position within a year the work of that analyst shall be reviewed.

ARTICLE 18

RECORD-KEEPING REQUIREMENTS

Iris H-Y Chiu

1. **ESG rating providers shall record their ESG rating activities. Those records shall contain the information listed in Annexes I and II.**
2. **ESG rating providers shall keep the information referred to in paragraph 1 for at least five years and in such a form that it is possible to replicate and fully understand the determination of an ESG rating.**

A. INTRODUCTION

18.01 This article provides for the mandatory obligations for ESG rating providers to keep records that can be produced for inspection and supervisory processes as required by ESMA. Mandatory record-keeping can be regarded as a cross-cutting regulatory rule that is found in many other pieces of EU financial regulation.[1]

18.02 Where regulation provides for authorization regimes of persons to carry out regulated activities, mandatory record-keeping can be regarded as one of the ongoing conditions of remaining authorized.

18.03 Often what needs to be recorded is prescribed in a granular fashion and is usually relevant to evidencing how the regulated entity has carried out regulated activities in a manner that complies with regulatory provisions. These are

1 Eg see Art 16(6), Markets in Financial Instruments Directive 2014/65/EU, also client transaction records, such as Art 25 relating to investment advice.

important sources of information for supervisory processes as well as investigations, if breach is suspected.

B. INFORMATION FOR APPLICATIONS

18.04 Part 1 of Article 18 refers to Annexes I and II as the information that ESG rating providers should keep records of. In particular, Annex I refers to information supplied by ESG rating providers when they make applications to be authorized by ESMA. Such information is usually biographic in nature, relating to the name, registered office and legal identity of the applicant. As firms are often the legal persons seeking authorization, application information often also includes the identities and profiles of senior management. Annex I is very extensive and includes information such as other parts of the applicant's business group, the numbers of analysts, employees and their relevant levels of qualifications and training. These pieces of information are uniquely demanded of ESG rating providers and are not commonly required elsewhere.[2] It is queried as to why these pieces of information are required as business lines and staff can be rather dynamic phenomena and subject to change. It is also noted that other authorization regimes in financial regulation often require significant ownership details to be provided, which is not mentioned in Annex I.

18.05 Annex I further provides for applicants to furnish ESMA with information regarding rating methodologies, conflicts of interest management and outsourcing plans, which are subject to ongoing conduct of business regulation discussed elsewhere in this Commentary. In this way the application information required serves as a means of ensuring that applicants are prepared to comply with the Regulation's provisions and understand what they need to achieve.

18.06 The authorization information requirements are in general consistent with EU financial regulation, which often requires applicants to show that they have in place systems, structures and procedures that are capable of producing ongoing regulatory compliance.

2 Not in the main legislations for investment services, *ibid* or banking services in the Capital Requirements Directive 2013/36/EU. The Regulation for credit rating agencies 1060/2009 does require rating agencies to ensure that employees are sufficiently knowledgeable and experienced, but these are not stipulated as information or conditions for authorization.

C. ONGOING RECORD-KEEPING

The provisions of Annex II set out the records required to be made and maintained by ESG rating providers in ongoing conduct of business. In particular, these relate to who were involved in rating methodological determination and application, and what methodologies were involved; as well as the person/s who issued the rating output and their approver/s. These records are intended to provide supervisors with a comprehensive view of the process trails for each rating issued by the provider. The process trails also include methodological matters as extensively set out in Annex II (1)(e) to (i). **18.07**

Ongoing record-keeping is intended to highlight potential financial or business circumstances or interests that could affect the ESG ratings produced. Hence, each rating's process trail must include whether it has been solicited or otherwise, and the accounting records relating to payment of fees for the rating. **18.08**

In light of the rather extensive conflict of interest regulation provided, it is queried why records of conflict of interest management for each rating process are not more extensively prescribed, such as compared with the regulation of credit rating agencies.[3] Indeed some commentators suggest that ESG rating providers face a greater range of conflicts of interests due to their issuer-pays and user-pays business models[4] and their plural relations with a range of input providers.[5] **18.09**

Ongoing record keeping also includes all complaints received and their relevant documentations. This allows ESMA to uncover potentially important supervisory information, as well as determine if the complaint-handling standards stipulated in the Regulation (commented elsewhere in this volume) are met. **18.10**

D. OUTSOURCING RECORDS

Annex II curiously provides for the conditions that ESG rating providers have to meet in order to carry out compliant outsourcing. These do not, on the face of it, show clearly what relationship there is to record keeping. Read with **18.11**

3 Annex I, Regulation 1060/2009.

4 Sung Eun (Summer) Kim, 'The Duality of Variance Among ESG Assessments' (2023) 88 *Missouri Law Review*, https://scholarship.law.missouri.edu/mlr/vol88/iss2/7.

5 Iris H-Y Chiu, 'Regulating ESG Rating and Data Product Providers: A Study of Regulatory Consistency and Gaps' (2024) *European Journal of Risk Regulation*, https://doi.org/10.1017/err.2024.53.

Article 18, it can be inferred that records should be kept by ESG rating providers to show that they are satisfied that the conditions for outsourcing are met. This interpretation is however not perfectly clear. Article 18 (1) can be read as requiring that records be kept to show that the ESG rating provider confirms the conditions of fulfilment for outsourcing, rather than explaining how these conditions are met. It can be made clearer to stipulate that records should be kept in order to provide evidence that the conditions for outsourcing are met, for example, showing why rating providers are satisfied that the outsourcee would be effective, as well as what arrangements rating providers have in place to effectively supervise them. Such record-keeping would be consistent with ESMA's need to have comprehensive information for the purposes of supervision.

E. SUPERVISORY PURPOSES

18.12 Part 2 of Article 18 requires records to be kept for five years. Further, records must be kept in a form to allow supervisors to fully see how an ESG rating has been produced. The provision stipulates that the form of the record must achieve this. Effective 'forms' of such records can include time stamped work processes and Excel documentation. It would also likely be important that such records be difficult to be tampered with or alter, for example, by managerial staff.

ARTICLE 19

COMPLAINT-HANDLING MECHANISM

Iris H-Y Chiu

1. ESG rating providers shall have in place and publish on their website procedures for receiving, investigating and retaining records concerning complaints made by users of ESG ratings, by rated items and by issuers of rated items. ESG rating providers shall also clearly provide information on their website about their complaint-handling mechanism and contact details.

2. The procedures referred to in paragraph 1 shall ensure that:
  - **(a) the ESG rating provider makes publicly available the complaint-handling policy;**
  - **(b) complaints are investigated in a timely and fair manner and the outcome of the investigation is communicated to the complainant within a reasonable period of time, unless such communication would be contrary to objectives of public policy or to Regulation (EU) No 596/2014 of the European Parliament and of the Council; and**
  - **(c) the inquiry is conducted independently of any personnel who have been involved in the determination of an individual rating about which the complaint is made.**

3. Complaints may be submitted in respect of any of the following:
  - **(a) the sources of data used for an individual ESG rating, factual errors and mistakes;**
  - **(b) the way in which the rating methodology in relation to an individual ESG rating has been applied;**
  - **(c) whether an individual ESG rating is representative of the rated item or the issuer of the rated item.**

A. INTRODUCTION

19.01 This Article provides for how ESG rating providers should engage in complaint-handling. In essence this article does not differ much from the complaint-handling obligation imposed on many other regulated financial services entities in EU legislation, making the conduct of complaint-handling a highly convergent cross-cutting regulatory rule.

19.02 The need for regulated financial services entities to provide a complaint-handling mechanism ensures that there is a hierarchy of dispute resolution between affected persons and the relevant financial services firm. A mechanism to receive and decide on complaints is instituted to allow the firm, as a first port of call, to neutralize a grievance against it before the matter is externalized.

19.03 Such complaint-handling is usually carried out by staff not involved in the complaint at hand. Part 2(c) of the regulation provides that complaint-handling should be carried out by staff not involved in the complaint, but does not make particular prescription as to the independent status of complaint-handling within the firm.

19.04 The existence of complaint-handling mechanisms at firm level is important as often, complainants have to show that they have exhausted the internal avenues for dispute resolution before proceeding to external avenues, such as the Financial Ombudsman in the UK.[1]

19.05 Further, the existence of a complaint-handling mechanism provides an efficient and cost-effective way for complainants to resolve a grievance. This is important particularly for financial consumers. However, an external form of dispute resolution is desirable so that consumers' justice is not only left to internal firm processes that can be seen as insufficiently independent. In the UK for example, there have been criticisms against firms' complaint-handling processes as being insufficiently robust and fair to affected consumers.[2] Hence, in the EU, financial ombudsmen have been instituted in Member States in

---

1 The UK Financial Ombudsman requires that complainants against regulated financial services firms must first exhaust the informal complaint-handling process at the firm, https://www.financial-ombudsman.org.uk/consumers/complaints-can-help.

2 'Merricks hits out at high-complaint firms' attitudes' (Money Marketing, 8 February 2007); 'FSA acts to stem tide of PPI complaints' (Money Marketing, 19 Sep 2008).

order to serve consumers' dispute resolution needs.[3] Judicial avenues are highly prohibitive due to cost.

Complaint records are useful sources of information for supervisory processes, as they can reveal the first signs of regulated firms' regulatory risks.[4] 19.06

B. THE CONDUCT OF COMPLAINT-HANDLING

The article provides that ESG rating providers must put in place a complaint-handling policy. This is a type of procedural regulation[5] whose nature is earlier discussed in relation to commentary on Article 15. Regulation stipulates that the firm must have certain systems or procedures to carry out a certain activity but the firm has the discretion as to how to implement it. Procedural regulation is often necessary because regulators cannot fully prescribe or micro-manage how a firm carries out a particular activity. In this case, the ESG rating provider determines its own complaint-handling mechanism as long as it meets the requirements that complaints must be handled in a timely and fair manner. 19.07

The qualities of being timely and fair are also prescribed in other regulation applicable to financial services firms' complaint-handling mechanisms. These are open-ended qualities and it can be argued that firms have the discretion as to how to determine what is timely and what is fair. Nevertheless regulators are able to scrutinize the complaint-handling policy as part of their supervisory process and they will be able to shape the conduct of the firm in terms of what might be timely and fair. 19.08

The ESG rating providers' complaint-handling mechanism must also be able to communicate an outcome to the complainant within the reasonable period 19.09

---

3 David Thomas and Francis Frizon, 'Resolving Disputes between Consumers and Financial Businesses: A Practical Guide Based On Experience In Western Europe' (Word Bank, 2012), https://documents1.worldbank.org/curated/en/169791468233091985/pdf/699160v10ESW0P0en0Vol10Fundamentals.pdf.

4 Such as discussed in Dame Elizabeth Gloster DBE, Report of the Independent Investigation into the Financial Conduct Authority's Regulation of London Capital & Finance plc (December 2020), https://assets.publishing.service.gov.uk/government/uploads/system/uploads/attachment_data/file/945247/Gloster_Report_FINAL.pdf.

5 Cary Coglianese and David Lazer, 'Management-Based Regulation: Prescribing Private Management to Achieve Public Goals' (2003) 37 *Law and Society Review* 691. At a higher level, such regulation of firms' requirements to institute their own systems and processes is often known as 'meta' regulation as regulation is fastened at a meta-level for firms to implement the required outworkings themselves. See Sharon Gilad, 'It Runs in the Family: Meta-regulation and its Siblings' (2010) 4 Regulation and Governance 485; Folarin Akinbami, 'Is Meta-Regulation All It is Cracked Up to Be? The Case of UK Financial Regulation' (2013) 14 *Journal of Banking Regulation* 16.

of time. Although it is not stated as to what the reasonable period of time is, a cross reference to Article 20 may suggest that a reasonable period of time could be within 30 working days.

19.10 Part 2 of this article provides that the communication of the outcome to the complainant need not be made if the communication will be contrary to public policy or to the specified regulation 596/2014 which refers to the Market Abuse Regulation. This means that the communication of the complaint outcome may not be made if the communication may result in a communication of inside information which could be in contravention of the provisions of the Market Abuse Regulation. It is possible to imagine a situation where certain investors might bring a complaint against the ESG rating provider about a particular issuer's ESG rating which affects these investors' interests. The outcome of such a complaint could involve the uncovering of certain inside or confidential information provided by the company which resulted in the rating provider issuing such a rating. In that case, communicating the outcome of the complaint could involve having to communicate the nature of such confidential or inside information to an investor which would be inappropriate. However, the ratings provider would be in the position to decide whether the communication of the outcome is adverse to public policy or may facilitate market abuse. Hence, the rating provider could justify itself in failing to give an outcome to the complainant. Such conduct may itself need investigation and supervisory support to see if it can be warranted.

19.11 The ESG rating providers' complaint-handling mechanisms must also be publicly published so that complainants may know how to access it. Further Part 1 of this article provides that ESG providers must publicly publish on their website procedures for receiving, investigating and retaining records of complaints.

19.12 Complaint-handling mechanisms are often mandated to be put in place for the benefit of consumers of financial services entities. ESG rating providers are however not likely to serve consumers directly. Indeed their business models are such that they would often be dealing with sophisticated parties. Many ESG rating providers are remunerated by subscription fees for supplying ESG data analytics ratings and scores to financial services providers.[6] These financial services providers may then use these ESG information products to design their own financial products usually in the form of collective investment

6 Found in IOSCO, Environmental, Social and Governance (ESG) Ratings and Data Products Providers (Final Report, November 2021).

funds.[7] Institutional investors can also subscribe to ESG data analytics ratings or scores in order to determine their equity allocations. ESG rating providers are not so much engaged in an issuer-pays business model. However it is observed that some of them are diversifying into the businesses or providing consultancy, compliance solutions or advice to issuers.[8] So in respect of the client base of ESG rating providers, these are likely the source of ESG rating providers' complaints.

It is queried whether sophisticated clients of ESG rating providers could use the complaint-handling mechanisms opportunistically to suit their own interests. These informal dispute resolution procedures could be used to create pressure on ESG rating providers to make changes to their processes or methodologies or to alter or review a rating. Policy makers could monitor how these complaint-handling mechanisms are actually used to determine whether or not they are useful, and a cost-effective form of informal dispute resolution, and what hazards they cause for ESG rating providers. **19.13**

C. SUBJECT MATTER FOR COMPLAINTS

Part 3 of the article provides for the range of subject matter for complaints to be received. First, relating to the sources of data used by the ESG rating provider, perhaps a complainant may challenge the ESG rating providers' omission of certain sources or selective use, or even the weighting given to certain sources over others. **19.14**

In relation to challenging factual errors and mistakes, this can be important in an era where 'fake' news and deep fakes can increasingly be generated by artificial intelligence. As some ESG rating providers use machine learning systems to analyze a vast range of information, the picking up of fake information by machine learning systems is not entirely unexpected. **19.15**

Complainants may also challenge ESG rating providers in relation to the manner of application of rating methodology. Where there is valid criticism that ESG rating providers' methodologies may be insufficiently transparent to **19.16**

7 Funds that are actively managed may carry an ESG themed label, and such fund managers may use ESG ratings or analytics in addition to in-house research and analysis, discussed in Matteo Gargantini and Michele Siri, 'Information Intermediaries and Sustainability: ESG Ratings and Benchmarks in the European Union' (ECMI Working Paper 2022). Passive fund managers may adhere to a selected ESG themed index, such as provided by MSCI, Bloomberg, FTSE Russell of S&P, and in this way, these benchmark providers influence financial allocations of passively managed funds.

8 IOSCO (2021).

users, and hence inscrutable as to whether they are designed or applied credibly, the complaint-handling mechanism can act as an accountability channel to compel rating providers to explain the credibility of their methodologies.

19.17 However the hazards for opening up complaint-handling as a channel for challenge against ESG rating providers' methodologies is that some challenges may be vexatious, based on a disagreement with a rating providers' conceptions and unique methods, rather than a constructive exercise that may assist in correcting flaws in rating providers' methodologies. Further, it is also possible for ESG rating providers' competitors to use the complaint-handling mechanism as a means to ferret out information regarding competitors' methodologies. This would be an opportunistic and disingenuous means of using the complaint-handling mechanism.

19.18 Part 3(c) provides that complaints can be made in relation to an ESG rating not being 'representative' of the rated item (usually a financial instrument) or an issuer. On the one hand, this provision is targeted at 'greenwashing' which is a representation of ESG credentials where controversies or ESG-harmful profiles of an issuer or rated item seem not addressed. Hence, the complaint-handling mechanism can be a way to compel rating providers to give a credible explanation as to how the rating is arrived at, or otherwise reconsider the rating. On the other hand, allowing challenge based on impressionistic terms can be burdensome for rating providers who may be developing unique or innovative conceptions or methodologies. Their ratings therefore reflect those differences. Complaint-handling mechanisms should not become a disincentive for ESG rating providers to diverge or engage in innovation in their conceptions and methodologies, as Preamble 36 supports the development of own methodologies by ESG rating providers. The Regulation does not intend to standardize rating methodologies.

D. PURPOSE

19.19 This commentary does raise the query whether it is necessary to institute a complaint-handling mechanism for ESG rating providers whose customers are unlikely to be financial consumers. The nature of this mechanism can be changed from accessible dispute resolution to an indirect accountability mechanism. It is queried then why accountability is not already achieved under mandatory transparency requirements (Articles 23–24, commented elsewhere in this volume). However, as complaints likely relate to specific matters, the existence of this mechanism is likely to serve the purposes of dispute resolution over that of requiring accountability.

ARTICLE 20

REASONED CONCERNS

Iris H-Y Chiu

1. **ESG rating providers shall have in place procedures for receiving reasoned concerns from stakeholders that provide their names and position.**
2. **ESG rating providers, with the exception of small ESG rating providers, within the meaning of Article 5(1) of this Regulation, shall endeavour to reply to the reasoned concerns within 30 working days of receipt thereof.**

A. INTRODUCTION

20.01 This article is unique to the Regulation on ESG rating providers as it is not found elsewhere in other EU financial regulation. It provides that ESG rating providers must put in place procedures to allow stakeholders to engage with them in respect of reasoned concerns. In this way stakeholders are provided with a right to engage with ESG rating providers whether or not they may have a contractual relationship with these providers. It is therefore surmised that Article 19 on complaint-handling should only apply to constituents with a contractual relationship with the ESG rating providers. Those without a contractual relationship would arguably be regarded as stakeholders and captured within the scope of this article.

20.02 What may be the basis of this particular article? It is questioned whether policymakers see ESG rating providers as not only providing a commercial service but their outputs have greater ramifications for society in general. This would be consistent with the EU's double materiality objective[1] which requires that the impact of corporate activities on the environment, society and good governance be evaluated separately from whether these factors affect a corporation's financial risk (i.e. single materiality). The double materiality objective could make ESG rating providers' output relevant more broadly for policymakers', society's, academics' and other interested stakeholders' evaluation of how economic activities affect non-financial priorities that are important to society and communities. In that way, even without contractual relationships, ESG rating providers' output would be salient to a broad range of stakeholders not captured within its commercial paradigms. Article 20 can therefore be seen as a social accountability channel as well as a form of social governance of ESG rating providers.

B. STAKEHOLDER RELATIONS

One question that can be asked is: who are the stakeholders who are entitled to raise reasoned concerns with ESG rating providers? The scope is not defined and therefore it seems that the article permits of a very broad scope of possible stakeholders as long as they provide their names and positions. As stakeholders that raise reasoned concerns cannot remain anonymous, this would allow ESG rating providers to deal with concerns that are hopefully genuinely raised. It would be important to spare ESG rating providers from dealing with spam or opportunistic ways of information-ferreting using artificial identities. In order to protect ESG rating providers from opportunistic or vexatious demands for their attention, it may be necessary to explicitly state that ESG rating providers do not need to provide a response if they cannot ascertain the identity of the stakeholder who has raised it. **20.03**

Another question that may be asked is: what is the meaning of reasoned concerns. If the concern raised to the ESG rating provider is not sufficiently or well-reasoned, is the ESG rating provider entitled to ignore it? On the one hand the need to have a reasoned concern is to allow stakeholders to genuinely engage with the ESG rating provider, showing the basis and the transparency regarding its concern. On the other hand, as the threshold for 'reasoned' is **20.04**

1 'The Challenge of Double Materiality' (Deloitte, undated), https://www2.deloitte.com/cn/en/pages/hot-topics/topics/climate-and-sustainability/dcca/thought-leadership/the-challenge-of-double-materiality.html; Andreas Engbert, 'ESG Ratings: Guiding a Movement in Search of Itself' (2023), https://www.ecgi.global/sites/default/files/working_papers/documents/esg.pdf on distinguishing between single and double materiality.

not defined, and the ESG rating provider is left to implement its determination as to whether the concern meets the threshold for a response, ESG rating providers could implement a high threshold in order to ignore concerns raised by stakeholders who may not have produced evidence or explanation to certain standards. The need to produce a certain level of evidence or explanation for certain stakeholders might then become a barrier to these stakeholders expressing their concerns.

20.05 This article is an example of the model of meta-regulation[2] that is often deployed in EU regulation. This regulatory model has been earlier discussed in the commentary to Article 15. Such regulation often requires the regulated firm to institute procedures for certain objectives, but the firm is left with the discretion as to how to implement these. There may be a need for ESMA the supervisor to ascertain how ESG rating providers carry out their stakeholder relations and to provide further guidance as best practices emerge with time.

C. RESPONSE

20.06 Part 2 of the article does not provide how ESG rating providers should respond to reasoned concerns, in terms of either time frame or format. There is only a provision that small rating providers be allowed to give their responses within a time frame that may possibly exceed 30 days. In this manner it can be surmised that all other rating providers should give a response within 30 days. It can be queried as to whether this time frame is too tight especially if there are matters that require further research or thinking. It is also possible for ESG rating providers to give a holding response within 30 days but not necessarily to provide an outcome or conclusion to the stakeholder within an efficient time frame. Anyway, the provision does not require ESG rating providers' response to necessarily be that of an outcome or determined conclusion.

20.07 This commentary makes some criticism of the shape that the article is in. If this article intends to provide a wider and public facing accountability channel for ESG rating providers, especially on the basis of their outputs on double materiality, then adopting a meta-regulation framework for how ESG rating providers manage non-contractual stakeholder relations and respond to their concerns seems to be rather ineffectual. This is because ESG rating providers

2 Sharon Gilad, 'It Runs in the Family: Meta-regulation and its Siblings' (2010) 4 *Regulation and Governance* 485; Folarin Akinbami, 'Is Meta-Regulation All It is Cracked Up to Be? The Case of UK Financial Regulation' (2013) 14 *Journal of Banking Regulation* 16, also see Colin Scott, 'Regulating Everything' (2010) 27 *Journal of Law and Society* 38 on the importance of meta-regulation as modern regulation.

can decide for themselves just how to implement these stakeholder relations. It is not necessary that they would engage with stakeholders on constructive terms or benefit from stakeholders' input, if they regard such reasoned concerns or inputs as being challenging for their competitive positions. There may be more rethinking that is needed on how to make stakeholder accountability and stakeholder engagement more robust, as well as accountable, for ESG rating providers.

ARTICLE 21

OUTSOURCING

Iris H-Y Chiu

1. **Outsourcing of important operational functions shall not be undertaken in such a way as to materially impair the quality of an ESG rating provider's internal controls and the ability of ESMA to supervise the ESG rating provider's compliance with its obligations under this Regulation.**
2. **ESG rating providers that outsource functions or any services or activities that are relevant for the provision of an ESG rating shall remain fully responsible for discharging all of their obligations under this Regulation and for disclosing the information referred to in Annex II.**

A. INTRODUCTION

21.01 Financial services firms often outsource a variety of functions and activities to third party suppliers. This is because it may be cost-effective and efficiency-enhancing to do so, when third party suppliers have certain specialist expertise,[1] such as in relation to information technology.[2] Further it is also possible to outsource the management of certain types of risks, such as using insurance arrangements.

1 Discussed in Dalvinder Singh, 'Outsourcing in Financial Services' (2005) 6 *Journal of Banking Regulation* 202.

2 Noted in Alessandra Chirico, 'Outsourcing in the Financial Services Industry' (2010) 21 *European Business Law Review* 89.

However, the risk with outsourcing is that financial firms may lose control of the activities that are outsourced while the third party supplier does not bear legal responsibility or liability. In this way, outsourcing can cause a regulatory implementation gap as well as a supervisory gap. Further, it can also be argued that financial services firms' outsourcing can be a way to evade legal responsibility for either implementation or supervision.[3] 21.02

The approach in EU financial regulation is to provide for the regulation of outsourcing carried out by firms. Hence regulating outsourcing is a cross cutting rule that applies in most EU financial regulation. Often, these regulatory rules provide that outsourcing needs to be well managed and supervised by the delegating financial services firm. Further, the delegating financial services firm retains primary legal responsibility and liability for the carrying out of those activities that are outsourced. Nevertheless, certain limits on outsourcing could also be introduced if activities are regarded as core, or highly significant to the meeting of regulatory objectives by the regulated entities.[4] 21.03

B. SCOPE OF OUTSOURCING

Part 3 of this article does not envisage any hard prohibitions on the areas that ESG rating providers should not outsource. However Annex II of the Regulation provides for a list of conditions that the ESG rating provider must fulfill in order to be able to outsource in a compliant manner. The only limit as to outsourcing is regarding important operational functions. These should not be outsourced in a manner that might impair the ESG rating providers' quality of internal control. This provision is the same as the one that applies to the regulation of credit rating agencies. 21.04

The above limitation on the outsourcing of important operational functions is consistent with the requirement that ESG rating providers ensure that they 21.05

3 See discussion in Ruth M. Evans, 'Outsourcing: The Regulatory Challenge for Financial Services Firms' (2005) 6 *Journal of Investment Compliance* 52.

4 Eg Art 19(6), Payment Services Directive 2015/2366 on payment services providers' outsourcing of operational activities. These can only be undertaken if the provider's internal control quality may not be impaired. Further Art 28 provides that payment services providers' outsourcing arrangements must be reported to their national regulators to enable supervisory scrutiny. The European Banking Authority's guidelines that implement the outsourcing governance provisions in the Capital Requirements Directive 2013/36/EU for credit institutions also shows that outsourcing governance is an important part of organizational and governance regulation to ensure that gaps are not unaddressed in the chain of supply of services to regulated firms, see EBA, Final Report on Guidelines on outsourcing arrangements (2019), https://www.eba.europa.eu/sites/default/files/documents/10180/2551996/38c80601-f5d7-4855-8ba3-702423665479/EBA%20revised%20Guidelines%20on%20outsourcing%20arrangements.pdf.

remain capable of supervising and intervening in the outsourced activities that the third party undertakes (Annex II of the Regulation). Hence, outsourced activities should not be unaccounted for by internal control functions in the ESG rating provider's firm nor be inscrutable because of distance from the third party. As ESG rating providers are required to institute an 'oversight function' under Article 15 (commented elsewhere in this volume), this function must presumably be able to oversee the activities carried out by the outsourcee, by having arrangements in place with the outsourcee.

C. CONDUCT OF OUTSOURCING

21.06 Annex II to this Regulation provides for the conditions that ESG rating providers must fulfill when outsourcing to third parties. These conditions can also be regarded as duties imposed on ESG rating providers to ensure that they conduct outsourcing appropriately and in a compliant manner. Annex II requires the ESG ratings provider to be satisfied that the third party is able to perform the activities to be outsourced in a reliable and professional manner. The ESG ratings provider remains responsible for supervising the outsourced entity and to manage all risks associated with this outsourcing.

21.07 In order to carry out outsourcing, the ESG ratings provider must put in place meta-level procedures, systems and arrangements to oversee and supervise the outsourced third party, as well as to be informed of any condition on the part of the third party that might impair performance. Even if the ESG ratings provider wishes to benefit from the efficiencies of outsourcing it must still have in place procedures, systems and arrangements in order to keep tabs on the ongoing performance of the third party. Evans[5] has opined that the requirement of hands-on supervision and awareness of how outsourced activities are being carried out could diminish the efficiency of outsourcing altogether. This is a difficult balance for firms to strike.

21.08 Further, as part of the ESG rating provider's adequate supervision of the third party, it needs to have in place contingency plans in case the third party fails to discharge or perform. The ESG ratings provider must also be able to terminate the outsourcing arrangements without significant disruption if necessary.

5 Evans (2005).

D. RESPONSIBILITY

Part 2 of this article clearly states that whether or not any functions or activities are outsourced, ESG ratings providers remain primarily responsible for discharging all of the obligations under the Regulation. Hence there is no way for an ESG ratings provider to disclaim responsibility by outsourcing particular functions or activities. In fact, not being able to be fully responsible for those activities would itself be in breach of the duties to supervise and to ensure that outsourcing risks are appropriately managed. **21.09**

ESG rating providers retain the legal risks for all the activities and functions that they carry out. Hence, they would have to consider whether or not it is still efficient to outsource, or whether the supervisory and management costs would be too high. This position is consistent with other outsourcing rules found elsewhere in EU financial regulation. The regulation of outsourcing impacts in a cross cutting manner on all regulated financial services entities in relation to their decisions on what activities or risks to retain in house. **21.10**

ARTICLE 22

EXEMPTIONS FROM GOVERNANCE REQUIREMENTS

Iris H-Y Chiu

1. An ESG rating provider may lodge a request with ESMA to be exempted from complying with the requirements laid down in Article 15(6), (8) and (10).

2. When assessing a request as referred to in paragraph 1 of this Article, ESMA shall verify whether the following conditions are met:

(a) the ESG rating provider is a small ESG rating provider, within the meaning of Article 5(1);

(b) the ESG rating provider has implemented measures and procedures, and in particular internal control mechanisms, reporting arrangements and measures, that ensure the independence of rating analysts and persons approving ESG ratings and that ensure effective compliance with this Regulation;

(c) the ESG rating provider has shown that its size has not been determined in such a way as to circumvent the requirements of this Regulation;

(d) the ESG rating provider has demonstrated with sufficient clarity that the requirements laid down in Article 15(6), (8) and (10) are not proportionate to the nature, scale or complexity of the business of that ESG rating provider or in view of the nature or range of the issuance of ESG ratings.

On the basis of those considerations, ESMA may exempt the ESG rating provider from all of the requirements laid down in Article 15(6), (8) and (10) or, in duly justified cases and based on the elements provided by the ESG rating provider pursuant to the first subparagraph, point (d), of this paragraph, from some of those requirements only.

A. INTRODUCTION

Regulating governance and organizational arrangements in financial services firms is a signature approach in EU financial regulation. Such a regulatory approach supports the substantive laws in the prudential or conduct regulation of financial services firms. By ensuring that firms have appropriate organizational structures, governance processes or policies, or the institution of certain personnel and positions, regulation intends to shape the behaviour of firms in an ex ante manner. Organizational and governance regulation forces firms to make sunk costs in investing in their set-ups, making the possibility of deviation or defection from compliance less likely. This regulatory approach supports the ex ante attainment of compliance with prudential and conduct of business regulations, so that regulatory objectives such as investor protection or financial stability can be achieved. Ex post remedial actions may not be sufficient to undo the damage of harms that can be prevented. More detail on the nature of organizational and governance regulation for ESG rating providers is found in the commentary on Article 15. **22.01**

This article provides for the possibility of ESG rating providers applying to ESMA for exemptions from various aspects of organizational and governance regulation. This is because the imposition of such regulations in an ex ante manner imposes upfront cost on firms and this may become a barrier to entry for firms into this industry, making the industry less competitive. Hence, the imposition of organizational and governance regulation has to strike a balance with pro-competition objectives. **22.02**

B. NATURE OF EXEMPTIONS

Exemptions can be applied in respect of the obligations under Articles 15(6), (8) and/or (10). These exemptions can apply to all three of those requirements or only in respect of some of them. **22.03**

Article 15(6) relates to the ESG rating provider's obligation to 'adopt and implement sound administrative and accounting procedures, internal control mechanisms, and effective control and safeguard arrangements for information processing systems.' This obligation is not found elsewhere, such as in the regulation of credit rating agencies or financial benchmarks. As the commentary to Article 14 points out, there is a lack of clarity as to what the 'administrative and accounting procedures,' 'internal control mechanisms' or 'effective control and safeguard arrangements' are. The commentary has offered possibilities **22.04** in interpretation to show how ESG rating providers may discharge the legal risks of complying with these requirements. ESG rating providers should ensure that the information processing systems they use, whether they relate to human frameworks or machine interfaces, are able to be compliant.

22.05 If an ESG rating provider can be exempted from complying with Article 15(6), it would mean that it does not need to put in place these procedures, systems or internal control specifically targeted at information processing systems. Is such an exemption sound given that risks associated with information processing, such as omission or corrupt data, would be detrimental to rating providers' products? Further, Article 14 points out that as ESG rating providers may find it beneficial and efficient to use artificial intelligence systems to process volumes of information, there may be specific risks of machine learning systems for information processing that need to be addressed.

22.06 It could, however, be argued that the conditions for exemption that will be discussed shortly are sufficient to mitigate against the lack of procedural controls for such information processing systems. In other words, exempt firms need not engage in costly installations of procedures or internal control at an ex ante point in time, but this does not mean that regulators are unable to scrutinize the robustness of their information processing systems on an ex post basis. Further, other regulatory provisions capture broadly the need for rating products to be independent and credible (such as Articles 15, 18 and 25) and it is arguable that the exemption only removes from the regulated entity a specific procedural regulation, leaving it with greater flexibility to determine how it would meet the fundamental regulatory demands that pertain to rating quality.

22.07 All regulated ESG rating providers still need to ensure that their ratings are methodologically sound, under the provisions regulating their methodological quality (Article 15(7)), and they need to institute systems, processes and internal controls sufficient for attaining compliance (Article 15(2) and (3)). Even if they may be exempt from specific controls and procedures for information processing systems, their need to institute overall compliant systems and internal control would allow these, and their rating outputs or methodologies affected by these, to be scrutinized.

22.08 Article 15(8) deals with ESG rating providers' obligations to review their ratings periodically, at least annually. Exempting firms from this provision would mean that there is no mandatory annual review imposed.

However, given the overriding regulation of methodological quality (Article 15(7)), the lack of timeliness and currency in the generation of ESG ratings may give rise to issues of methodological soundness, such as the lack of rigour or reliability. Hence, the exemption does not mean that exempt firms need not review ratings at all, but that such review, if any, would be expected to be undertaken by firms in their discretion in relation to how their methodological qualities would be met. **22.09**

Article 15(10) deals with ESG rating providers' obligation to institute a permanent, independent and effective oversight function to oversee all aspects of ratings production, for the purposes of complying with the Regulation. Again, such a provision entails cost for the firm, as suitable personnel need to be appointed to the oversight function, and certain organizational separations and protections need to be put in place, as discussed in the commentary to Article 15, to ensure that such oversight function can be effective and genuine. **22.10**

Exempting an ESG rating provider from Article 15(10) means that it would not be necessary for an oversight function to have the qualities of permanence and/or independence as stipulated. This does not mean that firms would not benefit from such a role. It could be envisaged that personnel from an internal control function can assume an equivalent role in the firm, which would not be compliant with the demands of Article 15(10), but would work for exempt firms. **22.11**

Even if firms do not institute any form of an oversight function, it would remain responsible for ensuring that the generation of its ratings complies with methodological regulation as well as conflict of interest management regulation (commented elsewhere in this volume). The exemption should be seen as a cost mitigating measure for exempt firms, rather than reducing the substantive quality of compliance with the Regulation. **22.12**

C. CONDITIONS FOR EXEMPTION

Part 2 provides for four conjunctive conditions for an exemption under this Article to be considered. Hence meeting the conditions does not as of right entitle an ESG rating provider to be exempt. It only opens the way for ESMA to consider if an exemption can be made. **22.13**

The first condition is that the ESG rating provider is a small undertaking or group, adopting the definition in Directive 2213/34/EU which is the Capital Requirements Directive applicable to credit institutions. A small undertaking **22.14** would meet at least two of the three criteria of: (i) having a balance sheet of 4,000,000 euros or below; (ii) having a net turnover of 8,000,000 euros or below and (iii) having an average number of employees not exceeding 50. Member States have the discretion to extend the balance sheet threshold to 6,000,000 euros and net turnover threshold to 12,000,000 euros.

22.15 Adopting a proportional approach to small undertakings is set out in Preamble 29 which reflects the pro-competition policy of fostering a market for ESG rating providers without undue barriers to entry. The Preamble also foresees that pre-existing small undertakings can benefit from a temporary regime for allowing their operations in the EU until formal authorization can be carried out with proportionate conditions.

22.16 The second condition relates to ESMA's overall satisfaction that the ESG rating provider has achieved sufficient internal control, reporting and oversight mechanism to ensure the independence of rating analysts and approvers. As mentioned above, this Commentary argues that the exemptions in Article 22, which relate to 'extra' and more sophisticated/costly procedures and systems, do not detract from the obligations for ESG rating providers to have in place 'core' systems and procedures for effective internal control and ensuring regulatory compliance. The second condition is therefore interpreted consistent with the basic expectation that ESG rating providers' core procedural compliance is regarded to be satisfactory. This would be judged especially in relation to protecting the independence of judgement in issuing ratings.

22.17 The third condition is that ESMA determines that the size of the ESG rating provider has not been deliberately structured in such a way as to avoid full regulatory compliance. In particular, small entities that are part of a larger group could be seen to benefit from deliberate asset partitioning and would not benefit from the possibility of these exemptions. This is explicitly stated in Preamble 48. This condition shows that those entities most likely to be able to ask for exemptions under this article are 'challenger' outfits that may be independent and not part of a larger group.

22.18 Since the early 2000s, specialist information and analytical providers such as Asset4, Refinitiv, Trucost and Viageo Eiris have been established as market providers of ESG information goods that traditional analysis and research may not have focussed on. The mainstreamization of material non-financial risks in investment management has changed the investment management business model.[1] Inflows into ESG investment funds have swelled since 2020[2] although this phenomenon may probably be better explained as the reframing and re-orientation of many conventional investment funds rather than necessarily the growth of a niche investment market. In this manner, the provision of ESG data, analytics, research and ratings is increasingly perceived to be mainstream financial infomediary business, and no longer so niche. The market structures for ESG rating providers have changed very much of late, as specialist providers have been merged with or acquired by large and influential financial market players such as stock exchanges, index providers and investment firms. For example, Asset4 was acquired by Thomson Reuters, which has since sold the business off to London Stock Exchange Group, which also acquired specialist ESG data firm Refinitiv. Leading credit rating agency S&P Global acquired Trucost while Moody's acquired Viageo Eiris. Although the market for ESG rating providers is not as oligopolistic as the market for credit ratings, policy-makers are watching the shifts in market structures to consider how ESG rating providers' power and influence are developing.

The final condition for exemption is that the obligations stipulated in Articles 15(6), (8) and/or (10) are not proportionate to the nature, scale or complexity of the business of the ESG rating provider or in view of the nature or range of the issuance of its ESG ratings. Again, the potential beneficiary of this article's exemptions may not only be a small entity but is likely to have fewer and less complex lines of business, or serve a limited market, therefore being limited in market power and influence as well. These features would make it proportionate for them not to be subject to too many demanding up-front procedural safeguards and set-ups, as compared to ESG rating providers with multiple lines of business. An ESG rating provider with both issuer-pays and user-pays models of revenue generation, for example, should do more in respect of having ex ante procedural and internal control safeguards to mitigate conflicts of interest, such as by complying with Article 15(10) and installing a permanent, effective and independent oversight function. **22.19**

1 UNEPFI, Fiduciary Responsibility: Legal and Practical Aspects of Integrating Environmental, Social And Governance Issues Into Institutional Investment (2009); PRI, UNEPFI and Generation Foundation, A Legal Framework for Impact: sustainability impact in investor decision-making (2021), https://www.unepfi.org/industries/investment/a-legal-framework-for-impact-sustainability-impact-in-investor-decision-making/.

2 A marked rise in ESG assets is seen from 2020, 'ESG assets projected to swell to as much as $30tn by 2030' (FN London, 22 December 2021), https://www.fnlondon.com/articles/esg-assets-projected-to-swell-to-as-much-as-30tn-by-2030-20211202.

22.20 Calibrating regulatory proportionality by broadly referring to the regulated entity's nature, scale, size and complexity of business is a norm very much applied in financial regulation. For brief purposes of cross-reference and comparison only, such proportionality is seen in the regulation of organizational and corporate governance in regulated banks and investment firms, as well as the regulation of remuneration policies in these entities and in investment fund managers.[3]

22.21 For the purposes of Article 22, the burden is placed on the entity requesting exemption to show 'with sufficient clarity' that the exemptions would be proportionate. This would be different from policy-makers' ex ante application of proportionality in determining the scope of regulatory application, which often sets out exemptible categories and criteria up front. ESMA would decide such exemption requests on a case by case basis.

3 Guido Ferranini, 'Compensation in Financial Institutions: Systemic Risk, Regulation, and Proportionality' in Danny Busch, Guido Ferrarini, Gerard van Solinge (eds), *Governance of Financial Institutions* (Oxford: Oxford University Press 2019), ch 11.

CHAPTER 2

TRANSPARENCY REQUIREMENTS

ARTICLE 23

DISCLOSURE TO THE PUBLIC OF THE METHODOLOGIES, MODELS AND KEY RATING ASSUMPTIONS USED IN ESG RATING ACTIVITIES

Irene-marié Esser

1. **ESG rating providers shall disclose on their website, as a minimum, the methodologies, models and key rating assumptions that they use in their ESG rating activities, including the information referred to in point (d) of Annex I and point 1 of Annex III. Such disclosure shall be made in a clear and transparent manner and identified in a separate section of the ESG rating provider's website.**

   The ESG rating provider shall disclose the information referred to in point 1 of Annex III at the latest when it starts issuing ESG ratings.
2. **Separate E, S and G ratings shall be provided rather than a single ESG rating that aggregates E, S and G factors. ESG rating providers shall provide the disclosures referred to in this Article and in Article 24 separately for each factor.**
3. **By way of derogation from paragraph 2 of this Article, ESG rating providers may provide a single ESG rating that aggregates E, S and G factors if they provide, without prejudice to further disclosure obligations under this Regulation, the information referred to in point (h) of point 1 of Annex III.**
4. **ESMA shall develop draft regulatory technical standards to specify further the elements to be disclosed in accordance with paragraph 1, first subparagraph. Those elements shall not include any additional disclosure requirements other than those listed in point 1 of Annex III.**

   ESMA shall submit the draft regulatory technical standards referred to in the first subparagraph of this paragraph to the Commission by 2 October 2025.

Power is delegated to the Commission to supplement this Regulation by adopting the regulatory technical standards referred to in the first subparagraph of this paragraph in accordance with the procedure laid down in Articles 10 to 14 of Regulation (EU) No 1095/2010.

5. **ESMA may develop draft implementing technical standards to specify the data standards, formats and templates that ESG rating providers are to use to present the information referred to in paragraph 1.**

ESMA shall submit the draft implementing technical standards referred to in the first subparagraph of this paragraph to the Commission.

Power is conferred on the Commission to adopt the implementing technical standards referred to in the first subparagraph of this paragraph in accordance with the procedure laid down in Article 15 of Regulation (EU) No 1095/2010.

A. INTRODUCTION

23.01 It is stated in the Parliament text[1] that 'As trust is pivotal in the functioning of financial markets, such lack of transparency and reliability of ESG ratings should be urgently addressed.'[2] Diverging measures and approaches could create obstacles to the detriment of the proper functioning of the internal market and have a negative impact on the ESG rating market. This Regulation complements the existing EU sustainability finance framework. Ultimately

1 April 2024, para 8.

2 The UK also published a Code of Conduct for ESG Ratings and Data Providers (2023), see https://www.irsg.co.uk/assets/DRWG/DRWG-Code-of-Conduct-for-ESG-Ratings-and-Data-Products-Providers.pdf, owned and operated by the International Capital Markets Association. The Code has six practices, aligned with the Final Report of the IOSCO, https://www.iosco.org/library/pubdocs/pdf/IOSCOPD690.pdf. In the context of transparency, it is stated in Principle 4 that 'ESG ratings and data products providers should make adequate levels of public disclosure and transparency a priority for their ESG ratings and data products, including their methodologies and processes to enable the users of the product to understand what the product is and how it is produced, including any potential conflicts of interest and while maintaining a balance with respect to proprietary or confidential information, data and methodologies.' This is a voluntary Code, which is different from this European Regulation. See, generally: https://www.cliffordchance.com/content/dam/cliffordchance/briefings/2024/07/esg-ratings-and-esg-data-regulation-and-practical-issues-in-the-equity-and-debt-capital-markets.pdf.

ESG ratings should facilitate information flows in order to facilitate investment decisions.[3]

23.02 ESG ratings provide an opinion on the sustainability profile of a company or financial instrument, i.e. by assessing the exposure to ESG risks (similar to credit ratings looking at credit risks).[4] There are limits when it comes to ESG ratings, especially with regards to transparency and the methodologies used to provide the rating.[5] This lack of transparency consequently leads to incomparability between ratings given by different providers.[6]

23.03 There is therefore a lack of trust in ESG rating systems[7] and that stems from the absence of transparency on methodologies and clarity over the operations of ESG rating providers. Investors and benchmark administrators increasingly use ESG ratings for pre-investment decision-making, post-investment analytics and attribution or as a basis for investment screening or for company engagement. On the other hand, companies use ESG ratings to look for and take account of operational risks and investment opportunities but also to see how they perform against ESG factors and compared to their peers.[8] Investors and companies claim that ESG rating providers do not gather and process data and information in an accurate, timely or reliable manner. Data reliability is thus problematic, this is due to, for example, a lack of quality assurance mechanisms, but also due to a lack of robustness when it comes to the information that the rating providers rely on, which is often backwards looking. Causation,

3 Preamble (14).

4 Credit ratings deal with the assessment of creditworthiness of debtors and debt instruments. EUSFiL Research Working Paper Series 2024 no. 3, Matteo Gargantini and Michele Siri, 'Information intermediaries and sustainability: the case of ESG ratings and benchmarks' (March 2024), p 6.

5 For instance, in feedback to the Commission by Norges Bank Investment Management they refer to some examples. Some ESG ratings aim to assess entities' exposure to financial risks tied to ESG issues (financial materiality), while others aim to assess whether companies' commitments and practices are aligned with societal goals, i.e. thinking about society and the environment (impact materiality). Also, some ESG ratings assess a company relative to rated entities in the same industry, while others compare it to all rated entities across industries. See https://www.nbim.no/en/publications/consultations/2023/feedback-to-the-european-commission-on-the-proposed-regulation-on-esg-ratings/.

6 See Florian Berg, Julian Kölbel and Roberto Rigobon, 'Aggregate Confusion: The Divergence of ESG Ratings' (2022) 26(6) *Review of Finance*, 1315 on the divergence of ESG ratings.

7 This was already identified in the Commission's 2018 Action Plan, European Commission 2018 (Action 6), again in the 2021 Action Plan and finally addressed in this Regulation, originally in 2023. See also EUSFiL (n 4), p. 5.

8 A survey conducted by Ninety One found that 88% of investment professionals use third-party ESG ratings as a part of their investment process, with 92% expecting to do so in the future. See https://ninetyone.com/en/united-kingdom/newsroom/ninety-one-survey-finds-european-fund-industry-overly-reliant-on-esg-scores. See also https://www.esma.europa.eu/sites/default/files/trv_2021_1-esg_ratings_status_and_key_issues_ahead.pdf.

with regard to ratings, is also at times questionable; it is not always clear how the rating is linked to the data inputs.[9]

B. DISCLOSURE

The ESG ratings regulation takes a disclosure-based regulatory approach, which, in theory, aims to make investors better informed when selecting and using ESG ratings and thereby discipline rating firms.[10] In that sense, the approach follows the general trend in the EU approach to ESG, whereby disclosure is the favoured approach, leaving investors to make informed decisions and markets to evolve according to the preferences of the ultimate investors.[11] Some argue that disclosure is not sufficient to address these concerns and facilitate investors to make informed decisions. It is argued that less sophisticated investors will still find it hard to examine or estimate the quality of ratings.[12] **23.04**

ESG ratings vary and that is not in itself a problem. Indeed, it is the view of the Commission that ESG ratings should not be standardized since diversity can be beneficial in meeting the ESG aspirations of investors.[13] This highlights the importance of disclosure in order to understand the methodologies used and the key assumptions which are made. Articles 23 and 24 contain the transparency requirements for ESG rating providers. Providers will be required to disclose on their websites the methodologies, models and key rating assumptions used in their ESG rating activities. This includes the limitations of the analysis and should explicitly disclose which dimension of the double materiality **23.05**

---

9 EUSFiL (n 4), p. 5, See also SustainAbility, 'Rate the Raters 2020: Investor Survey and Interview Results' (2020) 7 accessed 10 July 2023. In this survey it is held that 65% of investors surveyed use rating agencies at least once a week and they refer to more than one agency. The details of rating practices also vary significantly.

10 See Longjie Lu, 'Regulating ESG rating firms as the gatekeepers for sustainable finance' (2024) 19 *Capital Markets Law Journal*, 184–206. and her suggestion of a disgorgement scheme (rather than disclosure). This Regulation goes beyond disclosure as there is substantive regulation of oversight (see Article 15), independence and a rating process. For example, the quality and reliability of ESG ratings are ensured through rigorous, independent and systematic ratings methodologies. Transparency is achieved via disclosure of, e.g. methodologies, models and key rating assumptions. See for a discussion on this: https://www.cuatrecasas.com/en/spain/capital-markets/art/esg-ratings-eu-new-regulation.

11 Danny Busch, 'EU Sustainable Finance Disclosure Regulation' (2023) 18(3) *Capital Markets Law Journal* 303.

12 Lu (n 21), p196. It is argued that disclosure-based regulation will not work as it does not help with improving ex-post verifiability of the quality of ratings. It may instead incentivize rating forms to focus only on impression management through disclosures.

13 See also Preamble (36) where it is stated that this Regulation should not interfere with methodologies used by ESG rating providers, diversity in the methodologies of the ESR rating providers is important to ensure that broad requirements of users are met, and to promote competition in the market. See further the comments made on Article 15 at 15.040, 15.045, 15.049 and 15.073.

principle the rating addresses which enable users[14] of ESG ratings to perform their own due diligence when assessing whether to rely or not on those ESG ratings.[15] The information referred to in sub-section 1 should be disclosed when the rating provider starts issuing ESG ratings (see sub-section 5).

23.06 Article 1 of Annex III refers to what rating providers should disclose, as a minimum, on their website and through the European Single Access Point. It includes, *inter alia*, the methodology used and whether it is backwards looking or not, where the data used to make the rating is sourced from (i.e. whether the data is sourced from sustainability statements,[16] whether the data sources are public or non-public and an outline of data processes), whether the rating is assessing risks, impacts or both and whether it relates to the E, S and G or only some of the factors. The Regulations do not establish harmonized methodologies.[17] Some argue that this will 'prevent users from having more clarity regarding how raters assign ratings, allocate weights to each environmental (E), social (S), and governance (G) factor, and assess the data they use.'[18]

23.07 The nature of ESG ratings is not always the same, the rating can be based on an 'outside-in' approach (risk) or an 'inside-out' approach (impact), it is therefore important when it comes to disclosure to be clear on the nature of the rating.[19] With ESG ratings, linked to risk, due consideration of sustainability issues potentially improves the assessment of investments by including a broader range of factors into the analysis. With ESG ratings linked to impact, they do not only look at the quality of the investment, but also at the impact of those investments on ESG targets, regardless of the potential backlash for risks or financial returns.[20]

23.08 A further doubt cast on ESG ratings relates to the weight given to each factor. This has now been addressed in Article 23(2).[21] An aggregate rating (for E, S and G) can only be provided if any changes and deviations, such as these, relating to the methodology, are disclosed as per Annex III, (h). An aggregate

---

14 See further commentary on Articles 15 and 18.

15 See https://www.cuatrecasas.com/en/spain/capital-markets/art/esg-ratings-eu-new-regulation for an overview.

16 As required under Directive 2013/34/EU or from information disclosed under Regulation (EU) 2019/2088.

17 See further commentary on Articles 15 and 18.

18 https://www.transportenvironment.org/articles/do-the-eus-new-esg-rules-make-ratings-more-reliable.

19 As now dealt with in Annex III (f): '...information on the ratings' clearly defined objective and marking whether the rating is assessing risks, impacts, or both, according to the double materiality principle, or any other dimensions, and in the case of double materiality the proportion of the risk and impact materiality'.

20 EUSFiL (n 4), p. 4.

21 See also Annex III (g–i).

ESG rating can also only be provided if the provider discloses the weighting of each (E, S and G) factor and the explanation of the weighting method.[22] This section on the separate ESG factors was not in the original proposal.[23] Finally, the Regulation tasks ESMA with drafting implementing standards for the presentation of this information.

22 Parliament's rapporteur Aurore Lalucq (S&D) praised this part of the Regulation, stating that 'one of the most important achievements' of the deal – *not* featured in the original Commission proposal – is the requirement for rating agencies to "disaggregate" environmental, social, and governance criteria into three separate components.' 'Aggregating the scores for these three criteria didn't make any sense,' Lalucq said. 'An excellent score in one area could hide disastrous results in another. This is how we end up with companies in the oil sector very well rated, despite [the] environmental consequences of their activity.' See https://www.euractiv.com/section/economy-jobs/news/eu-agrees-historic-esg-regulatory-deal/.

23 This was the previous Article 21 (Amendment 48).

ARTICLE 24

DISCLOSURES TO USERS OF ESG RATINGS, RATED ITEMS AND ISSUERS OF RATED ITEMS

Irene-marié Esser

1. ESG rating providers shall disclose, as a minimum, the information referred to in point 2 of Annex III to users of ESG ratings, rated items and issuers of rated items on an ongoing basis.

2. An ESG rating provider shall ensure that when it authorises a user of ESG ratings to disclose an ESG rating, a link to the information referred to in point 1 of Annex III is attached to the ESG rating.

3. ESMA shall develop draft regulatory technical standards to specify further the elements that are to be disclosed in accordance with paragraph 1. Those elements shall not include any additional disclosure requirements other than those listed in point 2 of Annex III.

ESMA shall submit the draft regulatory technical standards referred to in the first subparagraph to the Commission by 2 October 2025.

Power is delegated to the Commission to supplement this Regulation by adopting the regulatory technical standards referred to in the first subparagraph of this paragraph in accordance with the procedure laid down in Articles 10 to 14 of Regulation (EU) No 1095/2010.

4. ESMA may develop draft implementing technical standards to specify the data standards, formats and templates that ESG rating providers are to use to present the information referred to in paragraph 1.

ESMA shall submit the draft implementing technical standards referred to in the first subparagraph of this paragraph to the Commission.

Power is conferred on the Commission to adopt the implementing technical standards referred to in the first subparagraph of this paragraph in accordance with the procedure laid down in Article 15 of Regulation (EU) No 1095/2010.

A. INTRODUCTION

24.01 This Article is also part of the chapter dealing with transparency. The previous article concerned disclosure of the methodologies, models and key assumptions used in ESG rating activities to the public. This Article concerns disclosure of ESG ratings and entities to users.

24.02 These ESG rating providers should make the information, as listed in Annex III, point 2 available, as a minimum, to users. Annex III deals with disclosure and Point 1 concerns the minimum disclosure requirements to the public.[1] Point 2, as referred to in this Article 24, concerns additional disclosure requirements to users and rated undertakings.[2] The rationale for additional disclosure, as provided for in Annex III, point 2, is not explained in the Preamble to the Regulation, but it is presumably due to the fact that these undertakings fall within the scope of the EU reporting regime. With the CSRD and CSDDD, large businesses in the EU are now required to disclose the impact of their operations on environmental issues, social concerns and governance practices. These rules also extend to the network of suppliers they use. ESG ratings and related disclosures therefore play an important role here by supplying relevant information to companies and their supply chain networks that will facilitate the process of due diligence.[3]

24.03 This additional disclosure information includes granular overviews[4] of the rating methodologies and the data processes used. The relevant Key Performance

1 See here the European Single Reference Point, https://www.european-financial-data-space.com/European_Single_Access_Point_(ESAP).html#:~:text=What%20is%20the%20European%20Single,%2C%20capital%20markets%20and%20sustainability%22.

2 David F. Larcker, Lukasz Pomorski, Brian Tayan and Edward M. Watts, 'ESG Ratings: A Compass without Direction' *Stanford Closer Look Series*, August 2, 2022 explains how ESG ratings have an impact on various groups like asset owners (as they are concerned about the ESG impact of the companies they invest in), institutional investors (as it is important to them as the creation of investment products and services should meet the needs of their clients) and companies, as they want to show the extent to which they invest in stakeholder-facing initiatives.

3 See Directive (EU) 2022/2464 of the European Parliament and of the Council of 14 December 2022 and Directive (EU) 2024/1760 of the European Parliament and of the Council of 13 June 2024 on corporate sustainability due diligence. Also see: https://www.forbes.com/sites/maryfoley/2024/05/22/esg-ratings-get-regulated-why-thats-a-good-thing-for-businesses/.

4 See subsection 2(a)(i): 'where applicable, scientific evidence and assumptions on which the ratings are based.' See Larcker et al for a detailed discussion of the problem of ESG ratings. In this article reference is made to the concerns with ESG ratings and the reliability of the assessments provided by the ESG rating providers. It is argued that ESG rating providers provide important insights on non-financial impacts but

Indicators for each factor (i.e. the E, S and the G) used should be disclosed as well as the weighting method used. In case of an aggregated ESG rating, it should be presented in a manner where comparison between the factors is possible. Any potential shortcomings should also be disclosed, and it should be indicated how this was addressed. Policies with regards to the revision of methodologies should also be indicated.[5]

24.04 Any upgrade or downgrade to the rating, changes to methodologies, models, key assumptions or data sources,[6] the reason for this and the implications for the rating should be disclosed.[7]

24.05 Other disclosure information includes engagement with the rated entity, if applicable, e.g. whether and how often on-site visits or reviews have taken place.[8] The artificial intelligence methodology used in data collection or rating process, if applicable, should be disclosed[9] and if a provider provides an unsolicited rating a prominent statement explaining this should be included.[10] In case of major, new information on a rated entity that will affect the rating, the provider shall inform how they used that information and how it affected the rating.[11]

24.06 All information referred to in Annex III, (2), shall be applicable to each rating.[12]

24.07 ESMA shall develop draft regulatory technical standards to specify further the elements that are to be disclosed in accordance with this Article 24

---

there are shortcomings re: methodologies used and objectives, which detract from the 'informativeness of their assessments.'

5 See Annex III, 2(a)(ii)–(v).

6 Including estimates.

7 See Annex III, 2(a)(vi).

8 Annex III, 2(c).

9 Annex III, 2(e). See, for example, AI ESG providers like Clarity AI (https://clarity.ai/) and ESG Book (https://www.esgbook.com/).

10 For example, was the entity aware that they would be rated, did it participate in the rating process and did the provider have access to relevant documents for the rated entity. Annex III (2)(d). See also here the commentary on Article 15(12) where it is stated that the ESG rating provider should inform the rated item or issuer of the rated item at least two full working days before the first issuance of the rating (see further para 15.070 for commentary on this section). It is important to give the rated item or the issuer of the rated item an opportunity to inform the ESG rating provider of any factual errors. The tricky relationship between ESG providers and issuers is discussed in 15.069. Closeness is good to gain information, but objectivity and independence should not be compromised.

11 Annex III, 2(f).

12 Annex III, 2(g).

(section 1), but it will not be any other information than those already listed in Annex III, (2).[13]

13 Article 24 (3).

CHAPTER 3

INDEPENDENCE AND CONFLICTS OF INTEREST

ARTICLE 25

INDEPENDENCE AND AVOIDANCE OF CONFLICTS OF INTEREST

Irene-marié Esser

1. ESG rating providers shall have in place robust governance arrangements, including a clear organisational structure with well-defined, transparent and consistent roles and responsibilities for all persons involved in the provision of an ESG rating.

2. ESG rating providers shall take all necessary steps to ensure that any ESG rating provided is not affected by any existing or potential conflict of interest, or by any business or other relationship, arising either from the ESG rating providers themselves or from their shareholders, managers, rating analysts, employees or any other natural persons whose services are placed at the disposal or under the control of the ESG rating providers, or any persons directly or indirectly linked to them by control or any third-party providers to whom functions or any services or activities have been outsourced.

3. Where there is a risk of a conflict of interest within an ESG rating provider due to the ownership structure, controlling interests or activities of that ESG rating provider, of any entity owning or controlling the ESG rating provider, of an entity that is owned or controlled by the ESG rating provider, or of any of the ESG rating provider's affiliates or third-party providers, ESMA shall take appropriate action. ESMA may require the ESG rating provider to take measures to mitigate that risk.

Where a conflict of interest as referred to in the first subparagraph is not adequately managed through the risk mitigation measures referred to in the first subparagraph, ESMA shall require the ESG rating provider to resolve that conflict of interest. If necessary, ESMA may require the ESG rating provider to cease the activities or relationships that create the conflict of interest, or to cease providing the ESG ratings.

4. A shareholder or a member of an ESG rating provider exercising significant influence within the meaning of Article 2, point (13), second sentence, of Directive 2013/34/EU over that ESG rating provider, or over an undertaking which has the power to exercise control or a dominant influence over that ESG rating provider, shall be prohibited from doing any of the following:

(a) exercising significant influence over any other ESG rating provider;

(b) having the right or the power to appoint or remove members of the administrative or supervisory board of any other ESG rating provider;

(c) being a member of the administrative or supervisory board of any other ESG rating provider.

The first subparagraph of this paragraph shall not apply to investments in other ESG rating providers belonging to the same group of ESG rating providers or to investments in ESG rating providers that are micro-undertakings or small undertakings according to the criteria laid down in Article 3(1) and Article 3(2), first subparagraph, respectively, of Directive 2013/34/EU.

5. ESG rating providers shall disclose to ESMA all existing or potential conflicts of interest, including conflicts of interest arising from the ownership or control of the ESG rating providers.

6. ESG rating providers shall establish and operate policies, procedures and effective organisational arrangements for the identification, disclosure, prevention, management and mitigation of conflicts of interest. ESG rating providers shall regularly review and update those policies, procedures and arrangements. Those policies, procedures and arrangements shall specifically prevent, manage and mitigate conflicts of interest due to the ESG rating provider's ownership or control or due to other interests in the ESG rating provider's group, or conflicts of interest that are caused by other persons that exercise influence or control over the ESG rating provider in relation to determining the ESG rating.

7. ESG rating providers shall review their operations to identify potential conflicts of interest at least annually.

A. INTRODUCTION

25.01

A. INTRODUCTION

In March 2018 the Commission published its Action Plan, 'Financing Sustainable Growth,' setting up its strategy on financial sustainability. As part of this plan a Study was commissioned, and it highlighted the existence of conflicts of interest.[1] Conflicts of interest among ESG providers is thus a central focus of this Regulation. ESG rating providers should ensure that they provide ESG ratings that are independent, impartial, systematic and of adequate quality. Various measures are put in place, in Articles 17, 25 and 26.[2] **25.01**

Generally, conflicts of interest should be avoided or managed if unavoidable. If there is a conflict it should be disclosed in a timely manner (see 5 above). It is important to have records of any threat to the independence of the ESG rating provider or its employees. It is important that providers have appropriate internal policies and procedures in place to ensure internal controls and an oversight function (see 6 above and 26(2)). **25.02**

This also includes measures to prevent conflicts of interest in the decision-making process, the prohibition of certain activities by employees involved in the assessment process of the rated item and requirements to identify risks of conflicts of interest within the ESG provider (e.g. through ownership structures or controlling interests) (see 3 above). **25.03**

The conflicts of interest provisions therefore include provisions on separation of activities (providers should separate their ESG rating business from other activities), internal controls, separate ratings, disclosure and supervision. **25.04**

While Article 17 deals with the conflicts of interest of rating analysts, Article 25 deals with conflicts of interest in a more general manner (see 25(2)), encompassing governance, structure, ownership, business relationships and outsourcing. It requires ESG rating providers to put in place a robust governance structure that defines roles clearly for all persons involved in ESG ratings. It also requires ESG rating providers to take all necessary steps to ensure that **25.05**

---

1 Page 2, Preamble. See footnote 9 for the study.

2 See ESG Briefing (February 2024) by Freshfields Bruckhaus Deringer, https://www.freshfields.com/493133/contentassets/5221ed3b8c1d41839d2a2c038161490b/esg-rating-providers.pdf. It is interesting to note that the mechanism of an independent oversight function was deleted in the Draft Regulation. It was originally part of the Benchmark Regulation. In this briefing it is stated that this would not have been a popular regulation for ESG rating providers, as 'the implementation of an oversight function that can influence the ratings business in a meaningful way without interfering with the competences of the management bodies of ESG rating providers and the tasks of the internal oversight function could have proved difficult given the large number of potential rating users with conflicting interests.'

any ESG rating provided is not affected by any existing or potential conflict of interest. Article 25(5) requires all existing or potential conflicts of interest to be disclosed to ESMA. Article 25(6) requires ESG rating providers to establish and operate policies, procedures, and effective organizational arrangements for the identification, disclosure, prevention, management and mitigation of conflicts of interest.

25.06 Where there is a risk of a conflict of interest ESMA is provided with powers to require that the risk is mitigated or ended. As a backstop, ESMA is also able to stop the provision of the relevant ESG ratings.

25.07 Significant shareholders (20%) of an ESG ratings provider are prohibited from doing any of the following:

(a) holding significant influence in any other ESG rating provider;
(c) having the right or the power to appoint or remove members of the administrative or supervisory board of any other ESG rating provider;
(d) being a member of the administrative or supervisory board of any other ESG rating provider.

25.08 This prohibition does not apply to holding in small ESG ratings providers.

ARTICLE 26

MANAGEMENT OF POTENTIAL CONFLICTS OF INTEREST ARISING FROM EMPLOYEES

Irene-marié Esser

1. ESG rating providers shall ensure that their employees and any other natural persons whose services are placed at their disposal or under their control and who are directly involved in the provision of an ESG rating:

(a) have the skills that are necessary for performing their tasks and duties and are subject to effective management and supervision;

(b) are not subject to undue influence or conflicts of interest;

(c) are not compensated and their performance is not evaluated in such a manner as to create conflicts of interest or otherwise impinge upon the integrity of the ESG rating determination process;

(d) do not have any interests or business connections that compromise the activities of the ESG rating provider;

(e) are prohibited from contributing to an ESG rating determination by way of engaging in bids, offers and trades on a personal basis or on behalf of market participants, except where such contribution is expressly required as part of the ESG rating methodology and is subject to specific rules laid down therein; and

(f) are subject to effective procedures to control the exchange of information with other employees involved in activities that might create a risk of conflicts of interest or with third parties, where that information might affect the ESG rating.

2. ESG rating providers shall establish specific internal control procedures to ensure the integrity and reliability of the employee or person determining the ESG rating, including internal approval by management before the distribution of the ESG rating.

A. INTRODUCTION

26.01 This Article overlaps with the general provisions on conflicts of interest in Article 25 and the specific provisions on rating analysts in Article 17. Its provisions apply more broadly to all employees and make explicit reference to the management of conflicts of interest by ensuring that compensation and performance arrangements do not give rise to conflicts of interest; that employees do not have any interests or business connections that compromise the activities of the ESG rating provider; and that ESG rating providers shall establish specific internal control procedures to ensure the integrity and reliability of the employee or person determining the ESG rating, including internal sign-off by management before the dissemination of the ESG rating.

ARTICLE 27

FAIR, REASONABLE, TRANSPARENT AND NON-DISCRIMINATORY TREATMENT OF USERS OF ESG RATINGS

Irene-marié Esser

1. **ESG rating providers shall take steps that are adequate to ensure that fees charged to clients are fair, reasonable, transparent and non-discriminatory.**
2. **For the purposes of paragraph 1 of this Article, ESMA may require ESG rating providers to provide it with documented evidence on their pricing policy, including the fee structure and pricing criteria. ESMA may take supervisory measures in accordance with Article 35, and may decide to impose fines in accordance with Article 36 where it finds that fees charged by ESG rating providers are not fair, reasonable, transparent and non-discriminatory.**

A. INTRODUCTION

27.01 This article concerns the charging of fees by ESG rating providers. The fees charged should be fair, reasonable, transparent and non-discriminatory.[1] There is no indication of what these steps should entail in the Regulation or the Preamble. Moreover, while this approach to pricing is familiar in other forms of EU regulation such as the Credit Rating Agencies Regulation (CRAR),[2]

1 Article 27(1). The previous version also stated, 'and not based on actual costs.'

2 Article 6.2 CRAR in conjunction with Annex I, Section B, par 3c.

the European Markets Infrastructure Regulation (EMIR)[3] and the Markets in Financial Instruments Regulation (MiFIR),[4] the precise formulations differ in each context and so it is not possible to extrapolate a consistent approach or interpretation. Relatedly, different business models and market structures may call for different priorities in the approach to regulation: thus for credit rating agencies the equivalent provision refers only to fees not being discriminatory and based on actual costs, with the objective being primarily to 'mitigate conflicts of interest' and 'facilitate fair competition in the credit rating market'[5] rather than any broader objective of ensuring equal access to prices for customers in similar positions. It should be noted also that the EU competition law will likely have a role to play in this context, especially in relation to any abuse of a dominant market position.[6]

27.02 ESMA may ask the relevant ESG provider to provide evidence concerning the pricing policy, fee structure and pricing criteria.[7]

27.03 Supervisory measures can be undertaken by ESMA or a fine imposed, if the fees are not fair, reasonable, transparent and non-discriminatory.[8]

3 Article 4.3a, referring to the price of clearing services.
4 Article 13(1), referring to the price of market data.
5 Recital 38 of Regulation 462/2013 amending CRAR.
6 See further Article 102 TFEU.
7 Article 27(2).
8 Article 27(2), see Article 35 and 36 for the supervisory measures (e.g. to withdraw or suspend the authorization or recognition of the ESG rating provider) and fines. The maximum amount of the fine shall be 10% of the total annual net turnover of the ESG rating provider, calculated on the basis of the most recent available financial statements approved by the management body of the ESG rating provider, Article 36(1). See also https://www.dlapiper.com/en-om/insights/publications/2024/05/european-parliament-adopts-regulation-on-esg-ratings for a good overview of this Regulation, also with regards to this Article.

CHAPTER 4

SUPERVISION BY ESMA

Section 1 General principles

ARTICLE 28

NON-INTERFERENCE WITH THE CONTENTS OF RATINGS OR METHODOLOGIES

Francesco De Pascalis

In carrying out their duties under this Regulation, ESMA, the Commission or any Member State public authorities shall not interfere with the content of ESG ratings or methodologies.

A. INTRODUCTION

28.01 Chapter 4 of the 'Proposal for a regulation of the European Parliament and of the Council on the transparency and integrity of Environmental, Social and Governance (ESG) rating activities' (the ESG ratings regulation) lays down a body of rules (Articles 28–46) on the rationale, structure and operation of the supervision of ESG rating providers. Before critically reviewing the contents and implications of these provisions, we need to acknowledge who is entrusted with ongoing control over the ESG rating providers' activities.

28.02 Recital 41 of the ESG ratings regulation explains the motives behind the appointment of the European Securities Market Authority (ESMA) as the unique ESG rating providers' supervisor. Given the increasing use of ESG ratings in global capital markets[1] and their significance for the creation of a

1 Recital 10 of Regulation (EU) No 2024/3005 of the European Parliament and of the Council of 27 November 2024 on the transparency and integrity of Environmental, Social and Governance (ESG)

sustainable finance market in the European Union (EU)[2] ongoing supervision is pivotal to ensure the achievement of the objectives of the ESG ratings regulation, such as independence, transparency, quality and reliability of ESG ratings.[3]

28.03 Nonetheless, Recital 41 does not refer to these grounds, including the circumstance that Member States do not regulate or supervise ESG rating providers' activities,[4] to justify ESMA's empowerment. The entrustment of supervisory duties is warranted because of the similarities between the activities of ESG rating providers and credit rating agencies (CRAs).[5]

28.04 Like credit ratings, ESG ratings are 'opinions' resulting from specific methodologies and reported on a letter or numeric basis.[6] However, the connection between ESG rating activities and credit rating activities would create alignments between this ESG regulation and the EU CRA regulation.[7] The EU CRA regulation consists of Regulation No 1060/2009, Regulation No 513/2011 and Regulation No 462/2013.

28.05 While Regulation No 462/2013 was issued to improve and expand the scope of Regulation No 1060/2009, Regulation No 513/2011 lays down supervisory requirements by designating ESMA as the principal supervisor of CRAs in the EU.[8] Accordingly, the EU CRA supervisory framework becomes the model to apply to supervise EU ESG rating providers. In other words, the complementarity between the activities of CRAs and ESG rating providers makes it necessary to make ESMA responsible for supervising ESG rating providers as much as it is the unique supervisor of CRAs. Moreover, some CRA supervisory rules are replicated in the present ESG rating providers regulation. In this way, harmonized and unformed supervision will also be achieved.[9]

28.06 Recital 41 finally clarifies that the mentioned motives are the sole reasons behind ESMA's supervisory powers over ESG rating providers. Such reasons

---

rating activities, and amending Regulations (EU) 2019/2088 and (EU) 2023/2859 OJEU.

2 Recital 11 of Regulation (EU) No 2024/3005.

3 Article 1 of Regulation (EU) No 2024/3005.

4 Recital 13 of Regulation (EU) No 2024/3005.

5 Recital 41 of Regulation (EU) No 2024/3005.

6 See, Article 3(1) of Regulation (EU) No 2024/3005 and Article 3(a) of Regulation (EU) 1060/2009 on credit rating agencies.

7 Recital 41 of Regulation (EU) No 2024/3005.

8 European Securities and Markets Authority (ESMA), 'Credit Rating Agencies', www.esma.europa.eu/esmas-activities/investors-and-issuers/credit-rating-agencies.

9 Recital 41 of Regulation (EU) No 2024/3005.

neither set a precedent nor establish practices/policies for attributing supervisory powers.[10]

Against this backdrop, Article 28 is the first rule to be analyzed within the 'General Principles' incorporated in Section 1 of Chapter 4 of the ESG ratings regulation entitled 'Supervision by ESMA.' **28.07**

B. THE NON-INTERFERENCE PRINCIPLE

1. Rating methodologies

Article 28 prohibits public authorities and institutions, including ESMA and the European Commission, from interfering with the contents of ESG ratings or underlying methodologies while performing their duties under the present regulation. Given the abovementioned alignments between this regulation and the CRA regulation, it is worth noting that Article 28 replicates Article 23 of CRA Regulation No 513/2011.[11] Consequently, the non-interference principle set out in Article 28 of the ESG ratings regulation can be construed in line with the interpretation of Article 23 of the CRA regulation. **28.08**

Preliminarily, it is important to explain the significance of 'rating methodologies' by recalling that in April 2024, ESMA launched consultations on possible amendments of Annex I of CRA Regulation No 1060/2009 and EU Delegated Regulation No 447/2012 relating to compliance with credit rating methodologies.[12] As the amendments are necessary to require CRAs to consider ESG risks in their credit ratings and rating outlooks, this subject matter will also have implications for ESG rating providers under the present regulation. In fact, ESMA proposes amendments to clarify the meaning of 'rating methodology' due to its vagueness.[13] In practice, the authority notes that lack of clarity depends on difficulties in identifying the elements that underpin a credit rating or rating outlook methodology. **28.09**

Consequently, ESMA proposes a definition that first consolidates the understanding of methodology as 'the framework that contributes to the **28.10**

---

10 *Ibid.*

11 See Article 23 of Regulation (EU) No 513/2011 ('Non-interference with content of ratings or methodologies').

12 ESMA, 'Consultation Paper. Proposed Revisions to Commission Delegated Regulation (EU) 447/2012 and Annex I of CRA Regulation' (2 April 2024), www.esma.europa.eu/sites/default/files/2024-04/ESMA84-2037069784-2112_Consultation_Paper_on_Changes_to_Delegated_Reg_447-2012_and_Annex_I_of_CRAR.pdf.

13 *Ibid.*

determination of a credit rating and rating outlooks'; and second, identifies the elements that are relevant for creditworthiness assessments (e.g. criteria, models, driving factors and key rating assumptions).[14]

28.11 Once finalized, the (proposed) definition of rating methodologies will guide the work of supervisors in the rating world, including the ESG rating area; and further explain the logic behind the principles of non-interference with rating contents or methodologies, which nurtures the operation of supervisors.

2. Rating providers and public authorities

28.12 At present, however, the more seasoned EU CRA regulation is the primary source for understanding the non-interference principle transposed in Article 28 of the ESG ratings regulation.

28.13 Since the preliminary discussions concerning the creation of the EU CRA regulation, there has been unanimous agreement on subjecting the operations of CRAs to rigorous control.[15] The principle of non-interference begins with the body of rules detailing the supervisory powers over CRAs. The same approach is then followed in the ESG rating providers regulation. Fundamentally, preventing public authorities from interfering with the rating process and methodologies responds to various needs, such as guaranteeing the independence of rating providers. Rating providers deploy their own, diversified, rating methodologies. This is particularly evident in the world of credit ratings, where the CRAs have different business models and use different methodologies to assess the creditworthiness of financial instruments or their issuers.[16]

28.14 The same can be seen in the ESG rating world, where there are several providers with their own approaches to evaluating firms' performance, ranging from qualitative and quantitative approaches to carbon footprint and energy efficiency focus or labour and human rights practices.[17] Furthermore, recent studies highlight congruities and divergences in the ESG ratings issued by six

---

14 *Ibid.*

15 See European Commission, 'Regulating credit rating agencies', https://finance.ec.europa.eu/capital-markets-union-and-financial-markets/financial-markets/regulating-credit-rating-agencies_en. See also The High-Level Group on Financial Supervision in the EU, *Report* (Brussels, 25 February 2009) 19, https://ec.europa.eu/economy_finance/publications/pages/publication14527_en.pdf.

16 See Standard & Poor's, 'Guide to Credit Ratings Essentials' (2022), www.spglobal.com/ratings/_division-assets/pdfs/guide_to_credit_rating_essentials_digital.pdf; see also Shourya Ghosh, 'A Study of Differences in Standard's & Poor's and Moody's Corporate Credit Ratings' (4 March 2013) The Leonard N. Stern School of Business, www.stern.nyu.edu/sites/default/files/assets/documents/con_041250.pdf.

17 Team Iris Carbon, 'A Beginner's Guide to ESG Rating Agencies and Methodologies' (*Iris Carbon*, 23 January 2023), www.iriscarbon.com/a-beginners-guide-to-esg-rating-agencies-and-methodologies/.

rating agencies and found that the latter are pervasive due to different factors and assessment methods.[18]

Such a variety of methods also results from the broad scope of the notion of ESG ratings. While acknowledging that the term includes a wide range of rating products, the International Organization of Securities Commissions (IOSCO) also included ESG scorings and ESG rankings, which imply different resources and methodologies despite pursuing the same objective of assessing ESG risk exposures.[19] **28.15**

Through this lens, non-interference with the contents of rating and methodologies means that public authority will not influence each provider's rating philosophy. Public authorities' non-interference is also necessary to avoid casting misleading messages to market participants. If public authorities had a strong say in the policies, methodologies and criteria applied by financial firms for issuing ratings, there would be the risk of rating users' misperceptions, as if the assigned ratings were faultless because the result from methodologies suggested or determined by regulators.[20] Overall, non-interference means that public authorities' will never be involved in the rating process. **28.16**

Nevertheless, non-interference does not mean that supervisory authorities do not have expectations. On the one hand, Recital 32 of the ESG ratings regulation clarifies that it is down to ESG rating providers to determine their own methodologies.[21] On the other hand, their rating methodologies should be rigorous, systematic, independent, continuous and capable of justification.[22] These requirements are then reiterated in paragraph 7 of Article 15 of the present regulation alongside the providers' duty to apply their rating methodologies **28.17**

---

18 Florian Berg, Julian F. Kölbel and Ricardo Rigobon, 'Aggregate Confusion: The Divergence of ESG Ratings' (2022) 26(6) *Review of Finance*, 1315.

19 International Organisation of Securities Commissions (IOSCO), *Environmental, Social and Governance (ESG) Ratings and Data Products Providers* (November 2021), www.iosco.org/library/pubdocs/pdf/IOSCOPD690.pdf.

20 House of Commons, Treasury Committee, 'Credit Rating Agencies: Written Evidence' (1 March 2012) 65, https://publications.parliament.uk/pa/cm201012/cmselect/cmtreasy/writev/1866/1866.pdf.

21 Recital 32 of Regulation (EU) No 2024/3005 provides as follows: 'To ensure the quality and reliability of ESG ratings, ESG rating providers should use rating methodologies that are rigorous, systematic, independent, continuous and capable of justification and that apply continuously and in a transparent manner. ESG rating providers should be encouraged to address both aspects of the double materiality principle. ESG rating providers should review ESG rating methodologies on an ongoing basis and at least annually, taking into account Union and international developments affecting the E, S or G factors. However, it is important to leave it to the ESG rating providers themselves to determine their own methodologies in accordance with those principles.' See also Recital 33 setting duties to disclose to the public methodologies, models and key rating assumptions used by ESG rating providers in their activities.

22 *Ibid.*

continuously and transparently.[23] Overall, the ESG regulation sets down the principles for assessing ESG rating methodologies but, under the non-interference principle of Article 28, does not empower ESMA and the public authorities to judge on the merit of the contents of ESG ratings or methodologies.

C. CONCLUSION

28.18 In conclusion, in line with the early EU CRA Regulation ESG rating providers shall retain their autonomy and independence regarding their rating methodologies. Their methodologies, however, need to demonstrate that certain criteria (rigorousness, systematicity, independence, continuous justification) are fulfilled. Assessing compliance with these criteria will be one of ESMA's supervisory duties. Public authorities' non-interference means, therefore, the freedom left to the ESG providers to design and put in place their own rating methodologies and the scope of the control exercised by ESMA, that is, the compliance of the ESG rating methodologies with specific criteria. The forthcoming definition of rating methodologies will finally be the model definition helping to clarify the contours of the perimeter of ongoing supervision.

23 See Article 15 in the present Commentary.

ARTICLE 29

ESMA

Francesco De Pascalis

1. **In accordance with Article 16 of Regulation (EU) No 1095/2010, ESMA shall issue and update guidelines on the cooperation between ESMA and the competent authorities for the purposes of this Regulation, including the procedures for, and detailed conditions relating to, the delegation of tasks.**
2. **In accordance with Article 16 of Regulation (EU) No 1095/2010, ESMA shall, in cooperation with EBA and EIOPA, issue and update guidelines on the application of the endorsement regime referred to in Article 11 of this Regulation by 2 October 2025.**
3. **ESMA shall publish an annual report on the application of this Regulation, including on the supervisory measures taken and fines and periodic penalty payments imposed by ESMA under this Regulation. That report shall contain, in particular, information on the evolution of the ESG ratings market in the Union and an assessment of the application of the third-country regimes referred to in Articles 10, 11 and 12. ESMA shall present the annual report referred to in the first subparagraph to the European Parliament, the Council and the Commission.**
4. **ESMA shall publish annually on its website a list of ESG rating providers included in the register referred to in Article 14(1), indicating their total market share in the Union. The publication shall take stock of the market structure, including concentration levels and the diversity of ESG rating providers.**
5. **For the purposes of paragraph 4, the market share shall be measured by reference to the annual turnover generated from ESG rating activities at group level in the Union.**
6. **ESMA shall cooperate with EBA and EIOPA in performing its tasks and shall consult EBA and EIOPA before issuing and updating guidelines and submitting draft regulatory technical standards under this Regulation.**

A. INTRODUCTION

29.01 The European Banking Authority (EBA), the European Insurance and Occupational Pensions Authority (EIOPA), and ESMA together form the European Supervisory Authorities (ESAs), a triptych of independent EU authorities in charge of micro-prudential supervision in their respective areas of competence: banking,[1] securities markets[2] and insurance corporations.[3] The three ESAs are part of a complex supervisory architecture, namely the European System of Financial Supervision (ESFS) built in the EU in the aftermath of the 2007–2009 financial crisis.

29.02 The creation of the ESFS represents a significant overhaul of the EU financial supervisory system. The founding regulations of the three ESAs clarify that such reforms were necessary to ensure better coordination, cooperation and consistent application of EU financial legislation against the inadequacies of nationally based supervisory models, unable to address the increased interconnection and integration of the EU financial markets and the cross-border reach of many financial institutions.[4]

29.03 Whereas the ESAs are micro-prudential authorities, macro-prudential oversight of the EU financial system is mandated to the European Systemic Risk Board (ESRB) within the ESFS.[5] Then, the ESFS architecture is completed through the Member States' national competent authorities, which are

1 Regulation (EU) No 1093/2010 of the European Parliament and of the Council of 24 November 2010 establishing a European Supervisory Authority (European Banking Authority), amending Decision No 716/2009/EC and repealing Commission Decision 2009/78/EC [2010] OJ L 331.

2 Regulation (EU) No 1095/2010 of the European Parliament and of the Council of 24 November 2010 establishing a European Supervisory Authority (European Securities and Markets Authority), amending Decision No 716/2009/EC and repealing Commission Decision 2009/77/EC [2010] OJ L 331.

3 Regulation (EU) No 1094/2010 of the European Parliament and of the Council of 24 November 2010 establishing a European Supervisory Authority (European Insurance and Occupational Pensions Authority), amending Decision No 716/2009/EC and repealing Commission Decision 2009/79/EC [2010] OJ L 331.

4 Recital 1 of Regulation (EU) No 1093/2010; Recital 1 of Regulation (EU) No 1095/2010; Recital 1 Regulation (EU) No 1094/2010.

5 Regulation (EU) No 1092/2010 of the European Parliament and of the Council of 24 November 2010 on European Union macro-prudential oversight of the financial system and establishing a European Systemic Risk Board [2010] OJ L 331.

responsible for the day-to-day supervision of their domestic markets and financial institutions.

Significantly, within this network of supervisory authorities, ESMA's supervisory mandate began with its designation as the sole supervisor of entities whose operations had pan-European reach. In 2011, ESMA was entrusted with the registration, ongoing supervision, and enforcement powers over credit rating agencies (CRAs) operating across the EU space. Since then, ESMA's direct responsibilities have expanded to include the registration and supervision of EU-based trade repositories and securitization repositories. Recently, ESMA's supervisory mandate has been extended to certain data reporting services providers, certain administrators of EU critical benchmarks and Tier 2 third-country central counterparties.[6] **29.04**

Like the EBA and EIOPA, ESMA operates against the objective of ensuring the stability and effectiveness of the EU financial system, financial markets transparency, and the protection of the involved players.[7] In so doing, ESMA strives to promote the consistent application of EU legislation among Member States by issuing regulatory technical standards and implementing technical standards that the European Commission will finally adopt as delegated or implemented acts.[8] Furthermore, ESMA can issue 'Guidelines and Recommendations' to promote convergence in supervisory practices across the ESFS.[9] **29.05**

B. SUPERVISORY COOPERATION

Accordingly, Article 29 of the ESG ratings regulation, entitled 'ESMA,' details how the authority shall operate and liaise with the other ESAs and Member States' national competent authorities within the ESG rating providers area. To this end, Article 29(1) relates to a key instrument ESMA uses in the exercise of its supervisory mandate: the 'guidelines.' As paragraph 1 of Article 29 specifies, ESMA's guidelines find their legal basis in Article 16 ('Guidelines and Recommendations') of Regulation (EU) 1095/2010, which governs the structure, powers and operation of ESMA in the EU. **29.06**

6 See ESMA, 'Home Page', www.esma.europa.eu/.

7 *Ibid.*

8 *Ibid.*

9 *Ibid.*

29.07 Article 16 of ESMA founding regulation, stresses that national competent authorities or financial market participants are the receivers of guidelines and recommendations.[10] The publishing of guidelines or recommendations may be preceded by public consultations ESMA can launch to seek views on their nature, scope and potential impact.[11] From the reading of Article 16, it is evident that the non-legally binding nature of guidelines and recommendations, which are finally based on the 'comply or explain' legal principle.[12] Competent authorities and market participants are expected to notify ESMA of their intention to comply with published guidelines or recommendations, or to explain in case they will not. The Authority will keep a record of non-compliance and, if necessary, publish the reasons for not complying.[13] Against this setting, ESMA will have to comply with the principles and procedures set down in Article 16 of Regulation (EU) 1095/2010 when issuing guidelines on cooperation with national competent authorities for achieving the aims of the ESG ratings regulation.

C. DELEGATION OF TASKS

29.08 ESMA's guidelines, where necessary, will need to be updated to cover the procedures and prerequisites for delegating supervisory tasks to the national competent authorities. As explained in the previous chapter, the delegation of tasks to national competent authorities underlines ESMA's primacy in the supervision of ESG rating providers.[14] Delegation of tasks is addressed in Article 43 of the ESG ratings regulation ('Delegation of tasks by ESMA to competent authorities').[15] Within the present discussion, it is worth recalling that given the alignment of the ESG ratings regulation with the CRA regulation, ESMA's delegation of tasks can be explained by referring to the consolidated meaning of the CRA supervisory rules.

29.09 'Delegation' means that supervisory tasks are undertaken by another authority in lieu of the responsible authority.[16] There can be various reasons behind a delegation. In the case of delegation from ESMA to national competent

10 See Article 16 of Regulation (EU) No 1095/2010.

11 *Ibid.*

12 ESAs 'Guidelines and recommendations are also defined as "non-legislative materials"'; see also Financial Conduct Authority (FCA), 'Brexit: Our Approach to EU Non-legislative Materials' (October 2020) 1, www.fca.org.uk/publication/corporate/brexit-our-approach-to-eu-non-legislative-materials.pdf.

13 See Article 16 of Regulation (EU) No 1095/2010.

14 Article 28 in the present Commentary.

15 Article 43 in the present Commentary.

16 See Recital 39 of Regulation (EU) No 1095/2010.

authorities, one of the principal reasons is that some tasks require certain knowledge and expertise that put national authorities in the best position.[17] In any case, delegation is vital for avoiding duplication of tasks, strengthening cooperation and calibrating supervisory burden within the ESFS.[18] Consequently, the ESMA guidelines contemplated by paragraph 1 of Article 29 will have to instruct the delegates on how to perform the tasks indicated in Article 43(a)(b) of the ESG ratings regulation (i.e. requests for information, investigations and on-site inspections).

D. ESAS COOPERATION

Article 16 of Regulation (EU) 1095/2010 is also the legal basis for issuing guidelines relating to the endorsement in the EU of ESG ratings published by providers established outside the Union, which the present regulation disciplines in Article 11. The possibility of endorsement is subject to strict conditions.[19] According to paragraph 2 of Article 29 of the ESG ratings regulation, any guideline on this subject matter must be issued by ESMA in tandem with the EBA and EIOPA by nine months from the entry into force of the ESG ratings regulation.[20] This requirement finds its reasons in the cross-sector implications that the endorsement of ESG ratings may have. In other words, joint supervisory efforts are necessary to coordinate in matters where each of the ESA may have supervisory stakes. ESG ratings and the activities of the providers have indeed cross-sectoral reach given their use by a variety of financial stakeholders.[21] **29.10**

Even though ESMA is the sole supervisor, such activities may also affect the areas and institutions supervised by the other two ESAs. Accordingly, paragraph 2 of Article 29 must also be read in conjunction with paragraph 6, which closes the circle of ESA supervisory cooperation duties by reinforcing that ESMA must cooperate and consult with the EBA and EIOPA regarding **29.11**

17 *Ibid.*

18 *Ibid.*

19 Article 11 in the present Commentary.

20 See Article 29 of Regulation (EU) No 2024/3005, para 2.

21 See Josefina Capdevila Panalva, 'Transparency and Integrity of Environmental, Social and Governance Rating Activities' (November 2023), European Parliamentary Research Services www.europarl.europa.eu/RegData/etudes/BRIE/2023/753185/EPRS_BRI(2023)753185_EN.pdf; see also Bryan Tayan, 'ESG Ratings: A Compass Without Direction' (*Harward Law School Forum on Corporate Governance*, 24 August 2022), https://corpgov.law.harvard.edu/2022/08/24/esg-ratings-a-compass-without-direction/.

the publishing and updating of guidelines and draft regulatory technical standards.[22]

E. MONITORING ACTIVITIES

29.12 Finally, paragraphs 3 and 4 of Article 29 complete the picture of the information ESMA is expected to produce in relation to ESG ratings.

29.13 Under Paragraph 3, ESMA, as the sole supervisor of ESG rating providers, is expected to monitor the application of the present legislation once it is in force. Annual reports published by ESMA and submitted to the European Parliament, the Council and the European Commission, will be a crucial source to digest the impact and outcomes of the present regulation. In its reports, ESMA must record any supervisory action taken against ESG rating firms, including fines, penalties and periodic penalty payments. Moreover, ESMA must analyze and produce data on the evolution of the ESG rating market and on the effective application of the equivalence and endorsement regimes governed in the present regulation.[23]

29.14 Paragraph 4 requires ESMA to provide updates on the number of registered ESG rating providers and their presence in the EU. Indeed, ESG rating providers are a diversified world comprising entities with different market structures and operations.[24] Accordingly, paragraph 4 of Article 29 requires ESMA to publicize, on its website, the list of the registered ESG rating providers and their total market share in the Union. The market structure of the ESG rating providers, their diversification and concentration level across the EU will be the parameters ESMA can refer to for the information requested under paragraph 3(a) of Article 29.

F. CONCLUSION

29.15 Article 29, as its title suggests, introduces the tasks ESMA is supposed to undertake as the direct supervisor of ESG rating providers. Its provisions clarify the importance of supervisory cooperation between ESMA and the

22 See Article 29 of Regulation (EU) No 2024/3005, para 6.
23 See Article 29 of Regulation (EU) No 2024/3005, para 3
24 Capdevila Panalma (n 21).

Member States' national competent authorities, including joint supervision with EBA and EIOPA. Overall, Article 29 provides an overview of direct supervision and, within the body of rules set out in Chapter 4 of the ESG ratings regulation, is the backbone of the subsequent rules governing ESMA's direct supervision more specifically.

ARTICLE 30

COMPETENT AUTHORITIES

Francesco De Pascalis

1. **By 2 April 2026, each Member State shall designate a competent authority for the purposes of this Regulation.**
2. **The competent authorities shall be adequately staffed, with regard to capacity and expertise, to be able to carry out their tasks under this Regulation.**

A. INTRODUCTION

30.01 Article 30 of the ESG ratings regulation is a general provision on Member States' national competent authorities. It sets a deadline for Member States (15 months after the entry into force of the ESG ratings Regulation) to designate the national authority that will have to cooperate with ESMA for the purposes of the ESG ratings Regulation. The prospective national competent authorities must be adequately staffed and have the necessary resources to carry out their tasks. By setting these two requirements, Article 30 is a very straightforward rule, which also replicates the wording of Article 22 of the EU CRA Regulation as evidence, once again, of the alignments between the ESG ratings and CRA regulations.[1] Nevertheless, Article 30 offers significant points of reflection.

1 See Article 22 Regulation (EU) No 1060/2009.

B. SHARING RESPONSIBILITIES

Within the ESFS, ESMA is the EU securities and financial markets regulator and supervisor. To pursue its role and mission to ensure the proper functioning of the EU financial markets and market infrastructures, guarantee investor protection and strengthen the stability of the financial system, ESMA needs to coordinate its activities with other EU authorities and institutions. In its 2023–2028 strategy, ESMA underlines the need to strengthen cooperation with the EBA and EIOPA given the increasing integration between various financial sectors across the EU.[2] Coordination is also achieved through ESMA's collaboration with bodies seeking to strengthen the stability of international financial markets, or with international standard-setting bodies dealing with financial regulation, including the Financial Stability Board (FSB) and the International Organisation for Securities Commissions (IOSCO); and other relevant bodies such as the International Monetary Fund (IMF), the Organisation for Economic Cooperation and Development (OECD), the International Financial Reporting Standards (IFRS) Advisory Council and non-EU securities regulators, including the Bank of England (BOE), the UK Financial Conduct Authority (FCA), the US Commodities and Futures Trading Commission (CFTC) and the Securities and Exchange Commission (SEC) in relation to the sectors that fall under its direct supervision.[3] 30.02

The relationship with the Member States' national competent authorities is also crucial for accomplishing the authority's strategic objectives. ESMA's supervisory process can develop through four key stages: registration, monitoring, investigation and sanctioning.[4] Within this context, the relationship between ESMA and the national competent authorities is one of shared responsibilities. As specified in the previous chapters, the spectrum of EU entities under the control of ESMA as the sole supervisor has grown considerably since 2011.[5] Consequently, shared responsibilities between ESMA and national competent authorities have different connotations depending on which authority is entrusted with direct supervision. 30.03

---

2 European Securities and Markets Authorities (ESMA), 'ESMA strategy 2023-2028' (September 2022) 6, www.esma.europa.eu/sites/default/files/library/esma_strategy_2023-2028.pdf.

3 ESMA, 'ESMA's role in European and international regulatory cooperation' (June 2012) ESMA/2012/367 <www.esma.europa.eu/sites/default/files/library/2015/11/2012-367_esmas_role_in_european_and_international_regulatory_cooperaiton_icsa_conference_copenhagen_-_verena_ross_12_june_2012.pdf>. See also ESMA, 'International Cooperation' <www.esma.europa.eu/about-esma/international-cooperation>.

4 ESMA, 'Home Page', www.esma.europa.eu/.

5 See Article 29 in the present Commentary.

30.04 In any case, shared responsibilities are essential for developing a 'common supervisory culture' in the EU. As Article 29 of the ESMA founding regulation clarifies, a 'common supervisory culture' depends on ensuring consistent supervisory practices, uniform procedures and approaches across the Union.[6] ESMA must actively engage to this end through a range of activities such as providing opinion to competent authorities, exchanging information with competent authorities, developing high-quality regulatory and implementing technical standards and reviewing their application, promoting uniform supervisory standards and encouraging sectoral and cross-sectoral training programmes.[7]

30.05 On the one hand, regarding the entities under the direct supervision of ESMA (entities whose operations have pan-European reach), national competent authorities must aid ESMA in achieving the objectives of ensuring utmost compliance with regulation by the supervised entities and conduct changes where necessary.[8] As the ESG ratings regulation shows, the national competent authorities' assistance is particularly detailed when ESMA exercises enforcement powers such as investigations and on-site inspections.[9] On the other hand, when supervision is left at the national level, shared responsibilities mean ESMA's duties to proactively promote supervisory convergence among national competent authorities.

C. SUPERVISORY CONVERGENCE

30.06 EU financial regulation aims at creating a level playing field between the Single Market's participants through a common framework guaranteeing the right to provide services in the EU and adequate investor protection.[10] The fulfilment of this objective requires, amongst other strategies, a consistent supervision of the financial entities operating in the EU space. ESMA undertakes this responsibility in cooperation with national competent authorities. Accordingly, financial supervision in the EU can be shared effectively between

6 See Article 29 of Regulation (EU) No 1095/2010.

7 *Ibid.*

8 ESMA Strategy 2023–2028 (n 2) 22.

9 Article 33 and Article 34 in the present Commentary.

10 ESMA, '2025 Annual Work Programme' (1 October 2024) ESMA22-50751485-1488, 6 <www.esma.europa.eu/sites/default/files/2024-10/ESMA22-50751485-1488_Annual_Work_Programme_2025.pdf>.

ESMA and the national competent authorities by fostering convergence of aims, priorities and strategies.[11]

Supervisory convergence entails enhancing coordination among national competent authorities, uniformly interpretating rules and sharing good practices to build a common supervisory culture in the EU.[12] There is no standardized approach to reach supervisory convergence. Strategies depend on the specific situations and the capabilities and means of the national competent authorities. Within this context, ESMA can therefore play various important roles. For example, through Common Supervisory Actions (CSAs), peer reviews, case discussions, practice sharing, supervisory colleges, trainings and workshops, as well as assessments of allegations of breach of EU law by national supervisors. Specifically, CSAs can be established through the 'Union-wide Strategic Supervisory Priorities' (USSPs) that ESMA drafts periodically. The USSPs help identify those financial areas/sectors where supervisory convergence should be maximized,[13] while supervisory colleges enhance convergence by promoting coordination in the supervision of entities operating across EU Member States.[14] Convergence can be also reached through the strengthening of information sharing between the ESMA and the national competent authorities' experts in enforcement cases. In this respect, ESMA strives to promote an effective common EU enforcement culture by laying down common enforcement approaches, tools and methods.[15] **30.07**

In addition, ESMA can be the first port of call for disseminating supervisory know-how and offering valuable guidance for planning and managing supervisory activities.[16] Facilitation roles also imply coordinator efforts to ensure a smooth, consistent and efficient performance of supervisory activities.[17] All things considered, within a context of shared responsibilities, ESMA and national competent authorities' activities complement each other. **30.08**

Regarding the EU ESG ratings sector, ESMA intends to foster supervisory convergence through the development of proper tools enabling the national supervisors to address effectively the risks posed by this sector. ESMA will **30.09**

---

11 ESMA, 'About ESMA' (9 April 2021) 2 <www.esma.europa.eu/sites/default/files/library/about_esma.pdf>.
12 See Recital 40 and Article 29 of Regulation (EU) No 1095/2010.
13 ESMA 2025 Annual Work Programme (n 10) 10.
14 *Ibid.*
15 *Ibid.*
16 ESMA Strategy 2023–2028 (n 2) 21.
17 *Ibid.*

support specialized training programmes for national supervisors, aiming at building up strong ESG knowledge, expertise and skills.[18]

D. AIMS OF ARTICLE 30

30.10 Against this backdrop, the purpose of Article 30 is to introduce the role of the Member States' national competent authorities within the ESG ratings regulation. Their presence is vital due to the absence of regulation and supervision of ESG rating activities at the national level.[19] Taking position for the designation of ESMA as the direct supervisor of ESG rating providers, this rule reveals their necessary presence as ESMA's adjuvants in the supervision of the EU ESG rating sector. To this end, Article 30 is the general rule leading to other provisions where shared responsibilities between the primary supervisor and the national competent authorities are specified.

30.11 Indeed, under Chapter 5 of the present regulation ('Cooperation between ESMA and national competent authorities'), Articles 43–46 discipline the interrelationship between ESMA and the national competent authorities, which can result in the delegation of tasks, exchange of information, notifications and requests of suspension and professional secrecy joint obligations.[20] These rules then intersect with Articles 32–34, which discipline the role and degree of assistance the national competent authorities will give when ESMA conducts investigations and on-site inspections.[21]

30.12 Article 30 declares, EU Member States must designate the authorities that will assist ESMA and thus contribute to the application of the ESG ratings regulation. Heads of the national competent authorities will be sitting on ESMA's Board of Supervisors.[22] The ESMA website lists Member States designated national competent authorities in charge of the supervision of securities and capital markets, which are likely to be appointed in relation to the ESG rating area as envisaged by Article 30.[23]

---

18 *Ibid*; see also Joint Committee of the European Supervisory Authorities, '2025 Work Programme' (7 October 2024) JC 2024 27 <www.esma.europa.eu/sites/default/files/2024-10/JC_2024_27_Joint_Committee_Annual_Work_Programme_2025.pdf>.

19 See Recital 13 of Regulation (EU) No 2024/3005.

20 Articles 43–46 in the present Commentary.

21 Articles 32–34 in the present Commentary.

22 Article 30 of Regulation (EU) No 2024/3005, para 1.

23 ESMA, 'Board of Supervisors', www.esma.europa.eu/about-esma/governance-structure/board-of-supervisors#NationalCompetentAuthorities.

E. CONCLUSION

ESMA and the national competent authorities are expected to join forces to ensure clarity, consistency and effective supervision in a growing sector such as the ESG ratings. The increasing interest in this sector by market participants will require constant assessment and monitoring of risks that can affect the financial markets. ESMA's role as the direct supervisor of certain service providers already represents a wealth of experience in setting up credible and effective supervisory responses in the ESG rating area. Interaction with the other EU institutions, international bodies and standard-setting bodies will also be critical to this end. In any case, as the ESMA 2023-2028 strategy recommends, the starting point of a profitable cooperation and, therefore, efficient supervision lies in the EU and national authorities' build-up of adequate capabilities to deal properly with the challenges posed by the ESG ratings.[24] **30.13**

24 ESMA Strategy 2023–2028 (n 2) 27.

ARTICLE 31

EXERCISE OF THE POWERS REFERRED TO IN ARTICLES 32, 33 AND 34

Francesco De Pascalis

The powers conferred on ESMA or on any official, or other person authorised by, ESMA by Articles 32, 33 and 34 shall not be used to require the disclosure of information or documents which are subject to legal privilege.

A. INTRODUCTION

31.01 Article 31 of the ESG ratings regulation precedes the rules relating to the investigation activities that ESMA, its official, or any other representative can perform as part of their supervisory powers. The rules in question are Article 32 ('requests for information'), Article 33 ('general investigations') and Article 34 ('on-site inspections'), which will be the subject of in-depth analysis in the following chapters. The intertwining between Article 31 and the mentioned rules is determined by a limit posed on ESMA when resorting to any of these supervisory tools. In essence, the power to request information, or conduct investigations, or on-site inspections at the premises of the supervised entities must never violate the legal privilege principle. Consequently, Article 31 should be interpreted as a warning to ESMA and its representatives against using their powers to ask for information or disclose information subject to legal privilege.

31.02 As legal privilege is the main subject of Article 31, it is necessary to analyze its meaning to understand its importance within the supervisory rules set in the ESG ratings regulation.

B. THE LEGAL PRIVILEGE

Often referred to as 'legal professional privilege' (LPP), the legal privilege pertains to the relationship between lawyers and their clients. As such, LLP aims to protect the confidentiality of legal advice and, therefore, shield communications between lawyers and their clients from external intrusion, even when public authorities may request or access this information.[1] While LPP is widely recognized in the EU, the absence of a harmonized, uniform discipline makes this subject the exclusive prerogative of EU Member States' national law.[2] Even though different approaches at the national level result in fragmentation, there are EU rules on LPP that contribute to scholarly discussions. These rules have been developed in the context of competition law, namely enforcement actions by the European Commission.[3] Formal requests for information or the so-called Commission's 'dawn raids' at firms' premises can be opposed by invoking the LPP.[4] Firms can deny the disclosure of information or provision of documents by claiming they are protected under the LPP.[5] **31.03**

C. RELEVANT CASE LAW

This subject matter could not escape the Court of Justice of the European Union's (CJEU) review. The Court's interpretation has offered numerous insights for clarifying the meaning and scope of the LPP.[6] **31.04**

The CJEU recognized and construed the LPP concept in the EU in the 1982 *AM & S v Commission* case.[7] The dispute involved the exchange of communication between lawyers and undertakings and whether these communications might have violated the prohibitions that Articles 101 and 102 of the Treaty on the Functioning of the European Union (TFEU) set on competition **31.05**

1 DLA Piper, *Legal Professional Privilege* (2024) Global Guide, 5th edition, www.dlapiperintelligence.com /legalprivilege/. See also Richard S. Pike, 'The English Law of Legal Professional Privilege: A Guide for American Attorneys' (2006) 4 Loyola University Chicago International Law Review 1, 51.

2 Giacomo Di Federico, 'Case C-550/07 P, *Akzo Nobel Chemicals Ltd and Akcros Chemicals Ltd v. European Commission* Judgment of the European Court of Justice (Grand Chamber) of 14 September 2010' (2011) 48 *Common Market Law Review* 2, 581.

3 *Ibid.* See also Theofanis Christoforou, 'Protection of Legal Privilege in EEC Competition Law: The Imperfections of a Case' (1985) 9 *Fordham International Law Journal* 1, 1; Ian Forrester, 'Legal Professional Privilege: Limitations on the Commission's Powers of Inspection Following the AM & S Judgment' (1983) 20(1) *Common Market Law Review*, 75.

4 *Ibid.*

5 *Ibid.*

6 See also European Court of Human Rights (ECHR), 'Legal Professional Privilege' (2024) Press Unit <https://www.echr.coe.int/documents/d/echr/fs_legal_professional_privilege_eng>.

7 Case 155/79 *Am & S v Commission* (1982) ECR 1575.

law (i.e. to engage in agreements, decisions, or concerted practices that prevent, restrict or distort competition in the internal market, and conducts constituting abuse of dominant position).[8]

31.06 In this case, the CJEU found in favour of the application of the LPP by stressing the confidentiality of the communications between the lawyers and their clients.[9] However, the absence of common principles and discipline, coupled with fragmentation at the national level, gave the CJEU limited room for manoeuvre. As a result, the CJEU brought forward strict conditions for the application of the LPP in enforcement actions by public institutions. Specifically, the LPP could be invoked only for correspondence concerning the client's defence strategies provided that the lawyer was an external one, namely admitted to practice in EU Member States and not employed as an in-house lawyer by the client claiming the application of the LPP.[10]

31.07 Clearly, the CJEU recognizes the LPP as a fundamental right to protect the confidentiality of the communications between the lawyers and their clients so that there are no intrusions and constraints affecting the lawyer-client relationship. Nevertheless, the right to invoke the LPP is not absolute as communications on defence strategies and the lawyer's independence requirement are decisive in applying the privilege.

31.08 The CJEU consolidated its stances in the 2007 case *Akzo Nobel Chemicals v Commission*.[11] Once again, the context is an investigation for possible competition law violations. In short, back in 2003, during on-site inspections at Akzo Nobel and Akcros Chemical, the Commission officers seized numerous documents. The dispute that followed concerned whether the protection under the LPP could be invoked in relation to the correspondence exchanged between a UK-based manager and a lawyer admitted to the Netherlands BAR but employed as an in-house lawyer at Akzo on a permanent basis.

31.09 By relying on the previous *AM & S* decision, the CJEU excluded in-house counselling from the LPP's scope.[12] In practice, the Court rejected the argument that the lawyer's independence was implied by their BAR registration. It

8 See Articles 101 and 102 'Consolidated Version of the Treaty of the Functioning of the European Union' (2012) OJEU C 326/49.

9 *Am & S v Commission* (n 6).

10 *Ibid.*

11 Joined Cases T-125 and 253/03, *Akzo Nobel Chemicals v Commission of the European Communities* [2007] ECR II-3523.

12 *Ibid.*

emphasized that the concept of independence applies to a lawyer who 'structurally, hierarchically and functionally is a third party in relation to the [client] receiving that advice.'[13] In-house counselling entails an employment relationship that excludes this interpretation. The CJEU also supported this argument by examining whether Member States' approaches to the scope of the LPP's protection could include situations similar to those in the Akzo case. The lack of unanimous consensus reinforced the Court's stance and led to the rejection of the claim that the correspondence in question was protected under privilege law.[14]

D. RECENT DEVELOPMENTS

Undeniably, the scope of the LPP remains controversial. While the decisions in *AM & S* and *Akzo Nobel* were not contradicted as to the rationale behind the exclusion of in-house lawyers from the scope of privilege, there are some important updates as to the object of the correspondence between the lawyers and their clients (legal defence strategies). In the *Orde van Vlaamse Balies* case concerning lawyers' disclosure duties in aggressive tax planning, the CJEU extended the scope of the LPP not only to the information the parties exchange for legal defence purposes but also to any legal advice.[15] **31.10**

Article 47 ('Right to an effective remedy and a fair trial') and Article 7 ('Protection of private communications, including between clients and their lawyers') of the Charter of Fundamental Rights of the European Union, read and applied in conjunction with Article 6 ('Right to a fair trial') and Article 8 ('Right to respect for private and family life') of the European Convention on Human Rights, are the legal basis under which the CJEU justified extending the scope of the LPP.[16] The outcomes of the *Orde* case are particularly relevant **31.11**

---

13 *Ibid.*

14 Di Federico (n 2). See also Arianna Andreangeli, 'The Protection of Legal Professional Privilege in EU Law and the Impact of the Rules on the Exchange of Information within the European Competition Network on the Secrecy of Communications between Lawyer and Client: One step forward, two steps back?' (2008) 2 The Competition Law Review 1, 31; Joris Cornelis, 'The Court of First Instance Findings in Akzo Nobel – Potential Repercussions on Claiming Protection under Legal Professional Privilege in EC Trade Defence Investigations' (2008) 3 Global Trade and Customs Journal 2, 85; Vincent Power, 'In-house Lawyers and the European Court: The Akzo v Commission Judgment' (2010) 45 Irish Jurist, 198; Luca Schicho, 'Legal Privilege for In-house Lawyers in the light of AKZO; A Matter of Law or Policy?' (2011) 5 Research Papers in Law, College of Europe, 3; Justine N Stefanelli, 'The Negative Implications of EU Privilege Law under Akzo Nobel at Home and Abroad' (2011) 60 International and Comparative Law Quarterly 2, 545.

15 Case C-694/20 *Orde van Vlaamse Balies and Others v Vlaamse Regering* (2022).

16 *Ibid.*

for dawn raids as they mean that public authorities can no longer oppose the invocation of the LPP on the grounds that the written exchange between the lawyers and their clients does not pertain to legal defence.[17]

E. CONCLUSION

31.12 Until now, the LPP has always been presented and analyzed as the counter-tool against the European Commission's investigatory powers in matters involving EU competition law. However, the applicability of privilege law is recognized in other areas where the European Commission can exercise investigatory powers, such as merger control and state aid matters.[18] In any case, it would be wrong to confine the LPP to the European Commission alone. The European Commission set the case law history of the LPP and, for these reasons, any discussion on the LPP must consider the enforcement actions of the European Commission in certain ambits as the starting point. However, the LPP is recognized as a principle applying to any EU public authority entrusted with investigative and sanctioning powers.

31.13 Article 31 of the Proposal confirms that ESMA's officials must consider the LPP in the event the exercise of the powers set out in Articles 32–34 involves the relationship between the controlled entities and their lawyers. Accordingly, the dos and don'ts of the LPP determined through the jurisprudential evolution of the CJEU are the basis for ESMA officials' actions.

17 Enrico Salmini Sturli and Thibault Henry, 'Extension of EU Legal Professional Privilege: Case C-694/20 Orde Van Vlaamse Balies' (2023) 14 Journal of European Competition Law and Practice 3, 165; Kristof Boel, 'Is the Privilege Too Privileged? the Orde van de Vlaamse Balies Case Revisited' (2024) 52 Intertax 11, 713.

18 DLA Piper (n 1).

ARTICLE 32

REQUESTS FOR INFORMATION

Francesco De Pascalis

1. **ESMA may by simple request or by decision require ESG rating providers, persons involved in ESG rating activities, rated items and issuers of rated items, third parties to whom ESG rating providers have outsourced operational functions or activities, and persons otherwise closely and substantially related or connected to ESG rating providers or ESG rating activities, to provide all information that it needs to carry out its duties under this Regulation.**
2. **When sending a simple request for information under paragraph 1 of this Article, ESMA shall:**
   - (a) **refer to this Article as the legal basis for the request;**
   - (b) **state the purpose of the request;**
   - (c) **specify what information is required;**
   - (d) **set a reasonable time limit within which the information is to be provided and the format in which the requested information is to be provided;**
   - (e) **inform the person from whom the information is requested that there is no obligation to provide the information but that any reply to the request for information must not be incorrect or misleading;**
   - (f) **indicate the fines provided for in Article 36, where the information supplied is incorrect or misleading.**
3. **When requiring the provision of information by decision under paragraph 1 of this Article, ESMA shall:**
   - (a) **refer to this Article as the legal basis for the request;**
   - (b) **state the purpose of the request;**
   - (c) **specify what information is required;**
   - (d) **set a reasonable time limit within which the information is to be provided and the format in which the requested information is to be provided;**
   - (e) **indicate the periodic penalty payments provided for in Article 37 where the requested information is not submitted within the set time limit or is incomplete;**
   - (f) **indicate the fines provided for in Article 36 where the information supplied is incorrect or misleading;**
   - (g) **indicate the right to appeal the decision before the Board of Appeal in accordance with Article 60 of Regulation (EU) No 1095/2010 and**

to have the decision reviewed by the Court of Justice of the European Union in accordance with Article 61 of Regulation (EU) No 1095/2010.

4. **The persons referred to in paragraph 1 or their representatives, and, in the case of legal persons or of associations having no legal personality, the persons authorised to represent them by law or by their constitution, shall supply the information requested. Lawyers duly authorised to act may supply the information on behalf of their clients. Those clients shall remain fully responsible if the information supplied by their lawyers is incomplete, incorrect or misleading.**
5. **ESMA shall, without delay, send a copy of the simple request or of its decision to the competent authority of the Member State where the persons referred to in paragraph 1 who are concerned by the request for information are domiciled or established.**

A. INTRODUCTION

32.01 Section 1 of Chapter IV ('Supervision by ESMA') of the ESG ratings regulation is completed by three rules (Articles 32–34) governing the initiatives ESMA can take towards the ESG rating providers. These actions are part of the investigation stage that, within the supervisory powers, can be triggered on suspicion of breaches of relevant regulation.

B. THE RATIONALE OF ARTICLE 32

32.02 Article 32 sets ESMA's right to request information from ESG rating providers and the requirements that must be observed while performing these duties. In practice, Article 32 is the legal basis of ESMA's right to request information from its supervised entities. Indeed, in any official demand addressed to the controlled entities, ESMA must specify that Article 32 constitutes the legal basis that legitimizes its action.

32.03 Against this backdrop, our analysis can be widened by considering the foundation of ESMA's powers to request information. Reference needs to be made, once again, to its founding Regulation (EU) No 1095/2010, in which some provisions deal with information requests, for example, Article 35 titled 'collection of information.' However, this rule concerns the relationship between ESMA and the national competent authorities. Article 35 lays down reciprocal duties and obligations to satisfy requests for information when it is necessary to carry out supervisory duties.[1] Article 35, therefore, should be construed as aiming to strengthen the relationship between ESMA and the national competent authorities through supervisory convergence.

Instead, Article 32 of the ESG ratings regulation relates to the relationship between a controlling authority and its controlled entities. As such, the rule finds its rationale within the powers the authority can exercise towards its supervisees. **32.04**

Nonetheless, in ESMA's founding regulation it is possible to identify a common basis for the authority's right to request information whether from national competent authorities or supervised entities. Recital 46 of Regulation No 1095/2010 states first that ESMA's right to request information is essential to performing its duties. Then, it identifies both national competent authorities and financial market participants as the receivers of the request.[2] **32.05**

Even though Recital 46 explicitly mentions reporting obligations, that is, information to be given periodically, it is also the milestone of the authority's powers to request or obtain information for investigatory purposes. Both national competent authorities and supervised entities are, therefore, supposed to submit to ESMA's request, no matter the contexts and aims.[3] **32.06**

---

1 See Article 35(1) of Regulation (EU) No 1095/2010: 'At the request of the Authority, the competent authorities of the Member States shall provide the Authority with all the necessary information to carry out the duties assigned to it by this Regulation, provided that they have legal access to the relevant information, and that the request for information is necessary in relation to the nature of the duty in question.' See also paragraph 2 of Article 35: 'Upon a duly justified request from a competent authority of a Member State, the Authority may provide any information that is necessary to enable the competent authority to carry out its duties.'

2 Recital 46 of Regulation (EU) No 1095/2010: 'In order to carry out its duties effectively, the Authority should have the right to request all necessary information. To avoid the duplication of reporting obligations for financial market participants, that information should normally be provided by the national supervisory authorities which are closest to the financial markets and financial market participants and should take into account already existing statistics. However, as a last resort, the Authority should be able to address a duly justified and reasoned request for information directly to a financial market participant where a national competent authority does not or cannot provide such information in a timely fashion. Member States' authorities should be obliged to assist the Authority in enforcing such direct requests. In that context, the work on common reporting formats is essential.'

3 *Ibid.*

C. THE REQUEST RECEIVERS

32.07 Article 32 empowers ESMA to request any information necessary for implementing its duties under the ESG ratings regulation. The rule has a hierarchical order of information request receivers, with the ESG rating providers on top of this pyramid. ESG rating providers are followed by persons involved in ESG rating activities, issuers of rated items, and more general categories such as third parties whose services have been outsourced by an ESG rating provider, and anyone substantially related or connected to the ESG rating area. In this case, the use of the adverb 'substantially' denotes that, for being receivers of information requests, these persons should be strongly connected with the ESG rating providers.[4]

D. SIMPLE REQUEST VERSUS REQUEST BY DECISION

32.08 Having identified and grouped together the receivers of information requests, Article 32 goes on by setting different requirements ESMA must comply with according on whether the information is simply requested or requested by decision. The distinction between 'simple request' or 'request by decision' denotes two different procedures for issuing information requests. These procedures are common in other regulations in which the ESMA acts as the unique supervisor.[5] Preliminarily, it must be recalled that ESMA's Board of Supervisors is the source of any action the authority can take towards the controlled entities.[6] As is known, the authority works through two arms, namely the Board of Supervisors and the Management Board. While the Management Board, as the name suggests, deals with the managing of the authority (i.e. budget, staff resources and multi-annual Work Programme),[7] the Board of Supervisors is the beating heart of the authority as it has decisions-making responsibilities on every aspect relating to the ESMA's supervisory duties, spanning draft technical standards, guidelines, opinions, reports, advice to European Institutions,

4 Article 32 of Regulation (EU) No 2024/3005, para 1.

5 See Article 23(b) of Regulation (EU) No 462/2013; see also Article 25(f) of Regulation (EU) No 648/2012 and Article 48b of Regulation (EU) No 1011/2016.

6 ESMA, 'About ESMA' (9 April 2021) 7, www.esma.europa.eu/sites/default/files/library/about_esma.pdf.

7 ESMA, 'Summary of Conclusions' (12 November 2024) Management Board <www.esma.europa.eu/sites/default/files/2024-11/ESMA22-1669215091-5831_Management_Board_October_2024_SoC.pdf>. See also, ESMA, 'Decision of the Management Board' (19 June 2014) ESMA/2014/MB/39 <www.esma.europa.eu/sites/default/files/library/2015/11/esma-2014-mb-39_-_decision_on_the_implementing_rules_to_the_financial_regulation_of_esma.pdf>.

enforcement powers and declaring crisis situations.[8] The Board of Supervisors' governance is quite complex, and several standing committees and working group support its operation.[9] Clearly, requests for information result from the Board of Supervisors.

Paragraphs 2 and 3 of Article 32 deal with a 'simple request' for information and a request for information 'by decision,' respectively. **32.09**

As demonstrated in the text of the rule, the requirements that ESMA must observe in both types of requests for information are almost similar. The difference is merely quantitative as paragraph 3 (request of supply of information by decision) adds one more requirement vis-à-vis paragraph 2 (request of supply of information by simple decision). Namely, in addition to requirements such as the indication of the legal basis behind the request, object of information, time-limit for providing the information and its format, paragraph 3 adds the requirement to make the receiver aware of the right to appeal against the decision before the Court of Justice of the European Union (CJEU) as provided by Articles 60 and 61 of ESMA's founding regulation.[10] **32.10**

It is, therefore, evident that a request 'by decision' is triggered because of more serious issues compared to a simple request. This difference is further reinforced by the fact that paragraph 3, in addition to the requirement to indicate the fines to be imposed if the answers provided by the receivers are incorrect or misleading, also contemplates the requirement to indicate the periodic penalty payments in case the production of the required information is incomplete.[11] **32.11**

Furthermore, requests for information by decision must be satisfied by the controlled entities, while simple requests leave room for discretion to the receivers. In fact, letter (e) of paragraph 2 states that the (simple) request must specify that there is no obligation for the receiver to provide the information. If the receiver decides to acknowledge ESMA's simple request, then the information shall be correct and genuine.[12] **32.12**

---

8 ESMA, 'Decision of the Board of Supervisors' (20 January 2025) ESMA22-1669215091-5867 <www.esma.europa.eu/sites/default/files/2025-01/ESMA22-1669215091-5867-_Rules_of_Procedure_Board_of_Supervisors.pdf>.

9 ESMA (n 6) 7.

10 See Article 60 ('Appeals') and Article 61 ('Actions before the Court of Justice of the European Union') of Regulation (EU) No 1095/2010.

11 Article 32 of Regulation (EU) No 2024/3005, para 3.

12 *Ibid*, para 2.

E. INFORMATION SUPPLY DUTIES

32.13 Paragraph 4 indirectly relates to the considerations made for the legal privilege under Article 31.[13] The ESG rating providers and the other persons specified in paragraph 1 of Article 32 may comply with the request for information through lawyers acting on their behalf. Save the invocation of the legal professional privilege in accordance with the principles set by the CJEU,[14] lawyers will have to supply the requested information. However, the liability for incomplete, incorrect, or misleading information rests upon their clients.

32.14 Finally, paragraph 5 of Article 32 concludes by posing further duties on ESMA. To facilitate supervisory convergence and coordination, ESMA must send a copy of a request for information, no matter whether they are simple or by decision, to the competent authorities of the Member States where the receivers are domiciled or established.[15]

F. CONCLUSION

32.15 ESMA's actions must always consider the size and risk of the supervised entities. Article 32, in its contents, is not different than the 'request for information' provisions that can be reviewed in other regulations empowering ESMA with direct supervision. However, the expansion of the direct supervisory powers through the inclusion of the EU ESG rating providers inevitably requires ESMA to enhance its enforcement supervisory powers. Timely and appropriate responses to possible ESG ratings regulation infringements are expected. The numerous challenges posed by the ESG rating market, which the present (new) regulation intends to address, demand efficient and effective enforcement tools. The expertise that ESMA has built up through its various mandates until now will be an important asset for dealing with the complexities of the ESG ratings world.

---

13 See Article 31 in the present Commentary.

14 *Ibid.*

15 Article 32 of Regulation (EU) No 2024/3005, para 5.

ARTICLE 33

GENERAL INVESTIGATIONS

Francesco De Pascalis

1. **In order to carry out its duties under this Regulation, ESMA may conduct all necessary investigations of the persons referred to in Article 32(1). To that end, the officials and other persons authorised by ESMA shall be empowered to:**
   (a) **examine any records, data, procedures and any other material relevant to the execution of their tasks irrespective of the medium on which they are stored;**
   (b) **take or obtain certified copies of or extracts from such records, data, procedures and other material;**
   (c) **summon and ask any person referred to in Article 32(1), or their representatives or staff, for oral or written explanations on facts or documents related to the subject matter and purpose of the investigation and to record the answers;**
   (d) **interview any other natural or legal person who consents to be interviewed for the purpose of collecting information relating to the subject matter of an investigation;**
   (e) **request records of telephone and data traffic.**
2. **The officials and other persons authorised by ESMA for the purposes of the investigations referred to in paragraph 1 shall exercise their powers upon the production of a written authorisation specifying the subject matter and purpose of the investigation. That authorisation shall also indicate the periodic penalty payments provided for in Article 37(1) where the production of the required records, data, procedures or any other material, or the information supplied by the persons referred to in Article 32(1), are not provided or are incomplete, and the fines provided for in Article 36 where the information supplied by the persons referred to in Article 32(1) is incorrect or misleading.**
3. **The persons referred to in Article 32(1) of this Regulation shall submit to investigations launched on the basis of a decision of ESMA. The decision shall specify the subject matter and purpose of the investigation, the periodic penalty payments provided for in Article 37 of this**

Regulation, the legal remedies available under Regulation (EU) No 1095/2010 and the right to have the decision reviewed by the Court of Justice of the European Union.

4. **In good time before the investigation, ESMA shall inform the competent authority of the Member State in whose territory that investigation is to be carried out of the investigation and of the identity of the persons authorised by ESMA for the purposes of the investigation. Officials of the competent authority concerned shall, upon the request of ESMA, assist those authorised persons in carrying out their duties. Officials of the competent authority concerned may also attend the investigation upon request.**
5. **If a request for records of telephone or data traffic referred to in paragraph 1, point (e), requires authorisation from a judicial authority according to national rules, such authorisation shall be applied for. Such authorisation may also be applied for as a precautionary measure.**
6. **Where an authorisation as referred to in paragraph 5 is applied for, the national judicial authority shall verify that the decision of ESMA is authentic and that the coercive measures envisaged are neither arbitrary nor excessive having regard to the subject matter of the investigation. When verifying the proportionality of the coercive measures, the national judicial authority may ask ESMA for detailed explanations, in particular relating to the grounds ESMA has for suspecting that an infringement of this Regulation has taken place, the seriousness of the suspected infringement and the nature of the involvement of the person subject to the coercive measures. However, the national judicial authority shall not review the necessity for the investigation or demand that it be provided with the information on ESMA's file. The lawfulness of ESMA's decision shall be subject to review only by the Court of Justice of the European Union following the procedure set out in Regulation (EU) No 1095/2010.**

A. INTRODUCTION

As anticipated in the previous chapter general investigations and on-site inspections, disciplined in Article 33 and Article 34 of the ESG ratings regulation, find their rationale in the extensive investigatory powers ESMA has in its capacity as the main supervisor of selected financial market participants. ESMA's investigations assume that the supervised entities might be non-compliant with their reference regulations.[1] Consequently, both general investigations and on-site inspections are the tools ESMA can use to verify potential regulatory breaches and take further actions.[2] Moreover, this toolkit allows ESMA to assess and measure the risks that the supervisees may be posing in the financial markets. Before commenting on each of these tools, it is important to review the characteristics and aims of ESMA's supervisory strategies. **33.01**

B. SUPERVISORY APPROACHES

Both general investigations and on-site inspections reflect ESMA's supervisory philosophy, which is defined as risk-based, data-driven, and outcome-focussed supervision.[3] **33.02**

Risk-based supervision has been the primary approach of ESMA since its foundation. In general, a risk-based supervisory approach involves identifying, assessing and mitigating potential risks.[4] Any supervisory response is calibrated to the seriousness of the identified and measured risk. Within the role and activities that ESMA pursues, a risk-based supervisory approach is necessary to the extent that it allows it to navigate through different risks associated with the activities of (different) supervised entities. In other words, a standard supervisory approach would not be suitable given the diversification of supervised entities. Instead, the level of risk each of them carries permits the selection of the most suitable supervisory action and tools. Against this backdrop, a risk-based approach is also regarded as 'forward-looking' to the extent that it **33.03**

1 ESMA, 'Investigations and Inspections' <https://www.esma.europa.eu/esmas-activities/supervision-and-convergence/investigations-and-inspections>.

2 *Ibid.*

3 European Securities and Markets Authorities (ESMA), 'ESMA strategy 2023-2028' (September 2022) 20, www.esma.europa.eu/sites/default/files/library/esma_strategy_2023-2028.pdf; see also ESMA, 'Supervision and Convergence,' www.esma.europa.eu/esmas-activities/supervision-and-convergence.

4 Deloitte, 'Navigating the Risk Based Supervision Process' (January 2014) 3 <www2.deloitte.com/content/dam/Deloitte/in/Documents/financial-services/in-fs-navigating-risk-based-supervision-noexp.pdf>. See also Torontocentre, 'Risk-Based Supervision' (March 2018) <www.torontocentre.org/videos/Risk-Based_Supervision.pdf>.

aims at preventing risks before they materialize.[5] In this case, the supervision directly influences the behaviour of the controlled entities.

33.04 Finally, a risk-based approach would have the advantage of being a flexible method. New risks can always materialize in the financial markets, and thus, a risk-based approach can allow the supervisory authorities to adapt their methods and techniques to the constant changes affecting the financial markets. To this end, ESMA periodically issues the 'Union strategic supervisory priorities' to provide the optimal strategy against crucial risks in the EU financial markets.[6]

33.05 If the risk at stake determines the appropriate action to be taken and the tool for performing it, data collection and analysis are crucial to identifying and assessing types of risk. For these reasons, risk-based approaches intertwine with data use.[7] In this respect, ESMA relies on market-wide and entity-level data to enhance its risk-based approach.[8]

33.06 Risk-based and data-driven supervisory methods are complemented through outcome focussed approaches. Supervisory activities must be tailored to realistic outcomes. To this end, valuable supervisory outcomes are achieved when compliance with regulation and positive changes to the conduct of the supervised entities are achieved.[9]

33.07 Supervisory enforcement powers and tools like general investigations and on-site inspections are instrumental to performing risk-based and data-driven supervision and ultimately gaining efficient supervisory outcomes.

---

5 ESMA strategy 2023–2028 (n 3).

6 *Ibid.*

7 Frank Elderson, 'Embedding a strong data culture in supervision - another stepping stone towards effective supervision' (5 July 2024) Bank for International Settlement (BIS) <www.bis.org/review/r240709e.pdf>.

8 ESMA, 'Data Strategy 2023–2028' (15 June 2023) ESMA50-157-3404, 3 <www.esma.europa.eu/sites/default/files/2023-06/ESMA50-157-3404_ESMA_Data_Strategy_2023-2028.pdf>. See also Natasha Cazenave, 'ESMA as a data driven regulator and supervisor' (8 October 2021) ESMA74-362-2159 <www.esma.europa.eu/sites/default/files/library/esma_74-362-2159_speech_natasha_cazenave_afme_2021.pdf>.

9 *Ibid.* See also Verena Ross, 'ESMA – driving forward high-quality supervision and transparency in a single EU capital market' (20 April 2022) ESMA80-187-945 <www.esma.europa.eu/sites/default/files/library/esma80-187-945_verena_ross_speech_at_ecmi-ceps_webinar.pdf>.

C. INVESTIGATORY POWERS

Against this background, Article 33 ('general investigations') can now be easily reviewed. ESMA officials can address all the persons mentioned under Article 32[10] for investigative purposes. It is worth recalling that the context in which the investigative duties are performed is one of possible infringements of regulation, which finally legitimate enforcement powers. Indeed, the duties under paragraph 1 of Article 33 refer to the actions the authority must take in situations involving possible regulatory breaches by the supervised entities. This context also justifies the list that Article 33 sets regarding the powers of authorized ESMA officials while performing investigatory duties. The importance of data-driven supervision is reflected in this list of powers, which distinguishes several ways for the collection and analysis of information, ranging from the examination of stored data, requests of extract or certified copies of materials, requests for oral or written explanations to the persons mentioned in Article 32 (or their representatives) and interviews to requests to make available records of telephone and data traffic.[11] **33.08**

D. WRITTEN AUHORIZATION

Paragraph 2 of Article 33 aims to mitigate the exercise of the investigative powers through several requirements of ESMA officials.[12] Such conditions are pretty much the same as those explained in connection with the request for information.[13] Paragraph 2 mentions the periodic penalties that can be inflicted if the information specified in paragraph 1 is not provided or is incomplete or the fines if the replies to the requested information are incorrect or misleading. In any case, these requirements must be satisfied in a written authorization the ESMA officials must produce every time they conduct general investigations. In this way, paragraph 2 intends to emphasize the importance of clear communication between ESMA and supervised entities by demanding the production of a written statement certifying that the officials are acting on behalf of a supervisory authority and that their operations are conducted within certain limits. Accordingly, the supervised entities will have full knowledge of the situation and be put in a position to cooperate at best. **33.09**

10 See Article 32 in the present Commentary.
11 See Article 33 of Regulation (EU) No 2024/3005, para 1.
12 See Article 33 of Regulation (EU) No 2024/3005, para 2.
13 See Article 32 in the present Commentary.

E. LEGAL BASIS

33.10 Paragraph 3 complements the observations made in relation to paragraph 2. It recalls that behind the performance of an investigation there is a decision taken by the Boards of Supervisors, which must set out the subject and purpose of the investigation, indicate the possible imposition of periodic penalties and the right of persons under investigation to challenge the decision before the Court of Justice of the European Union (CJEU).[14] Overall, paragraph 3 of Article 33 reiterates that ESMA's decision to launch an investigation is the legal basis under which the ESG rating providers and the other stakeholders listed in Article 32 are obliged to submit to general investigations.

F. NATIONAL COMPETENT AUTHORITIES

33.11 Paragraph 4 involves the exchange of information between ESMA and the competent authorities of the Member State where the investigation will take place. This paragraph reflects the aim of building a proper supervisory culture through convergence and cooperation among authorities. This aim is crucial when authorities like ESMA are entrusted with primary supervision of entities whose activities have cross-border reach.[15] Convergence and cooperation are achieved not only by informing the national competent authorities of all the details of the investigation (persons subject to investigation and ESMA's officials conducting the operations) but also by requesting to aid ESMA officials in the investigation process where needed. In this case, the support from the officials of the national competent authorities may entail their direct participation in the investigations, if requested.[16]

G. LIMITS TO INVESTIGATORY POWERS

33.12 Paragraph 5 of Article 33 sets further limits to ESMA's powers when the investigations target records of telephone or data traffic. Given the sensitivity of these data, paragraph 5 provides for ESMA to obtain such information through authorization from national judiciary authorities if national

14 See Article 33 of Regulation (EU) No 2024/3005, para 3.
15 See Article 29 in the present Commentary.
16 See Article 33 of Regulation (EU) no 2024/3005, para 4.

legislation imposes such a procedure. Clearly, the national judiciary authority is an important filter for ESMA's action when data protection and privacy matters are at stake.[17]

H. ARBITRARINESS AND PROPORTIONALITY CHECKS

Nonetheless, in their dealing with ESMA's applications, national judiciary authorities are not immune from limitations. This is the subject matter of paragraph 6 of Article 33, which sets the dos and don'ts of the judicial authority's intervention by taking position from the context governed by paragraph 5. While first assessing the authenticity of ESMA's application, the judicial authorities have the power to scrutinize the proportionality of the ESMA's coercive measures. To this end, they can ask for clarifications about the suspected breach of regulation, particularly as to the solidity of their suspicions, the seriousness of the violation and the degree of involvement of the persons that may finally undertake coercive measures. This is the only room for manoeuvres the judicial authority has against an authorization requested by ESMA. In other words, the national judiciary authority cannot discuss the opportunity of ESMA's decision to launch an investigation as any control of legitimacy falls under the remit of the CJEU.[18] **33.13**

I. CONCLUSION

Article 33 provides ESMA's officials with a wide spectrum of powers when they conduct general investigations. At the same time, the exercise of these powers is subject to specific limits to make it fair and proportionate. Indeed, Article 33 articulates the list of the officials' powers with a series of procedural steps that must be taken to legitimize their actions. Any launched investigation is underpinned by an ESMA's decision, which also authorizes the officials to act. The protection of the entities under investigation is ensured through their right to challenge the lawfulness of the decision before the CJEU. The judicial authorities operating in the Member State in which the entity under investigation is located are also involved to have an additional layer of protection. In fact, Article 33 requires them to check the authenticity and proportionality of **33.14**

17 See Article 33 of Regulation (EU) No 2024/3005, para 5.

18 See Article 33 of Regulation (EU) No 2024/3005, para 6.

the decision of ESMA. Overall, Article 33 sets an adequate balance between the involved parties. Like Article 32, Article 33 is the duplication of rules designed in other areas of which ESMA has direct supervision. Again, the experience the Authority has gained in these areas, particularly in the credit rating sector, will be a valuable know-how to be transferred to the ESG ratings area.

ARTICLE 34

ON-SITE INSPECTIONS

Francesco De Pascalis

1. In order to carry out its duties under this Regulation, ESMA may conduct all necessary on-site inspections at the business premises of the legal persons referred to in Article 32(1). Where the proper conduct and efficiency of the inspection so require, ESMA may carry out the on-site inspection without prior announcement.
2. The officials and other persons authorised by ESMA to conduct an on-site inspection may enter any business premises and land of the legal persons subject to an investigation decision adopted by ESMA and shall have the powers provided for in Article 33(1). They shall also have the power to seal any business premises and books or records for the period of, and to the extent necessary for, the inspection.
3. The officials and other persons authorised by ESMA to conduct an on-site inspection shall exercise their powers upon production of a written authorisation specifying the subject matter and purpose of the inspection. That authorisation shall also indicate the periodic penalty payments provided for in Article 37 where the persons concerned do not submit to the inspection. In good time before the inspection, ESMA shall give notice of the inspection to the competent authority of the Member State where it is to be conducted.
4. The persons referred to in Article 32(1) of this Regulation shall submit to on-site inspections ordered by decision of ESMA. The decision shall specify the subject matter and purpose of the inspection, the date on which it is to begin, the periodic penalty payments provided for in Article 37 of this Regulation, the legal remedies available under Regulation (EU) No 1095/2010 and the right to have the decision reviewed by the Court of Justice of the European Union. ESMA shall take such decisions after consulting the competent authority of the Member State where the inspection is to be conducted.

5. Officials and other persons authorised or appointed by the competent authority of the Member State where the inspection is to be conducted shall, upon the request of ESMA, actively assist the officials and other persons authorised by ESMA. To that end, they shall enjoy the powers set out in paragraph 2. Officials of the competent authority of the Member State concerned may also attend the on-site inspections upon request.

6. ESMA may also require the competent authorities to carry out specific investigatory tasks and on-site inspections on its behalf, as provided for in this Article and in Article 33(1). To that end, the competent authorities shall enjoy the same powers as ESMA as set out in this Article and in Article 33(1).

7. Where the officials and other persons authorised by ESMA find that a person opposes an inspection ordered pursuant to this Article, the competent authority of the Member State concerned shall afford them the necessary assistance, requesting, where appropriate, the assistance of the police or of an equivalent enforcement authority, so as to enable them to conduct their on-site inspection.

8. If the on-site inspection provided for in paragraph 1 or the assistance provided for in paragraph 7 requires authorisation by a judicial authority according to national rules, such authorisation shall be applied for. Such authorisation may also be applied for as a precautionary measure.

9. Where an authorisation as referred to in paragraph 8 is applied for, the national judicial authority shall verify that the decision of ESMA is authentic and that the coercive measures envisaged are neither arbitrary nor excessive having regard to the subject matter of the inspection. When verifying the proportionality of the coercive measures, the national judicial authority may ask ESMA for detailed explanations, in particular relating to the grounds ESMA has for suspecting that an infringement of this Regulation has taken place, the seriousness of the suspected infringement and the nature of the involvement of the person subject to the coercive measures. However, the national judicial authority shall not review the necessity for the inspection or demand to be provided with the information on ESMA's file. The lawfulness of ESMA's decision shall be subject to review only by the Court of Justice of the European Union following the procedure set out in Regulation (EU) No 1095/2010.

A. INTRODUCTION

On-site inspections complete ESMA's supervisory toolbox disciplined under Section 1 of Chapter V of the ESG ratings regulation. Article 34 is the point of reference for understanding and analyzing the principles underlining the on-site inspection procedure. Though adapted to the specific context of on-site inspections, Article 34 replicates part of the contents of Article 33 on general investigations. Like Article 33, Article 34 subjects the actions of all those involved in on-site inspection procedures to well-defined limits. Conduct rules are established for those who initiate (and perform) on-site inspections and those who submit to the inspections. Given the similarities with Article 33, it is opportune to engage in a comparative analysis to highlight the peculiarities of Article 34 prior to any critical discussion. **34.01**

B. ARTICLE 33 VERSUS ARTICLE 34

Like in general investigation procedures, the actors involved in on-site inspections are ESMA officials or their representatives, the ESG rating providers and the other stakeholders listed in Article 30, Member States' competent authorities, national judiciary authorities and the Court of Justice of the European Union (CJEU). Among them, the national judicial authorities and the CJEU have an indirect involvement to the extent that they can be addressed only under specific conditions. Within this context, the similarities with Article 31 lie in the scope of action granted to the national judicial authorities and the CJEU when ESMA submits requests for on-site inspections. Once again, on top of the national judicial authorities' engagement there must be national rules imposing ESMA to seek authorization for on-site inspections before national courts.[1] **34.02**

When an authorization request is submitted, the judges' controls are subjected to the same limits provided in paragraph 6 of Article 33: checks on the authenticity of ESMA's decision, checks on the arbitrariness and proportionality of ESMA's possible coercive measures and the power to ask for any clarification as to the seriousness of the suspected infringement. Then again, checks on the **34.03**

1 See Article 34 of Regulation (EU) No 2024/3005, para 8.

lawfulness of ESMA's requests to take action are the sole competence of the CJEU.[2]

34.04 Looking now at the role of the Member States' competent authorities, Article 34 expands further their role in comparison to Article 33 on general investigations. In addition to the duty to help ESMA officials or their representatives conduct the inspections by, for example, requesting the assistance of the police in case of impediments to perform the inspections and attending the inspections at the business premises, national competent authorities' representatives may also conduct investigations and on-site inspections on behalf of ESMA. Such delegations will give them the same powers and obligations as ESMA officials or representatives when they conduct general investigations or on-site inspections.[3]

34.05 As to ESMA's obligations, any power to conduct on-site inspections must be justified through a written authorization to be shown to the firms submitting to the inspections. Then, like in Article 33, Article 34 sets down the same requirements to specify the subject matter, purpose of inspection and periodic penalties and to inform the competent authorities of the Member State as to the location of the inspection. Like in requests for general information, on-site inspections find their rationale in an investigation decision taken by ESMA. The actions that can be taken during on-site inspections are wide as they also include the power to seal the business premises and seize books or records. Furthermore, inspections can be conducted without prior announcement if the investigation requires to act promptly and with urgency.[4]

34.06 Save their right to challenge ESMA's decision before the CJEU, ESG rating providers or the other involved stakeholders mentioned in paragraph 1 of Article 32 must submit to on-site inspection orders and offer their cooperation.

C. AUTHORIZATION REQUEST

34.07 Having clarified the contents of Article 34, there is room for further reflection. To this end, it is useful to focus on the relationship between ESMA and the Member States' national judicial authorities under paragraph 9 of Article 34. It must be recognized that on-site inspection cases involving entities ESMA has direct supervision of have been rare until now. Nonetheless, it is possible

2 See also Article 33 in the present Commentary.

3 See Article 34 of Regulation (EU) No 2024/3005 paras 5, 6 and 7.

4 See Article 34 of Regulation (EU) No 2024/3005 paras 1 and 2.

to see the implementation of the procedures spelt out in Article 34 by referring to some early requests for authorizations ESMA submitted before national judicial authorities.

In 2015, when the United Kingdom (UK) was still part of the EU, ESMA sought authorization before the Chancery Division of the England and Wales High Court to carry out inspections at the premises of a UK-based trade repository ('DTCC Derivatives Repository Limited').[5] Significantly, this was a case in which there was no suspicion of regulatory breach behind ESMA's request. The inspection was justified by 'general supervisory functions.'[6] 34.08

This aspect highlights subtle differences between the general investigation (Article 33) and on-site inspection (Article 34) supervisory tools. While in general investigations the recourse to the judicial authority is necessary if ESMA requests records of telephone or data traffic and there is national legislation imposing to refer to the national judicial authority in these circumstances,[7] instead, in case of on-site inspections, it is the instrument on its own (the inspection), coupled with national legislation requiring the liaising between ESMA and the judicial authority, that imposes a request of authorization before national courts. Therefore, on-site inspections appear to be a more delicate context, where requirements are stricter than general investigations despite the respective rules having the same wording. 34.09

In the DTCC case, even conducting on-site inspections for general supervisory functions needed the authorization filter of the national judicial authority.[8] The national legislation requiring to liaise with the judicial authority was 'The Financial Services and Markets Act 2000 (Over the Counter Derivatives, Central Counterparties and Trade Repositories) Regulations 2013 (S.I. 2013/504) ('The Domestic Regulations').' Within the Regulations 2013, Regulation 17 required ESMA to obtain authorization from the High Court before any of its representatives initiate an on-site inspections.[9] At the hearing, 34.10

---

5 On-site Inspections were conducted under Article 63 of Regulation (EU) No 648/2012 of the European Parliament and of the Council of 4 July 2012 on OTC derivatives, central counterparties and trade repositories (2012) OJEU L 201/1.

6 Case HC-2015-001218 *European Securities and Markets Authority & DTCC Derivatives Repository Limited* [2015] EWHC 1085 (Ch).

7 See Article 33 in the present Commentary.

8 *European Securities and Markets Authorities* (n 6) para 1.

9 The Financial Services and Markets Act 2000 (Over the Counter Derivatives, Central Counterparties and Trade Repositories) Regulations 2013, Regulation 17: 'The High Court may grant authorisation for the purposes of paragraph (1) or (2) if satisfied, on an application made to the High Court in accordance with rules of court by ESMA or the FCA, that – (a) ESMA has initiated an Article 63 inspection; and (b) the Article 63 inspection would be neither arbitrary nor excessive having regard to the subject matter of the

Mrs Justice Rose reviewed ESMA's request along with the documents that needed to be produced (e.g. decision, names of ESMA officials, notification to national competent authorities, and mail exchange between ESMA and DTCC legal and compliance office director). Mrs Justice Rose finally granted authorization but warned to respect the legal privilege while conducting on-site inspections.[10]

D. LOOKING AHEAD

34.11 This case of a request for authorization for on-site inspections stimulates reflections in connection with the supervision of the ESG rating providers. Given the assistance that Member State competent authorities' officials can provide to ESMA officials or authorized representatives when conducting on-site inspections, future steps will be the draft of national laws to enable the competent authority representatives to exercise their powers effectively, even when they might be acting on behalf of ESMA and therefore having the same rights and obligations as envisaged in paragraph 6 of Article 34. Then, the requirement of liaising with national judicial authorities through a request of authorization if Member States' law requires so raises the issue of the differences among Member States' laws. In this respect, there are ongoing discussions among scholars. Some authors point out these differences and underline that despite the CJEU's urge to strengthen the authorization requirements, some Member States were proactive in establishing or reinforcing them while others did not even contemplate this possibility.[11]

34.12 Other authors, in considering the specific ambit of ESMA's on-site inspection powers, argue that such differences can potentially lessen ESMA's accountability as, in some Member States, there would not be judicial control over

---

inspection. The High Court must conduct the assessment referred to in paragraph (3) in accordance with Article 63(9) of the EMIR regulation and may exercise the powers conferred by that paragraph for the purposes of making its assessment,' www.legislation.gov.uk/uksi/2013/504/regulation/17/made.

10 *European Securities and Markets Authorities* (n 6) para 13: 'Having seen all this documentation I am satisfied that it is appropriate to grant authorisation for this inspection. I made one amendment to the draft order that was provided, in exercise of my power to ensure that the inspection would be neither arbitrary nor excessive having regard to its subject matter. That amendment was to state in the order that the inspection is subject to Article 60 of the EMIR relating to the non-disclosure of legally privileged information and documents. I consider that a reference should be made to this important safeguard on the face of the documents which are presented to the company.'

11 Laura Wissink, Ton Duijkersloot and Rob Widdershoven, 'Shifts in Competences between Member States and the EU in the New Supervisory System for Credit Institutions and their Consequences for Judicial Protection' (2014) 10(5) *Utrecht Law Review*, 92.

the arbitrariness of the decision to conduct on-site inspections.[12] Having the same wording and structure as the supervisory rules of other EU regulations where ESMA is entrusted with direct supervision, the rules of the ESG ratings regulation are likely to keep the discussion on these issues alive.

It remains to be seen how national laws may develop or change regarding the interaction between principal supervisors, national supervisors and (where needed) judicial authorities in the critical area of ESG ratings. **34.13**

12 Marloes van Rijsbergen and Miroslava Scholten, 'ESMA Inspecting: The Implications for Judicial Control under Shared Enforcement' (2016) 7(3) *European Journal of Risk Regulation*, 569.

Section 2 Supervisory measures and penalties

ARTICLE 35

SUPERVISORY MEASURES BY ESMA

Andrea Miglionico

1. **Where ESMA finds that an ESG rating provider has not complied with its obligations under this Regulation, it shall take one or more of the following supervisory measures:**
   (a) **suspend or withdraw the authorisation or recognition of the ESG rating provider;**
   (b) **temporarily prohibit the ESG rating provider from publishing or distributing ESG ratings, until the infringement has been brought to an end;**
   (c) **require the ESG rating provider to bring the infringement to an end;**
   (d) **impose fines pursuant to Article 36;**
   (e) **issue public notices.**
2. **ESMA may also take one or more of the supervisory measures referred to in paragraph 1, points (b) to (e), of this Article in respect of any ESG rating provider that operates in the Union pursuant to Article 2(1):**
   (a) **without complying with Article 4, or where ESMA has suspended or withdrawn the ESG rating provider's authorisation or recognition referred to in that Article;**
   (b) **without complying with the conditions to benefit from any exclusion set out in Article 2(2).**
3. **ESMA may also take the supervisory measure referred to in paragraph 1, point (e), in the event that an ESG rating activity of an ESG rating provider operating in the Union poses a serious threat to market integrity or to investor protection in the Union.**

   In order to verify whether a person is operating in the Union pursuant to Article 2(1), ESMA may use the powers conferred on it by Articles 32, 33 and 34 in respect of the person concerned or any third parties who enable the person concerned to carry out the ESG rating activity.
4. **The supervisory measures referred to in paragraph 1 shall be effective, proportionate and dissuasive.**

5. **When taking any of the supervisory measures referred to in paragraph 1, ESMA shall take into account the nature and seriousness of the infringement, having regard to the following criteria:**
   (a) **the duration and frequency of the infringement;**
   (b) **whether financial crime has been committed or facilitated or is otherwise attributable to the infringement;**
   (c) **whether the infringement has been committed intentionally or negligently;**
   (d) **the degree of responsibility of the person responsible for the infringement;**
   (e) **the financial strength of the ESG rating provider, as indicated by its total annual net turnover;**
   (f) **the impact of the infringement on the interests of investors and on other users of ESG ratings;**
   (g) **the importance of the profits gained and losses avoided by the ESG rating provider or the losses for third parties derived from the infringement, insofar as such profits and losses can be determined;**
   (h) **the level of cooperation of the ESG rating provider with ESMA, without prejudice to the need to ensure the disgorgement of profits gained or losses avoided by that ESG rating provider due to the infringement;**
   (i) **any previous infringements by the ESG rating provider;**
   (j) **measures taken after the infringement by the ESG rating provider to prevent its repetition.**

   For the purposes of the first subparagraph, point (c), an infringement shall be considered to have been committed intentionally if ESMA finds objective elements which demonstrate that a person acted deliberately to commit the infringement.
6. **ESMA shall notify any decision to take a supervisory measure pursuant to paragraph 1 to the person responsible for the infringement without undue delay. ESMA shall publish any such decision on its website within 10 working days of the date when it was adopted.**

   The publication referred to in the first subparagraph shall contain all of the following:
   (a) **a statement affirming the right of the ESG rating provider to appeal the decision;**
   (b) **where relevant, a statement affirming that an appeal has been lodged and specifying that such an appeal does not have suspensive effect;**
   (c) **a statement asserting that it is possible for ESMA to suspend the application of the contested decision in accordance with Article 60(3) of Regulation (EU) No 1095/2010.**
7. **ESMA may also require the infringing ESG rating provider to inform the users of its ESG ratings of any supervisory measure taken by ESMA pursuant to paragraph 1.**

A. INTRODUCTION

Section 2 of Chapter 4 of the Regulation provides specific supervisory measures and enforcement mechanisms over the rating providers' activities. The article stipulates that ESG rating providers have to be authorized by the European Securities and Markets Authority (ESMA) and are subject to its supervision, while complying with transparency obligations, in particular regarding the methodology used and the sources of information. The article points that ESMA is the authority responsible of overseeing its implementation, ensuring uniform standards for all ratings providers operating in the EU. Further, ESMA has authority to investigate or request information from ratings providers, and maintains a public registry of authorized ratings providers. Specifically, ESMA has significant powers of supervision in relation to compliance with the Regulation, such as the power to carry out on-site inspections, withdraw or suspend the relevant provider's authorization, and issue public notices or impose fines. The supervisory and enforcement mechanisms designed to ensure the quality of ratings have been introduced after the concerns raised by ESMA on the reliability and quality of ESG ratings providers in the assessment of sustainable investments.[1] On this view, the increasing demand for ratings that provide insights on an entity's ESG profile should be aligned with safeguards measures that ensure the information is transparent and the evaluations are in order to prevent the risk of greenwashing. ESMA called for more stringent monitoring on ESG ratings given their specific role in the financial system as part of the Strategy for Financing a Transition to a Sustainable Economy.[2] **35.01**

The intent to reduce the risk of conflicts of interest and ensure the objectivity and quality of ratings is the major challenge for regulators.[3] In this context, ESMA adopts a risk-based approach to supervising rating agencies and **35.02**

1 ESMA letter to EC on ESG ratings (28 January 2021), ESMA30-379-423, https://www.esma.europa.eu/document/esma-letter-ec-esg-ratings.

2 ESMA, 'CRAs and Sustainability,' https://www.esma.europa.eu/esmas-activities/sustainable-finance/cras-and-sustainability.

3 Sung Eun (Summer) Kim, 'The Duality of Variance Among ESG Assessments' (2023) 88(2) *Missouri Law Review* 409.

improving compliance with the provisions of the Regulation.[4] ESMA's activities include formal requests for information, the conduct of inspections and investigations as well as enforcement actions in appropriate cases.[5] However, supervision of ratings providers' internal governance (clarity regarding staff roles and responsibilities, and the involvement of ratings analysts in business development) seems a difficult task for regulators.[6] This risk-based approach aims to enhance the oversight of ESG ratings and to improve the application of different supervisory tools. Therefore, ESG ratings providers need to put in place effective internal controls to ensure that these tools are adequately resourced.[7] As the EU Commission stated, 'a key requirement of forming sustainable investment strategies is access to high-quality sustainability-related data, ratings and research.'[8] A lack of transparency leads to a lack of understanding on the content of rating and presents a risk that investors rely on sustainability ratings without making their own judgements and considering whether and how well a rating represents a valuable indicator for investors to meet their sustainability investment objectives.[9] There is need to provide more data granularity, data quality, consistency and timeliness, so investors can better integrate this into their own financial analysis. There is also a lack of clear and consistent terminology used and a need for clearer and standardized definitions for sustainability-related products and services. This includes terms such as ESG, sustainability and responsible investment; also there is no consensus on a set of standards and principles for sustainability-related products and services, or how to measure and verify the implementation of them. These issues have implications for investor protection and resources misallocations. Empirical studies have demonstrated that Investors react to ESG rating information not related to firms' fundamentals and investors incorporate ESG rating information not related to fundamentals into stock prices.[10] Further,

---

4 ESMA, 'ESMA's supervision of credit rating agencies, trade repositories and monitoring of third country central counterparties' (3 February 2017), 7.

5 ESMA, 'Supervision of Credit Rating Agencies and Trade Repositories' (16 February 2015), Annual Report and Work Plan, 6–7.

6 Gudula Deipenbrock, 'After CRA III – Achievements and Challenges from the Legal Perspective,' paper presented at the 'Proceedings of the Workshop on Credit Rating Agencies – Implementation of Legislation,' European Parliament, Brussels, 18 March 2014.

7 ESMA, 'Supervision of credit rating agencies and trade repositories' (5 February 2015), 6.

8 EU Commission, 'Study on Sustainability-Related Ratings, Data and Research' (November 2020), https://op.europa.eu/en/publication-detail/-/publication/d7d85036-509c-11eb-b59f-01aa75ed71a1.

9 Hendrik Garz and Claudia Volk, 'The ESG Risk Ratings: Moving up the innovation curve' (October 2018) Sustainalytics White Paper – Volume 1, p.8–9, https://connect.sustainalytics.com/esg-risk-ratings-whitepaper-volume-one.

10 Aleksandra Rzeźnik, Kathleen Hanley and Loriana Pelizzon, 'Investor Reliance on ESG Ratings and Stock Price Performance' (May 2024) SAFE Working Paper No. 310, http://dx.doi.org/10.2139/ssrn.3801703.

it is argued that the lack of transparency of sustainability ratings may lead to sub-optimal allocation of capital in the markets, even in the presence of arbitrageurs.[11] The Regulation empowered ESMA of stringent scrutiny over the governance of ESG ratings providers to avoid practices of misleading sustainability reports which turn into greenwashing.[12]

35.03 According to ESMA, ESG ratings providers are required to disclose their rating approach through the balance between cyclical or more permanent elements, although compliance with this could not be demonstrated typically because policies and procedures did not describe in sufficient detail the different steps of the process followed or did not clearly allocate roles and responsibilities.[13] Closer examination of ESMA's supervisory duties leaves the impression that rating methodologies are not monitored effectively. Similarly to the credit rating industry, ESMA enhanced the validation and review of raters' internal models in order to enhance investigation measures, such as 'discriminatory power,' 'predictive power,' 'historical robustness' and 'limited quantitative evidence.'[14] In terms of ratings accuracy, a parallel can be made with the Credit Rating Agencies Technical Committee which provides support to ESMA by promoting supervisory convergence and technical standards concerning policy in the area of credit rating agencies (CRAs).[15] It is worth noting that ESMA issued a final report on proposed amendments to the Delegated Regulation and Annex I of the Credit Rating Agencies (CRA) Regulation.[16] The high demand for ESG ratings reflects the desire of investors to understand how the labelling 'sustainable' can influence the companies' performance and stock prices.[17] The proposed amendments aim to enhance the incorporation of ESG factors into credit rating methodologies and improve disclosures on the relevance of ESG factors for individual credit rating actions.

---

11 *Ibid.*

12 Christopher P. Buttigieg and Sarah Pulis, 'Strategic initiatives to address greenwashing' (2024) 25 *ERA Forum*, 327–328.

13 ESMA, 'Reply to ESRB letter on procyclical impact of downgrades of corporate bonds on markets and entities across the financial system' (29 March 2021), ESMA80-195-858.

14 ESMA, 'Open Hearing on Discussion Paper on the Validation and Review of Credit Rating Agencies' Methodologies' (25 January 2016), ESMA/2016/96.

15 ESMA, 'Terms of Reference. Credit Rating Agencies Technical Committee (CRA TC),' 27 January 2016, ESMA/2016/219; ESMA, 'Guidelines on the validation and review of Credit Rating Agencies' methodologies' (15 November 2016), ESMA/2016/1575; ESMA, 'A Common Approach to the CRA Regulation's Provisions for Encouraging the use of Smaller CRAs' (6 April 2017), ESMA33-9-158.

16 ESMA, 'Technical Advice on Revisions to Commission Delegated Regulation (EU) 447/2012 and Annex I of CRA Regulation. Final Report' (18 December 2024), ESMA84-2037069784-2196.

17 Daniel Cash, *Sustainability Rating Agencies vs Credit Rating Agencies: The Battle to Serve the Mainstream Investor* (Palgrave Macmillan 2021) 69–70.

As a result, CRAs would need to identify in press releases or reports when ESG considerations are a key element of a credit rating or rating outlook.

B. THE SUPERVISORY REGIME

35.04 The ESMA's power of supervision can overlap with the ratings providers' compliance procedures. The upshot is that ESG Ratings providers can continue their activity largely unmonitored within the areas of conflicts of interest and market concentration.[18] The risk is that ESG ratings continue to respond to the incentives of the rating business with the result that they are driven mostly by changes in business cycle variables rather than changes in the sustainability decisions of individual firms.[19] The internal control system of the rating agencies should comply with ESMA monitoring measures in order to identify and eliminate conflicts of interest and to disclose to markets. In this context, ESMA supervisory actions are directed to ensure transparency of the ESG ratings providers' activities and to prevent potential collusive behaviour from influencing the quality of ratings. ESMA launched a call for evidence on market characteristics for ESG Rating Providers in the EU examining the size, structure, resourcing, revenues and product offerings of the different ESG rating providers operating in the European Union.[20] The outcome of the call for evidence highlighted the need to address the insufficient granularity of data, complexity and lack of transparency around of ratings methodologies.[21] ESMA also pointed on some degree of shortcoming in the interactions between entities and rating providers, most notably on the level of transparency as to the basis for the rating, the timing of feedback and the correction of errors. Further, the results showed that the predominant business model of ESG ratings is investor-pays and the operation of the same rating providers indicates a degree of concentration in the market. Large parts of conflicts of interest stem from ESG data giants' reliance on data produced by the

18 Kristyn Noeth, *The ESG and Sustainability Deskbook for Business: A Guide to Policy, Regulation, and Practice* (Los Angeles: Apress Media LLC 2024) 333–334.

19 ESMA, 'Thematic Report. On fees charged by Credit Rating Agencies and Trade Repositories' (11 January 2018), 2.

20 ESMA, 'Call for evidence on Market Characteristics for ESG Rating Providers in the EU' (3 February 2022), ESMA80-416-250, https://www.esma.europa.eu/document/call-evidence-market-characteristics-esg-rating-providers-in-eu.

21 See Outcome of ESMA Call for Evidence on Market Characteristics of ESG Rating and Data Providers in the EU (24 June 2022), ESMA22-328-603, https://www.esma.europa.eu/sites/default/files/library/esma80-416-347_letter_on_esg_ratings_call_for_evidence_june_2022.pdf.

companies they rate, and the potential for either investors or companies to influence the final score.[22]

According to the Regulation, rating agencies are required to show that ratings are sufficiently independent from their business interests and are not allowed to offer consulting, auditing or other financial services. Ratings providers are also required to divest from any conflicting activities, such as consulting or offering insurance to businesses they rate, and risk being fined if conflicts of interest persist.[23] ESMA found disclosure inconsistencies of ESG factors in ratings: the growing investor interest in ESG evaluations does not square with the granularity of the E, S or G category.[24] Main objective of the supervisory regime is to ensure that ESG ratings used for pre-investment decision-making, post-investment analytics and attribution or as a basis for investment screening or for company engagement are consistent, comparable and understandable when assigning a scoring to a particular product. The aim is to create harmonized standards for raters through transparency and supervisory actions which would increase the utility of ESG ratings providers and eliminate opacity in dubious assessments. ESG ratings operate as a benchmark for investors decision-making process which rely on the score attributed to companies, however the variety of sources and different metrics used to elaborate assessments can lead to arbitrary reports.[25] Companies could receive a high ESG score from a ratings provider because they are milking raters to issue a good report about the sustainability factors but they might not have a committed environmental policy.[26] These issues are exacerbated by the fact that there is confusion between the perception of what ESG ratings assess and what they actually demonstrate. It has been observed that 'the scores are not designed to measure corporate performance on carbon emissions or pollution, instead, the raters measure how well a company is managing environmental, social and governance risks to their own bottom line, for example from hurricanes **35.05**

22 Xuanbo Li, Yun Lou and Liandong Zhang, 'Do Commercial Ties Influence ESG Ratings? Evidence from Moody's and S&P' (2024) 62(5) *Journal of Accounting Research*, 1901.

23 ESMA, 'ESMA fines Scope EUR 2,197,500 for breaches of conflict of interest obligations' (22 March 2024), ESMA43-1868696574-745, https://www.esma.europa.eu/press-news/esma-news/esma-fines-scope-eur-2197500-breaches-conflict-interest-obligations.

24 ESMA TRV Risk Analysis, 'Text mining ESG disclosures in rating agency press releases' (10 February 2022), ESMA 80-195-1352, https://www.esma.europa.eu/press-news/esma-news/esma-finds-high-level-divergence-in-disclosure-esg-factors-in-credit-ratings.

25 See 'What is the point of ESG ratings?' *Financial Times* (26 January 2024), https://www.ft.com/content/9082d21b-dde5-4228-abfe-d4e4cd0f9b12.

26 Alice Ross, 'Can sustainable investing survive Trump 2.0?' *Financial Times* (17 January 2025), https://www.ft.com/content/14ee5968-79de-42bf-80a4-811531e80de7.

or carbon taxes.'[27] ESG ratings providers publish detailed narrative analysis in their credit rating reports which should ensure transparency on ESG credit factors material to their rating analysis, however the ESG descriptions remain subjective and it is difficult to verify the quality of data that form the corporate credit scores. The subjectivity of ratings influence which stocks and bonds are marketed as sustainable although it is questioned the reliable raw data that investors can then integrate into their view of a company's prospects. The Regulation should improve the scrutiny on rating analysts and incentivize them to work on audited financial statements.

C. THE ENFORCEMENT MECHANISMS

35.06 The article establishes that ESMA is the competent authority responsible for authorising ESG rating providers to operate in the EU, assessing equivalence for third-country regimes, and supervising compliance with the Regulation. The article also sets specific enforcement mechanisms which are acted by the ESMA in case ratings providers are non-compliant with their obligations under the Regulation. Pervasive and strict investigative powers allow to request information from providers, conduct general investigations, and carry out unannounced on-site inspections. Within this enforcement armoury, ESMA can review records, interview relevant individuals, and even request telephone and data traffic records, subject to judicial authorization where necessary. The article empowers ESMA to suspend or withdraw the provider's authorization or recognition, temporarily prohibiting the publication or distribution of ESG ratings, requiring the infringement to be rectified, issuing public notices, and imposing fines.

27 Kenza Bryan, 'ESG ratings: whose interests do they serve?' *Financial Times* (3 October 2023), https://www.ft.com/content/fbe10867-fea1-4887-b404-9f9e301e102e.

ARTICLE 36

FINES

Andrea Miglionico

1. Where ESMA finds that an ESG rating provider, or, where applicable, its legal representative, has, intentionally or negligently, infringed this Regulation, it shall adopt a decision imposing a fine. The maximum amount of the fine shall be 10% of the total annual net turnover of the ESG rating provider, calculated on the basis of the most recent available financial statements approved by the management body of the ESG rating provider.
2. Where the ESG rating provider referred to in paragraph 1 of this Article is a parent undertaking or a subsidiary of a parent undertaking which is required to prepare consolidated financial accounts in accordance with Directive 2013/34/EU, the relevant total annual net turnover shall be either the total annual net turnover, or the corresponding type of income in accordance with applicable Union law in the area of accounting, according to the most recent available consolidated accounts approved by the management body of the ultimate parent undertaking.
3. When determining the level of a fine pursuant to paragraph 1 of this Article, ESMA shall take into account the criteria set out in Article 35(5).
4. Notwithstanding paragraph 3, where the ESG rating provider referred to in paragraph 1 has directly or indirectly benefitted financially from the infringement, the amount of the fine shall be at least equal to that benefit.
5. Where an act or omission of an ESG rating provider constitutes more than one infringement of this Regulation, only the higher fine calculated in accordance with paragraph 2 and relating to one of those infringements shall apply.

A. INTRODUCTION

36.01 Under Article 36, ESMA can impose fines on ESG rating providers or their legal representatives for intentional or negligent breaches of the Regulation.[1] Specifically, fines can reach up to 10% of the provider's total annual net turnover, based on the most recent financial statements, or the corresponding income in the case of consolidated financial accounts. If the provider has financially benefitted from the infringement, the fine will be at least equal to the benefit gained.

36.02 The article provides that ESMA, in its supervisory role, can issue fines over ESG ratings providers when they intentionally or negligently do not comply with the requirements set in the Regulation. This provision defines the enforcement tool of ESMA when considering the sanctions applicable to raters: the element of intention or negligence is relevant to determine the fine. The legislator indicates the amount of 10% of the total annual net turnover of the ESG rating provider as appropriate level of the fine based on the most recent available financial statements approved by the management body of the ESG rating provider. The calculation of the fine refers to the infringement of raters which in case of a parent undertaking or a subsidiary of a parent undertaking relates to the consolidated accounts approved by the management body of the ultimate parent undertaking. The criteria to determine the nature and seriousness of the infringement are indicated in Article 35(5) which considers various factors when taking the supervisory measures. Interestingly, paragraph 4 of the provision regulates the case where the ESG rating provider has directly or indirectly benefitted financially from the infringement and indicates the amount of the fine which should be at least equal to that benefit. The aim of this sanction is to reduce the incentive of raters to engage with profitable activities in breach of the Regulation in particular when conflicts of interest arise. As noted in the doctrinal debate, the sanctions resemble the enforcement mechanism provided for the supervision of CRAs which seems a duplication of the ESMA administrative duties.[2] Paragraph 5 of the article points

1 See 'EU Adopts ESG Ratings Regulation: Strengthening Transparency and Reliability in Sustainable Finance' (10 December 2024), https://www.wilmerhale.com/en/insights/client-alerts/20241210-eu-adopts-esg-ratings-regulation-strengthening-transparency-and-reliability-in-sustainable-finance.

2 Catherine Malecki, 'The EU proposal for a Regulation on the transparency and integrity of ESG rating activities on 13 June 2023: the missing piece of sustainable finance regulation' (2023) 17(2) *Law and*

on act or omission of an ESG rating provider constituting more than one infringement of this Regulation which are sanctioned only with the higher fine calculated according to the criteria set out in paragraph 2 and relating to one of those infringements.

The rationale to impose fines over ratings providers reflects the need to ensure the quality and transparency of assessments which have been at the centre of criticisms for dubious relationships between issuer and clients. The concern often raised about ESG data is a lack of internal firewalls clearly separating analysis, sales and consultancy teams: the major issue is that analysts paid to assess a company's climate performance could be more lenient if their colleagues also need the company's help to hit a sales target.[3] Reliance on ratings providers poses challenges for regulators and supervisory authorities because of the impact of assessment on company's exposure to potentially material ESG risks, the quality of companies' management systems and governance structures to mitigate such risks, and the provision of products and services that have a positive environmental or social contribution. The ratings providers which score companies on climate and governance risk have largely been left to their own devices, the ESMA enforcement framework would likely introduce more regulatory scrutiny on how these data providers operate. The sanctions will address conflicts of interest, market concentration and whether companies should get a "right to reply" if inaccurate data is used about them to build a rating. **36.03**

B. THE NATURE OF SANCTIONS

The category of sanctions introduced by the Regulation covers a significant number of cases of ratings businesses' infringements for blurred analysis and negligent screening of companies' performance. However, the problem is that ESG is a composite set of subjective assessments based on variable arbitrary data that allow financial firms to say they are ESG compliant.[4] There is risk that the fines issued by ESMA will have scant effect as there are many providers and methods and it is difficult to draw meaning from various rankings. The situation can be worse whether 'external sources, bemoaning how many of the **36.04**

Financial Markets Review 168.

3 Patrick Temple-West and Kenza Bryan, 'The coming crackdown on the ESG ratings industry' *Financial Times* (31 May 2023), https://www.ft.com/content/2284893d-dc6d-4681-8a12-fc08f9f94c1a.

4 Agnes Sipiczki, 'A critical look at the ESG market' (April 2022) CEPS Policy Insights No 2022-15, p. 7–8, https://cdn.ceps.eu/wp-content/uploads/2022/04/PI2022-15_A-critical-look-at-the-ESG-market.pdf.

largest raters use "black box" algorithms to screen for ESG issues and do not provide access to the backing data.'[5] ESG rating providers will maintain full control of the methodologies they use and will remain independent when it comes to the choice of those methodologies. The Regulation allows a variety of approaches which are available in the ESG ratings market although this can be an obstacle for the effectiveness of sanctions. It seems that, on the one hand, the EU legislator established a strict framework of fines but, on the other side, it adopts a moral suasion tool when it comes to strengthen the internal governance of providers. It is fundamental to ensure supervisory and enforcement convergence and facilitates greater transparency on sanctions. The ESMA regime needs to be complemented with timely enforcement intervention on the decision-making process of ESG ratings to avoid immune positions in case of misleading allegations.

5 Alan Livsey, 'Boom in ESG ratings leaves trail of confusion' *Financial Times* (19 March 2022), https://www.ft.com/content/c34fe314-838b-4b00-ae25-9a4f0d93f822.

ARTICLE 37

PERIODIC PENALTY PAYMENTS

Andrea Miglionico

1. **ESMA shall, by decision, impose periodic penalty payments to compel**
   (a) **an ESG rating provider to put an end to an infringement in accordance with a decision taken pursuant to Article 35(1), point (c);**
   (b) **the persons referred to in Article 32(1):**
      (i) **to supply complete information which has been requested by a decision taken pursuant to Article 32(3);**
      (ii) **to submit to an investigation and in particular to produce complete records, data, procedures or any other material required and to complete and correct other information provided in an investigation launched by a decision taken pursuant to Article 33(3);**
      (iii) **to submit to an on-site inspection ordered by a decision taken pursuant to Article 34(4).**
2. **A periodic penalty payment shall be effective and proportionate. ESMA shall impose the periodic penalty payment on a daily basis until the ESG rating provider or person concerned complies with the relevant decision referred to in paragraph 1.**
3. **Notwithstanding paragraph 2, the amount of the periodic penalty payments shall be 3% of the average daily turnover in the preceding business year or, in the case of natural persons, 2% of the average daily income in the preceding calendar year. It shall be calculated from the date stipulated in the decision imposing the periodic penalty payment.**
4. **A periodic penalty payment shall be imposed for a maximum period of six months following notification of ESMA's decision referred to in paragraph 1. Following the end of the period for which the periodic penalty payment is imposed, ESMA shall review the measure.**

A. INTRODUCTION

37.01 The article empowers ESMA to impose periodic penalty payments to compel compliance with its decisions. These penalties can be up to 3% of the average daily turnover for businesses or 2% of the average daily income for individuals. ESMA is required to publicly disclose fines and penalty payments unless such disclosure exposes financial markets or causes disproportionate harm which can determine a reputational damage for non-compliant ratings providers. The rationale of the provision is to enforce ratings providers to comply with the requirements set up in the Regulation in particular on the transparency of information which form part of the investigation conducted by the ESMA. This provision resembles Article 36b ('Periodic penalty payments') of the Credit Rating Agencies Regulation,[1] which seems an oxymoron given the fact that under the legislation credit ratings provision is incompatible with ESG ratings provision with a view to preventing conflicts of interest. However, several provisions in Section 2 ('Supervisory measures and penalties') are similar to those contained in the CRAR. This raises the question about the relationship between ESG ratings and credit ratings to which the Regulation does not provide a clear answer. The ESG factors are embedded into credit ratings within the framework of the CRAR without making any reference to the ESG rating Regulation. The credit rating agency had been providing ESG credit indicator scores for publicly rated entities in some sectors and assets classes with little scrutiny of the independent scores for the credit impact of E, S and G factors.[2] As a result, the issue of transparency regarding the integration of ESG factors, their analysis and their influence on the credit rating result remains unresolved in a context where the Regulation should have provided clarity and certainty around the provisions. It seems that the EU legislator instead of keeping separate and standalone ESG ratings as such opted for the integration of ESG data into credit ratings. A missed opportunity for the drafters of Regulation to address a grey area in the ESG rating market which raises concerns on the ESG content in rating reports published by CRAs. This leads to the consideration whether and to which extent CRAs measure ESG in their credit risk analysis and how this affects decision making in capital

1 Regulation (EC) No 1060/2009 of the European Parliament and of the Council of 16 September 2009 on credit rating agencies.

2 Laurène Chenevat, 'ESG ratings: at last regulated, at risk of growing competition with raw data' (5 November 2024), https://gsh.cib.natixis.com/our-center-of-expertise/articles/esg-ratings-at-last-regulated-at-risk-of-growing-competition-with-raw-data

markets.[3] ESMA published technical advice on sustainability considerations in the credit rating market and a set of guidelines on disclosure requirements applicable to credit ratings.[4] Specifically, ESMA assessed the level of consideration of ESG factors in both specific credit rating actions, and the credit rating market in general. It found that, while CRAs are considering ESG factors in their ratings, the extent of their consideration can vary significantly across asset classes, according to each CRA's methodology. ESMA pointed that given the specific role of credit ratings in the EU regulatory framework for the purposes of assessing credit risk, it would be inadvisable to amend the CRA Regulation to explicitly mandate the consideration of sustainability characteristics in all rating assessments.[5] The guidelines serve as a regulatory tool for CRAs to harmonize disclosure of ESG considerations on disclosure requirements for credit ratings and improve the overall quality and consistency of CRAs' press releases related to their rating activity. The guidelines provide detailed guidance as to what CRAs should disclose when they issue a credit rating to ensure a better level of consistency in terms of the critical information included in CRAs' press releases; and require greater transparency around whether ESG factors were a key driver of the credit rating action. The guidelines constitute a catalogue for users of ratings to better assess where ESG factors are affecting credit rating actions.

The ESMA is required to issue effective and proportionate periodic penalty payment on a daily basis until the ESG rating provider is compliant with the decisions taken in accordance with paragraph 1. When taking the supervisory measures, ESMA should consider the nature and seriousness of the infringement. ESG ratings have an obligation to process requests in a timely and independent way. Periodic penalty payments are one of the enforcement measures available to the ESMA under the Regulation. They are established to get ratings providers to comply, as soon as possible, with requirements laid down in ESMA supervisory decisions. Periodic penalty payments are administrative measures to compel ESG ratings providers or the relevant persons to comply with previously issued decisions, requests for information, or investigation and inspections. Similar scope is found in the enforcement of the rules concerning **37.02**

3 Florian Kiesel and Felix Lücke, 'ESG in credit ratings and the impact on financial markets' (2019) 28(3) *Financial Markets, Institutions & Instruments* 263.

4 ESMA, Guidelines on Disclosure Requirements Applicable to Credit Ratings. Final Report (18 July 2019), ESMA33-9-320, https://www.esma.europa.eu/sites/default/files/library/esma33-9-320_final_report_guidelines_on_disclosure_requirements_applicable_to_credit_rating_agencies.pdf.

5 ESMA, 'ESMA advises on credit rating sustainability issues and sets disclosure requirements' (18 July 2019), Press Release, ESMA71-99-1199, https://www.esma.europa.eu/sites/default/files/library/esma71-99-1199_press_release_for_cra_sustainability.pdf.

the scope of the CRA Regulation where ESMA shall impose periodic penalty payments in order to compel the credit rating agency to put an end to the infringement of issuing credit ratings without being registered by ESMA, and impose fines where appropriate, in accordance respectively with Articles 36(b) and 36(a) of the CRA Regulation.[6]

37.03 The article identifies a maximum period of six months for imposing a periodic penalty payment. ESMA is responsible to review the administrative measure after the cessation of the period for which the periodic penalty payment is imposed. The provision leaves to ESMA the discretion to decide whether the penalty is sufficient to instil compliance with the Regulation: it indicates the specific amount of 3% of the average daily turnover in the preceding business year or, in the case of natural persons, 2% of the average daily income in the preceding calendar year. However, the amount of the periodic penalty payment seems standardized and related to the ESMA enforcement regime provided in other EU Regulations.[7]

B. THE ADMINISTRATIVE MEASURES OF ESMA

37.04 The ESMA's sanctioning powers over the ESG ratings providers involve responsibilities and powers to deal with possible infringements.[8] The enforcement framework operates along the supervisory investigation: ESMA teams perform supervisory work with the purpose of ensuring that the entities under their supervision comply with the requirements under the applicable legislation.[9] Where, as part of their investigations in a given case, ESMA supervisors find serious indications of possible facts liable to constitute infringements of the ESG ratings Regulation, the case is referred for further investigation to an independent investigating officer ('IIO') appointed within ESMA. The IIO has investigative powers whereby for example they may require information and documents, summon and interview persons, and execute on-site inspections. The IIO will make findings as to the commission of infringements and may recommend measures or fines to be imposed for those infringements. The

6 ESMA, 'Guidelines and Recommendations on the Scope of the CRA Regulation' (30 July 2013), ESMA/2013/720, p. 7, https://www.esma.europa.eu/sites/default/files/library/2015/11/2013-720_en.pdf.

7 See Article 66 of the EMIR Regulation No 648/2012 of the European Parliament and of the Council of 4 July 2012 on OTC derivatives, central counterparties and trade repositories.

8 See ESMA's Enforcement Role, https://www.esma.europa.eu/sites/default/files/library/esmas_enforcement_role.pdf.

9 ESMA, 'Sanctions and Enforcement,' https://www.esma.europa.eu/esmas-activities/supervision-and-convergence/sanctions-and-enforcement.

supervised entity will be given the opportunity to make submissions on the IIO's findings and the IIO will duly consider such submissions before submitting any findings and the file on which they are based to ESMA's Board of Supervisors. On the basis of the file and findings submitted by the IIO, and after having heard the person subject to investigation, the Board of Supervisors independently decides whether any infringements have been committed, adopts appropriate supervisory measures for infringements found and imposes fines for the infringements that have been found to be committed negligently or intentionally. When ESMA finds that a Credit Rating Agency has negligently or intentionally committed an infringement, the Authority calculates the fines to be imposed using a two-step methodology. This methodology is determined by Article 36a of the CRA Regulation and ESMA cannot deviate from it. The two-step methodology consists of the setting of a basic amount for the fine; and the adjustment, if necessary, of that basic amount.[10]

10 ESMA, 'Information on the methodology to set fines,' https://www.esma.europa.eu/sites/default/files/esma_-_information_regarding_methodology_to_set_fines.pdf

ARTICLE 38

DISCLOSURE, NATURE, ENFORCEMENT AND ALLOCATION OF FINES AND PERIODIC PENALTY PAYMENTS

Andrea Miglionico

1. **ESMA shall disclose to the public every fine and every periodic penalty payment that it has imposed pursuant to Articles 36 and 37 of this Regulation, unless such disclosure would seriously jeopardise Union financial markets or cause disproportionate damage to the parties involved. Such disclosure shall not contain personal data within the meaning of Regulation (EU) 2018/1725.**
2. **Fines and periodic penalty payments imposed pursuant to Articles 36 and 37 shall be of an administrative nature.**
3. **Fines and periodic penalty payments imposed pursuant to Articles 36 and 37 shall be enforceable. Enforcement of fines and periodic penalty payments shall be governed by the rules of procedure in force in the Member State or third country in which the fines and periodic penalty payments are enforced.**
4. **Fines and periodic penalty payments shall be allocated to the general budget of the Union.**

A. THE ESMA ENFORCEMENT ACTIVITIES OVER ESG RATINGS PROVIDERS

38.01 The article regulates the disclosure and publicity of fines and periodic penalty payments imposed by the ESMA. The provision aims to gives notice of the activities of supervisory and enforcement regime over the ESG ratings.

The Regulation requires to protect personal data of parties involved and to avoid the disclosure in case of serious reputational damage or disruption of the markets. It is an obligation to preserve the integrity and stability of the ESG industry and protect market participants from potential failures caused by the enforcement decisions. The article makes clear the administrative nature of supervisory measures and the enforceability of sanctions, which need to be regulated by national rules and procedures. This highlights the coercive powers of ESMA in collaboration with Member States that need to make enforceable the actions taken against ratings providers. The provision indicates the allocation of administrative sanctions to the general budget of the Union, which responds to the principle of transparency in the decision-making process. ESMA publishes extensive and detailed public versions of its enforcement decisions in order to provide more details on the reasons for its findings.[1] This has a number of benefits, including more legal certainty for entities supervised by ESMA and a better understanding of ESMA's enforcement role by stakeholders, including CRAs, investors and issuers. The public versions of enforcement decisions need to comply with the applicable rules regarding the protection of professional secrecy and personal data and so may be redacted. For that purpose, a confidentiality check takes place with the entity concerned before publication.

The provision reflects the content of Article 36d of the CRAR which is a **38.02** standardized rule for ESMA. As noted in the doctrinal debate, the purpose of fines is to penalize infringements and ensure that undertakings in general and specifically the infringing undertaking refrain(s) from hampering Commission investigations.[2] In case of periodic penalty payments, their central objective is to induce undertakings by way of a financial incentive to take, or refrain from taking, certain action. The Commission seeks to ensure the effectiveness of the investigatory process, and in particular to avoid that decisions on substance are taken on the basis of incomplete, incorrect, or misleading information. Formal enforcement decisions related to ESG ratings need to be tested. National competent authorities (NCAs) have addressed most irregularities in ongoing supervision and favour a gradual approach in the implementation of the new regulatory framework for sustainability-related matters. Unclear or ambiguous definitions may also contribute to difficulties in detecting infringements.

1 ESMA, 'Transparency of decisions,' https://www.esma.europa.eu/esmas-activities/supervision-and-convergence/sanctions-and-enforcement.

2 Ralf Sauer and Luis Ortiz Blanco, 'Procedural Infringements: Fines and Periodic Penalty Payments' in Luis Ortiz Blanco (ed), *EU Competition Procedure* (4th edn, Oxford: Oxford University Press 2022) 478–479.

NCA feedback to ESMA will include the importance of ex-ante reviews as an important safeguard from potential inaccuracy of ratings. ESMA aims to coordinate national enforcers' supervision through its Working Group which brings together representatives from the various EEA countries, providing them with a forum to discuss and share their experiences with the application and enforcement of ESG ratings Regulation requirements.

38.03 The article provides a summary of the ESMA's activities in its role of supervisor over the ESG ratings. It points on the ESMA supervision and enforcement to entities that form essential parts of the financial market infrastructure. This means that ESMA may act as supervisor either where the national competent authorities cannot intervene effectively, or where EU legislation confers a specific competence to act as the single supervisor.[3] ESMA supervises these entities through a strong common supervisory culture, approach and methodology across all mandates.[4] ESMA's supervisory activities target a positive supervisory outcome, aiming for high compliance standards and appropriate changes to the behaviour of the supervised entities where warranted. For those entities that are supervised at national level, ESMA takes an active role to promote sound, efficient, and consistent supervision, and effective coordinated supervision across the EU. As supervisory convergence, the purpose of promoting supervisory convergence is to ensure a level playing field of high-quality regulation and supervision without regulatory arbitrage or a race to the bottom between Member States. Supervisory convergence implies developing consistent interpretation of rules, building sound and effective supervisory capabilities, coordinating approaches and activities, conducting concerted supervisory actions across the EU, and reviewing and sharing good practices. ESMA applies different supervisory tools to its convergence work: it takes a consistent approach through its supervision and convergence work, by applying commonly shared principles of risk-based, outcome-based and data-driven approaches. ESMA developed its supervisory and enforcement actions to the type of risk or challenge at stake, taking into account its urgency, size and complexity and the history of the supervised entity.[5]

---

3 Marloes van Rijsbergen and Marta Simoncini, 'Controlling ESMAs enforcement powers' in Miroslava Scholten and Alex Brenninkmeijer (eds), *Controlling EU Agencies. The Rule of Law in a Multi-jurisdictional Legal Order* (Edward Elgar 2020) 272–273.

4 ESMA, 'Supervision and Convergence,' https://www.esma.europa.eu/esmas-activities/supervision-and-convergence.

5 Pierre Schammo, 'The European Securities and Markets Authority: Lifting the veil on the allocation of powers' (2011) 48(6) *Common Market Law Review* 1879.

ESMA can conduct investigations, ongoing inspections and impose fines directly on ratings providers that breach European Union rules. The new legislation conferred competence on ESMA for matters relating to the ongoing supervision of registered ESG ratings and delegated specific supervisory tasks to national authorities, including powers to request information, launch investigations and perform on-site inspections. Similar to CRAs, ESMA is also responsible for the endorsement of the 'as stringent as' test for ratings produced by credit rating agencies outside the EU.[6] However, the fact that ESMA is not an independent institution when it comes to monitoring rating performance may generate some doubts as to whether any objective improvements will be made in terms of the transparency of ESG ratings. ESMA is an authority with legal basis in the EU Treaty with mandate to develop regulatory technical standards which have no legally binding power while the Commission holds the discretionary power to endorse, partly endorse and amend these standards.[7] As noted, in its role as direct supervisor of rating agencies in the Union ESMA is considered the single capital markets supervisor.[8] The limited enforceability of ESMA's regulatory standards is found in the *Meroni* doctrine concerning the delegation of powers to a non-institutional body.[9] Specifically, the *Meroni* case clarified the principle of upholding the balance of powers among institutions established by the Treaties limiting the possibility to delegate tasks to regulatory agencies that operate beyond the provisions of Treaty. The risk-based approach of enforcement mechanisms is likely enhance the oversight of ESG ratings and to improve the internal governance of providers namely clarity regarding staff roles and responsibilities, and the involvement of ratings analysts in business development. **38.04**

6 Marloes van Rijsbergen and Jonathan Foster, '"Rating" ESMA's accountability: "AAA" status' in Miroslava Scholten and Michiel Luchtman (eds), *Law Enforcement by EU Authorities. Implications for Political and Judicial Accountability* (Edward Elgar 2017) 53–54.

7 Regulation (EU) No 1095/2010 of the European Parliament and of the Council of 24 November 2010 establishing a European Supervisory Authority (European Securities and Markets Authority), amending Decision No 716/2009/EC and repealing Commission Decision 2009/77/EC [2010] OJ L331/84.

8 Gudula Deipenbrock, 'Direct Supervisory Powers of the European Securities and Markets Authority (ESMA) in the Realm of Credit Rating Agencies – Some Critical Observations in a Broader Context' (2018) 29(2) *European Business Law Review* 169–170.

9 Case 9/56, *Meroni & Co., Industrie Metallurgiche, S.A.S. v High Authority of the European Coal and Steel Community* [1957–1958] ECR 133.

Section 3 Procedures and review

ARTICLE 39

PROCEDURAL RULES FOR TAKING SUPERVISORY MEASURES AND IMPOSING FINES

Andrea Miglionico

1. **Where ESMA finds that there are serious indications of a possible infringement of this Regulation, ESMA shall appoint an independent investigation officer within ESMA to investigate the matter. That investigation officer shall not be directly or indirectly involved or have been directly or indirectly involved in the supervision of the ESG ratings to which the infringement relates and shall perform his or her functions independently from ESMA's Board of Supervisors.**
2. **The investigation officer referred to in paragraph 1 shall investigate the alleged infringements, take into account any comments submitted by the persons who are subject to the investigation, and submit a complete file with his or her findings to ESMA's Board of Supervisors.**
3. **The investigation officer shall have the power to request information in accordance with Article 32 and to conduct investigations and on-site inspections in accordance with Articles 33 and 34.**
4. **When carrying out his or her tasks, the investigation officer shall have access to all documents and information that have been gathered by ESMA in its supervisory activities.**
5. **The rights of defence of the persons subject to the investigation shall be fully respected during investigations under this Regulation.**
6. **Upon submission of the file with his or her findings to ESMA's Board of Supervisors, the investigation officer shall notify the persons who are subject to the investigation.**
7. **On the basis of the file containing the investigation officer's findings, and where requested by the persons concerned after having heard those persons in accordance with Article 40, ESMA's Board of Supervisors shall assess whether one or more persons subject to the investigation have committed the infringements concerned and shall, where it comes to the conclusion that such infringements have been committed, take a supervisory measure as referred to in Article 35 and impose a fine in accordance with Article 36.**

8. The investigation officer shall not participate in the deliberations of ESMA's Board of Supervisors or in any other way intervene in the decision-making process of ESMA's Board of Supervisors.

9. The Commission shall adopt delegated acts in accordance with Article 47 to supplement this Regulation by adopting further rules of procedure for the exercise of ESMA's power to impose fines or periodic penalty payments, including provisions on rights of defence, temporal provisions and the collection of fines or periodic penalty payments, and by adopting detailed rules on the limitation periods for the imposition and enforcement of fines and periodic penalty payments.

10. ESMA shall refer matters for criminal prosecution to the national authorities concerned where, in carrying out its tasks under this Regulation, it finds that there are serious indications of the possible existence of facts liable to constitute criminal offences. ESMA shall refrain from imposing fines or periodic penalty payments where a prior acquittal or conviction arising from an identical fact or facts which are substantially the same has already acquired the force of res judicata as the result of criminal proceedings under national law.

A. INTRODUCTION

39.01 Section 3 of the Regulation provides detailed rules on procedural matters of supervisory and enforcement measures with respect to three main stages: monitoring, investigation and sanctioning. If there is a risk that an entity may not be compliant with a relevant legislation, ESMA may decide to open an investigation.[1] For this scope, ESMA uses its investigatory powers to assess potential regulatory breaches, including investigations and on-site inspections. This part deals with the ESMA's activities of investigation in case of serious indications of a potential breach of a rule. In this scenario, ESMA's Executive Director appoints an Independent Investigating Officer (IIO) for further enforcement action. The IIO conducts an independent review of the case and submits his/her findings on potential infringements to the Board of Supervisors, who is the ultimate decision maker. On the basis of the file and findings submitted by the IIO, and after having heard the person subject to investigation, the Board of Supervisors independently decides whether any

1 ESMA, 'Investigations and Inspections,' https://www.esma.europa.eu/esmas-activities/supervision-and-convergence/investigations-and-inspections.

infringements have been committed, adopts appropriate supervisory measures for infringements found, and imposes fines for the infringements that have been found to be committed negligently or intentionally.

Investigations and on-site inspections aim to provide an in-depth analysis of various risks and ascertain compliance with the relevant legislation. These activities are conducted with a predefined scope and time frame and generally they are risk-based, proportionate, forward looking and action oriented. In the course of investigations and on-site inspections, ESMA collects relevant evidence through requesting information from and interviewing supervised entities. ESMA may also contact third parties such as third persons to whom supervised entities have outsourced certain functions or activities to obtain information necessary for the investigation. ESMA not always gives prior notice of its on-site inspections. This is the case where ESMA believes that announcing the opening of an on-site inspection may impair the effectiveness of the gathering of information. ESMA leverages digital forensics tools and data analysis skills to collect, extract, correlate and contextualize a myriad of data points across information requested from supervised entities, engagement with key stakeholders, regulatory reporting as well as information extracted from past and on-going supervisory actions. When collecting and analyzing data, ESMA adopts arrangements to ensure the protection of personal data in accordance with the EU rules and exclusion of documents covered by legal privilege (according to the case law of the CJE). The provision resembles Article 23e of the CRAR ('Procedural rules for taking supervisory measures and imposing fines') where similar investigatory powers are attributed to ESMA over credit ratings. **39.02**

B. THE INVESTIGATION OFFICER

The IIO has investigative powers whereby may require information and documents, summon and interview persons, and execute on-site inspections. The IIO will make findings as to the commission of infringements and may recommend measures or fines to be imposed for those infringements. The supervised entity will be given the opportunity to make submissions on the IIO's findings and the IIO consider such submissions before submitting any findings and the file on which they are based to ESMA's Board of Supervisors. In the course of investigation, the IIO examines the suspected infringements and may use the same powers as ESMA's supervision teams, i.e. requesting information, carrying out general investigations and conducting on-site inspections. The IIO presents the findings of investigation along with the comments of the persons **39.03** subject to the procedure which form the content of the file, on the basis of which the Board of the Supervisors deliver its decision.

39.04 The process of investigation is complemented with thematic reviews which are generally exploratory activities in areas where ESMA does not have sufficient information to establish firm practice norms, market-wide risks, or its own expectations. They are often triggered by amounting risks, macroeconomic developments or new trends in a particular process or area. The purpose of this supervisory activity is to gather further information and enable ESMA to compare industry practices and to reflect on potential policy evolutions. The risks and trends identified in a review feed into the risk framework of each supervised entity. Specifically, thematic reviews might trigger follow-up targeted investigations on particular supervised entities or areas, and the publication of a report flagging risks to the market. To complete the process, ESMA conducts perimeter monitoring for identifying providers that are providing ratings without having registered with the authority. This is done via Internet searches, as well as referrals from outside entities and other stakeholders. If a provider is found to be issuing ratings as defined by the ESG Regulation, it will be compelled to apply for registration, and the case can then be referred for potential enforcement actions.

C. THE ESMA'S BOARD OF SUPERVISORS

39.05 The policy decisions of ESMA are executed by the Board of Supervisors.[2] The Board informs the work of the Authority and has the ultimate decision-making responsibility regarding a broad range of matters including the adoption of ESMA Technical Standards, Opinions, Guidelines and the issuance of advice to the EU institutions. The Board is supported by a number of ESMA standing committees and working groups who are dealing with technical issues. In addition to the ESMA Chair, the Board of Supervisors is composed of the heads of the NCAs in the EU and the EEA responsible for securities regulation and supervision with non-voting representatives from the European Commission, the ESRB, the EBA, the EIOPA and the European Free Trade Association Surveillance Authority (EFTA Surveillance Authority). The Board of Supervisors meets at least twice a year. According to Article 44(3) of the ESMA Regulation 1095/2010, the Board of Supervisors has adopted Rules

2 ESMA, 'Board of Supervisors,' https://www.esma.europa.eu/about-esma/governance-structure/board-of-supervisors.

of Procedure.[3] Voting by the Board of Supervisors is undertaken on a simple majority basis (one vote per national member) for all matters except guidelines and technical standards. In the case of guidelines and standards, voting will be done by qualified majority as set out under the Treaty on the European Union. In the sanctioning phase, the Board assesses the IIO's findings, whether the infringements have been committed with negligence or intent; and the legal and factual grounds on which the findings are based. ESMA's Board issues a final decision whether the person under investigation did indeed commit one or more infringements and whether it will impose a supervisory measure and/or a fine. ESMA can thus impose penalties without the involvement of the European Commission as it is in fact the only agency with a direct sanctioning power.[4] The ESG ratings Regulation provides an articulated framework of ESMA supervisory and enforcement powers which align with the accountability regime of EU agency composition.[5]

3 ESMA, 'Decision of the Board of Supervisors' (20 January 2025), ESMA22-1669215091-5867, https://www.esma.europa.eu/sites/default/files/2025-01/ESMA22-1669215091-5867-_Rules_of_Procedure_Board_of_Supervisors.pdf.

4 Miroslava Scholten, 'EU enforcement agencies' in Miroslava Scholten (ed), *Research Handbook on the Enforcement of EU Law* (Edward Elgar 2023) 152–153.

5 Elizabeth Howell, 'EU agencification and the rise of ESMA: are its governance arrangements fit for purpose?' (2019) 78(2) *Cambridge Law Journal* 324.

ARTICLE 40

HEARING OF PERSONS SUBJECT TO INVESTIGATIONS

Andrea Miglionico

1. **Before taking any decision imposing a supervisory measure, fine or periodic penalty payment pursuant to Article 35, 36 or 37, ESMA shall give the persons subject to the investigations the opportunity to be heard on its findings. ESMA shall base its decisions only on findings on which the persons subject to the investigations have had an opportunity to comment.**

   The first subparagraph shall not apply where urgent action pursuant to Article 35 is needed to prevent significant and imminent damage to the financial system. In such a case, ESMA may adopt an interim decision and shall give the persons concerned the opportunity to be heard as soon as possible after taking its decision.
2. **The rights of defence of the persons subject to the investigations shall be fully respected during the investigations. They shall be entitled to have access to ESMA's file, subject to the legitimate interest of other persons in the protection of their business secrets. The right of access to the file shall not extend to confidential information or ESMA's internal preparatory documents.**

A. INTRODUCTION

40.01 The procedural matter of sanctions is completed with the hearing of persons subject to the investigations process. This article mandates ESMA to give the persons subject to the investigations the opportunity to be heard on its findings in case of any comment or disagreement with the outcome of investigation. However, the provision allows an exemption when a supervisory measure needs to be taken urgently to prevent significant and imminent damage to the financial system. The rule aims to protect the rights of defence of the persons subject to the proceedings during the proceedings.[1] This responds to the principle of transparency of procedure which is fundamental in the right of access ESMA's file, subject to the legitimate interest of other persons in the protection of their business secrets, although it does not extend to confidential information or ESMA's internal preparatory documents. The article reflects the need to ensure good administrative practices and high standards of public access to documents, taking into account the specific nature of the ESMA's supervisory and enforcement activities.[2]

The article highlights the principle of transparency which is one of the core values underpinning the supervisory regime of ESMA.[3] In this context, to enable citizens to effectively exercise their right of public access to documents, ESMA makes accessible through the ESMA Library several types of documents, related to all of its areas of activity. For example, public users of the ESMA website are invited to use the search and filter options of the ESMA Library to find specific documents such as summaries of conclusions of meetings of its Board of Supervisors, Management Board and Securities and Markets Stakeholder Group, Consultation Papers, Reports, Opinions, Letters, Advice, Q&As and many other types of documents such as documents providing information about the contractors of ESMA, its powers in relation to breach of Union law, or its budget.[4] The annual reports on the activities of ESMA include a dedicated section on public access to documents requests, including information on the number of requests handled by ESMA in a given year and the outcome achieved. **40.02**

B. THE RIGHT TO ACCESS PUBLIC DOCUMENTS

The Charter of Fundamental Rights of the EU and the Treaty on the Functioning of the EU (TFEU) state that EU citizens and residents have a **40.03**

1 Similar scope is found in Article 25 of the CRAR ('Hearing of the persons concerned').

2 Marloes van Rijsbergen and Miroslava Scholten, 'ESMA Inspecting: The Implications for Judicial Control under Shared Enforcement' (2016) 7(3) *European Journal of Risk Regulation* 569.

3 Elizabeth Howell, 'The evolution of ESMA and direct supervision: Are there implications for EU supervisory governance?' (2017) 54(4) *Common Market Law Review* 1027.

4 ESMA, 'Transparency and Access to Documents,' https://www.esma.europa.eu/about-esma/transparency-and-access-documents.

right to access documents in the possession of EU institutions, bodies, offices and agencies. EU institutions must grant access to requested documents, except in certain circumstances set out in European law and rules. Specifically, the principle of transparency and the right of individuals to access documents of EU Bodies and Institutions are laid down in both Article 15 of the TFEU and Article 42 of the Charter of Fundamental Rights of the EU. The general rules giving effect to this right are set out in Regulation 1049/2001 on public access to EU documents which applies directly to the European Commission, the Council of the EU and the European Parliament. The European Council also applies Regulation 1049/2001 and the relevant rules of procedure of the Council of the EU. The three other EU institutions (the Court of Justice of the EU, the European Court of Auditors and the European Central Bank) apply separate rules that differ to varying degrees although are generally inspired by Regulation 1049/2001. Any EU citizen, any person residing in an EU Member State or any 'legal person' registered in an EU Member State (such as a company, organization or association) has a right to request public access to an EU document. An institution is entitled to ask for your contact details for the purpose of processing your request for access, including verifying if you are an EU resident or citizen. The term 'document' implies any content (words, numbers, symbols, computer code, pictures, sounds) in any format (such as paper or electronic documents, emails, text messages or sound, visual or audio-visual recordings). The right of public access to documents applies to documents relating to the policies, activities and decisions under the institution's sphere of responsibility. According to Regulation 1049/2001, all institutions are required to keep a register of documents they hold. Individuals can request access to documents that they know to exist but can also request access to any documents held by an institution related to a specific, defined matter, without knowing the exact description of the documents in question. While there is no limit to the amount of documents which can be requested, according to Regulation 1049/2001, EU institutions may refuse to deal with a request for very large documents or a very large number of documents. However, in such cases, they should first try to reach a fair solution with the person requesting access.

40.04 Requests for access to documents should clearly mention the full name of the requester and their contact details (notably email or postal address), and sufficiently describe at least the nature of the document to enable ESMA to identify it. In case a request is unclear, ESMA will contact requesters and ask them to better clarify the scope of their request. ESMA has 15 working days from receiving a clear request for access to documents to assess and respond to it.

This deadline may be extended pursuant to Regulation (EC) No 1049/2001 by a further 15 working days in exceptional cases, for example in the event of an application relating to a very long document or to a very large number of documents. Request for access to documents may be refused or partially refused where ESMA considers that one or more of the exceptions referred to in Regulation (EC) No 1049/2001 apply.[5] In such cases, requesters can ask ESMA to review its initial assessment by submitting a confirmatory application. The same timeline applies as to the initial request. Decisions that ESMA takes according to Article 8 of Regulation (EC) No 1049/2001 may be the subject of a complaint to the Ombudsman or of proceedings before the Court of Justice of the European Union, following an appeal to the Board of Appeal, as appropriate, in accordance with the conditions laid down in Articles 228 and 263 TFEU, respectively. For the purposes of handling requests for access to documents, certain personal data needs to be provided to ESMA. Such data will be processed in line with Regulation (EU) 2018/1725.[6]

5 Regulation 1049/2001 sets out certain exceptional circumstances under which an EU institution may refuse access to documents (Article 4 of the Regulation). These exceptions include if the institution considers disclosure would undermine the public interest in certain sensitive areas or would undermine the privacy of individuals (consistent with EU data protection law). The exceptions also cover the protection of ongoing decision-making procedures, legal procedures or commercial interests. In invoking these exceptions to withhold access, the institution must demonstrate that there is no overriding public interest that would justify disclosing the documents.

6 ESMA, 'Legal Notice and Data Protection,' https://www.esma.europa.eu/about-esma/governance-structure/legal-notice-data-protection.

ARTICLE 41

REVIEW BY THE COURT OF JUSTICE OF THE EUROPEAN UNION

Andrea Miglionico

The Court of Justice of the European Union shall have unlimited jurisdiction to review decisions of ESMA imposing a fine or a periodic penalty payment. It may annul, or reduce or increase the amount of, the fine or periodic penalty payment imposed.

A. THE ROLE OF THE COURT OF JUSTICE IN THE ENFORCEMENT REGIME

41.01 The article defines the role of the Court of Justice of the EU (CJEU) over the enforcement decisions of ESMA. It is a general provision on the jurisdiction of the Court against the sanctions imposed to ESG ratings in the case of ex post judicial control. The rule establishes that the CJEU may intervene to review the nature and amount of administrative measures after discussing the matter with both parties.[1] The scope of article is to provide scrutiny on ESMA's legal acts in the context of accountability of the EU agencies.[2] In substance, the article empowers the CJEU to dispute the legality of ESMA's decisions by requesting information and carrying out a general investigation or inspection with regard to the agency's final decisions to impose a fine. The intervention of the CJEU responds to the need to ensure consistent application of rules

1 Similar provision is found in Article 36e of the CRAR ('Review by the Court of Justice of the European Union').

2 Marloes van Rijsbergen and Miroslava Scholten, 'ESMA Inspecting: The Implications for Judicial Control under Shared Enforcement' (2017) 7(3) *European Journal of Risk Regulation* 569–570.

through a rapid and effective mechanism of judicial review.[3] The CJEU displays the role of guarantor of the Treaties and guardian of the rule of law in the Union by monitoring the correct application of the EU legislation.[4] The article delineates the judicial accountability of enforcement actions in which ESMA is involved and reflects the principle of certainty in the administrative discretion to issue fines and penalties.[5] The provision is relevant within the relationship between the CJEU and the ESAs and for the legal boundaries of the CJEU on the powers and the accountability mechanisms of ESMA.[6]

The CJEU consists of two courts, the Court of Justice proper and the General Court, and it offers various means of redress, as laid down in Article 19 of the Treaty on European Union, Articles 251–281 of the TFEU, Article 136 Euratom, and Protocol No 3 annexed to the Treaties on the Statute of the Court of Justice of the European Union.[7] The CJEU is responsible for the jurisdiction of the European Union.[8] The courts ensure the correct interpretation and application of primary and secondary EU law in the EU.[9] They review the legality of acts of the EU institutions and decide whether Member States have fulfilled their obligations under primary and secondary law. As noted, 'judicial review of legislative, administrative, and judicial decisions can be more or less intense. It can range from a very limited review which leaves almost everything to the discretion of the legislative, administrative, or lower judicial authority, to a full and comprehensive – and thus very intense – review of all aspects of the decision in question.'[10] The Court of Justice also provides **41.02**

3 Dominique Ritleng, 'Judicial Protection against the European Securities and Markets Authority (ESMA)' in Carl Fredrik Bergström and Magnus Strand (eds), *Legal Accountability in EU Markets for Financial Instruments: The Dual Role of Investment Firms* (Oxford: Oxford University Press 2021) 79–80.

4 Koen Lenaerts, 'The Court of Justice of the European Union as the guardian of the authority of EU law: A networking exercise' in Wolfgang Heusel and Jean-Philippe Rageade (eds), *The Authority of EU Law. Do We Still Believe in It?* (Springer 2019) 21–22.

5 Rob Widdershoven, 'The European Court of Justice and the Standard of Judicial Review' in Jurgen de Poorter, Ernst Hirsch Ballin and Saskia Lavrijssen (eds), *Judicial Review of Administrative Discretion in the Administrative State* (Springer 2019) 39–40.

6 Takis Tridimas, 'Financial Supervision and Agency Power: Reflections on ESMA' in Niamh Nic Shuibhne and Laurence W. Gormley (eds), *From Single Market to Economic Union: Essays in Memory of John A. Usher* (Oxford: Oxford University Press 2012) 55–56.

7 European Parliament, 'Competences of the Court of Justice of the European Union,' https://www.europarl.europa.eu/factsheets/en/sheet/12/competences-of-the-court-of-justice-of-the-european-union%29.

8 The composition of the Court of Justice and of the General Court is unchanged (Article 19 TEU): the Court of Justice consists of one judge from each Member State and the General Court includes at least one judge per Member State. The Civil Service Tribunal continues to consist of seven judges.

9 Michal Bobek, 'The Court of Justice of the European Union' in Damian Chalmers and Anthony Arnull (eds), *The Oxford Handbook of European Union Law* (Oxford: Oxford University Press 2015) 153–154.

10 Allan Rosas, 'Standard of Review: Court of Justice of the European Union (CJEU)' in *Max Planck Encyclopaedia of International Procedural Law* (Oxford: Oxford University Press 2019).

interpretations of EU law when requested by national judges. The Court gives a ruling on proceedings against states or institutions that have not fulfilled their obligations under EU law.[11] Proceedings against the EU institutions for annulment and for failure to act in cases where the applicant seeks the annulment of a measure supposedly contrary to EU law (annulment: Article 263 TFEU) or, in cases of infringement of EU law, where an institution, body, office or agency has failed to act (Article 265 TFEU). Actions may be brought by the Member States, the institutions themselves or any natural or legal person if the actions relate to a measure (in particular a regulation, directive or decision) adopted by an EU institution, body, office or agency and addressed to them. The Court declares the act void or declares that there has been a failure to act, in which case the institution at fault is required to take the necessary measures to comply with the Court's judgment (Article 266 TFEU).

11 R. Daniel Kelemen, 'The court of justice of the European Union in the twenty-first century' (2016) 79(1) *Law and Contemporary Problems*, 117–118.

Section 4 Fees and delegation

ARTICLE 42

SUPERVISORY FEES

Andrea Miglionico

1. ESMA shall charge proportionate fees to ESG rating providers in accordance with the delegated acts adopted pursuant to paragraph 2. Those fees shall fully cover ESMA's necessary expenditure relating to the supervision of ESG rating providers and the reimbursement of any costs that the competent authorities might incur when carrying out tasks pursuant to this Regulation, and in particular as a result of any delegation of tasks in accordance with Article 43.

2. The amount of an individual fee shall be proportionate to the annual net turnover of the ESG rating provider concerned.

By 2 January 2026, the Commission shall adopt delegated acts in accordance with Article 47 to supplement this Regulation by specifying the type of fees, the matters for which fees are due, the amount of the fees and the respective justification, the manner in which they are to be paid and, where applicable, the way in which ESMA is to reimburse the competent authorities in respect of any costs that they might incur when carrying out tasks pursuant to this Regulation, in particular as a result of any delegation of tasks as referred to in Article 43. Those delegated acts shall establish fees which are proportionate and appropriate to the size of ESG rating providers and to the extent of their supervision, in particular when they are categorised as small ESG rating providers.

A. THE SUPERVISORY FEES REGIME OF ESMA

42.01 The article regulates the expenditures for supervisory actions taken by ESMA, and indicates the amount of fees necessary to cover the costs sustained by competent authorities for administrative tasks. The provision establishes that the fees need to be proportionate to the annual net turnover of the ESG rating provider concerned which means that the ESG ratings providers have to pay supervisory fees to ESMA in proportion to their annual net turnover. On the amount and type of fees, the Regulation provides that the Commission will be in charge for the procedural matters of reimbursement. Delegated acts will be adopted to complement the Regulation in order to indicate the fees which are proportionate and appropriate to the size of ESG rating providers and commensurate of their supervision. The delegated acts will ensure that ESMA meets the regulatory obligation to charge fees that cover its costs whilst remaining proportionate to the revenues of the firms supervised. Similar to credit ratings, ESMA will provide comments and technical advice on the calculation and administration of registration fees, annual supervisory fees and certification fees of supervisory mandates.[1] The aim of delegated acts is to align the approach to collecting ESG ratings supervisory fees with the approach taken under ESMA's other supervisory mandates so that the fee collection process becomes easier to administer in future. The intended scope is to assess the compliance of supervised entities with the relevant cost-related provisions in the ESG ratings market and the obligation of not charging providers with undue costs. The delegated acts will indicate the calculation and the collection of supervisory fees which consist in a fixed registration fee and an annual supervisory fee of turnover to ratings providers with a range of annual revenues.[2] These fees reflect the costs of registering and granting certification status to ESG ratings as well as the costs of ESMA's ongoing supervision of providers issuing, certifying and endorsing ratings for use in the EU.

42.02 The Regulation requires the Commission to adopt delegated acts on supervisory fees to determine the different types of fees payable, the amount of fees

1 ESMA, 'Fees charged to Credit Rating Agencies by ESMA' (29 January 2021), Consultation Paper, ESMA 80-196-5019, https://www.esma.europa.eu/press-news/esma-news/esma-consults-changes-cra-supervisory-fees; ESMA, 'Technical Advice on Fees Charged to CRAs by ESMA' (21 June 2021) Final Report, ESMA80-196-5170, https://www.esma.europa.eu/document/final-report-technical-advice-fees-charged-cras-esma.

2 Specifically, the Commission Delegated Acts will regulate ESMA's budgetary and fee collection process, registration fees, annual supervisory fee, the calculation of ESG ratings' applicable turnover and certification fees. These fees also allow ESMA to reimburse national competent authorities for any costs they incur in carrying out work under the ESG ratings Regulation on ESMA's behalf.

payable, the modalities of payment and the reimbursement of fees to national competent authorities. ESMA is required to play an active role in building a common supervisory culture by promoting common supervisory approaches and practices. The delegated acts will ensure a fair and clear allocation of fees which reflected ESMA's administrative and supervisory costs whilst not being unduly burdensome for new market entrants. In order to achieve this, the delegated acts will be based on the calculation of supervisory fees on ESG providers' turnover from ratings and ancillary services. Similar to credit ratings, ESG ratings should not circumvent the fair allocation of fees by reallocating revenues to other entities within their group to reduce their fee contributions. The delegated acts will regulate the exemption thresholds and the amounts of registration and certification fees payable that should be reviewed as necessary to ensure that they reflect industry developments. They will make rating entities more transparent about the fees that they are charging to users of ESG ratings by disclosing their fee structures and that ESMA should ensure that the fees charged by ESG ratings providers are proportionate to the work they undertake.

42.03 The article points on the scope of delegated acts which will explain how ESMA calculates its budget for ESG ratings supervision and how it applies fees received from rating agencies against the expenses incurred. ESMA will publish a detailed overview of its costs so that ESG ratings and other stakeholders could better understand the basis for the sums budgeted against ESMA's expenses and how surpluses and shortfalls are accounted for in subsequent years. ESMA's budget for ESG ratings supervision in any given year will be driven by the activities that ESMA has planned for that year. Where increases are foreseen in ESMA's annual supervisory budget this may be due to increases in direct costs, such as staff numbers as well as increases in indirect costs, such as the costs of shared services like legal or information technology services. As the EU ESG rating industry is evolving it is normal that ESMA's supervisory costs may increase over time to reflect these changes. ESMA applies a universal budgeting approach, which means that income from fees is treated as general revenue. This is in line with the principle of universality defined in the EU Financial Regulation and is the standard practice of other partially fee funded EU agencies, as recommended by DG Budget of the European Commission. The main purpose of the rule is to ensure that the delegated acts accurately reflect ESMA's budgetary process and are consistent with the fees collection process across ESMA's supervisory mandates.

CHAPTER 5

COOPERATION BETWEEN ESMA AND THE COMPETENT AUTHORITIES

ARTICLE 43

DELEGATION OF TASKS BY ESMA TO THE COMPETENT AUTHORITIES

Andrea Miglionico

1. Where necessary for the proper performance of a supervisory task, ESMA may delegate the following supervisory tasks to the competent authority of a Member State in accordance with the guidelines issued by ESMA pursuant to Article 16 of Regulation (EU) No 1095/2010:
   (a) the power to request information in accordance with Article 32 of this Regulation;
   (b) the power to conduct investigations and on-site inspections in accordance with Articles 33 and 34 of this Regulation.

2. Prior to the delegation of a task in accordance with paragraph 1, ESMA shall consult the relevant competent authority about:
   (a) the scope of the task to be delegated;
   (b) the timetable for the performance of the task; and
   (c) the transmission of necessary information by and to ESMA.

3. ESMA shall reimburse the relevant competent authority for costs incurred as a result of carrying out delegated tasks. The costs to be reimbursed shall comprise all fixed costs, as well as variable costs related to the performance of the delegated tasks or the assistance provided by the competent authority to ESMA.

4. ESMA shall review any delegation made in accordance with paragraph 1 at appropriate intervals. ESMA may revoke a delegation at any time.

5. A delegation of tasks shall not affect the responsibility of ESMA nor limit ESMA's ability to conduct and oversee the delegated activity. ESMA shall not delegate supervisory responsibilities, including authorisation decisions, final assessments and follow-up decisions concerning infringements.

A. INTRODUCTION

43.01 The article provides a detailed and comprehensive overview on the process of delegation of supervisory duties by ESMA to national competent authorities (NCAs). It is a relevant provision which responds to the principles of collaboration and cooperation between ESMA, the competent authorities and the sectoral competent authorities, including the procedures and detailed conditions relating to the delegation of tasks. Paragraph 2 of the article establishes that ESMA needs to consult the relevant authorities before the delegation of a task in order to ensure the timeline and correct performance of duties. The article refers to the ESMA Regulation for the procedural matters on how NCAs request information and conduct investigations and on-site inspections. Paragraph 4 of the article regulates the costs of the delegated actions which need to be reimbursed to the NCA of a Member State for the performance of the delegated tasks or the assistance provided by the competent authority to ESMA. Interestingly, the provision makes clear that ESMA retains the power to review any decision to delegate tasks and to revoke a delegation at any time; further, the NCAs' supervisory delegated activities should not be an obstacle to ESMA's supervisory responsibilities. Paragraph 5 of the article highlights ESMA's central role to issue authorization decisions, final assessments and follow-up decisions concerning infringements. The aim of the provision is to allow NCAs to support ESMA in the supervision and enforcement regime when cases of ESG ratings require the direct intervention of NCAs. Similar scope is found in Article 30 of the CRAR ('Delegation of tasks by ESMA to competent authorities').

43.02 The provision ensures the fair and transparent delegation of supervisory tasks to avoid possible conflicts of interest and support objective supervision and decision-making. The main purpose is to establish a cooperation framework between ESMA, the competent authorities and the sectoral competent authorities for the purposes of the Regulation and of the relevant sectoral legislation, without prejudice to their respective supervisory powers. Proper consideration should not only be given to the fulfilment of the main objectives of supervision but also to the governance around the supervisory processes and functioning of the supervisory authority through which these decisions are made. Good governance is therefore required for the way supervisors are managed, assessed and held accountable.[1] The delegation of a task may be considered necessary if the proper performance of the specific supervisory task requires knowledge and experience with respect to local conditions, where these are available at the competent authority. The competent authority may perform delegated supervisory tasks with its own resources and capabilities or by using the services of third parties appointed by them. Before a delegation of a specific supervisory task, ESMA needs to consult the relevant competent authority. Similar to credit ratings, consultation generally will take place as soon as is practicable and at least nine weeks before performance of the task is to commence unless the parties agree to reduce this period.[2] ESMA will also provide details of the ESMA staff who will be responsible for coordinating the delegated task. ESMA will seek to resolve any concerns raised in the consultation before deciding to delegate the task, if necessary transferring the matter to senior staff in ESMA and the competent authority. In resolving the concerns raised, particular regard will be given to the resource available at the competent authority.

B. PROCEDURAL MATTERS OF THE DELEGATION OF TASKS

43.03 The cooperation framework is intended to build on the obligation of ESMA, the competent authorities and the sectoral competent authorities to cooperate where it is necessary for the purposes of the Regulation.[3] It also builds on ESMA's ability to delegate specific supervisory tasks to a competent authority. In this process, ESMA will provide the relevant competent authority with such information and guidance as may prove helpful to carry out the delegated task in good time. During the performance of the task, the competent authority may ask ESMA for any information that is necessary for the proper performance of the delegated task. ESMA will either provide the necessary information promptly or provide a reason why this is not possible and an indication of when the information will be provided. Usually, the competent authority performing the task should communicate any significant findings

---

1 For a commentary see Christopher P. Buttigieg, 'EU regulation and supervision of securities business: a critical analysis of the challenges faced by the National Competent Authorities of small EU and EEA EFTA Member States' (2020) 14(1) *Law and Financial Markets Review* 5–6.

2 ESMA, 'Cooperation including delegation between ESMA, the competent authorities and the sectoral competent authorities under Regulation (EU) No 513/2011 on credit rating agencies' (10 January 2012), Guidelines and Recommendations, ESMA/2011/188, https://www.esma.europa.eu/sites/default/files/library/2015/11/2011-188.pdf.

3 Federica Cacciatore, 'Patterns of Networked Enforcement in the European System of Financial Supervision: What is the New Role for the National Competent Authorities?' (2019) 10(3) *European Journal of Risk Regulation* 502–503.

to ESMA without undue delay. Upon completion of the task, the competent authority concerned should pass to ESMA all relevant information it obtained and do its best to provide prompt answers to any additional questions ESMA may have. When ESMA is planning an on-site inspection, it will notify the relevant competent authority as soon as ESMA has decided to conduct the inspection where possible. ESMA will inform the competent authority of the scope of the general investigation or of the on-site inspection and the expected level of assistance required. Except in urgent cases, the competent authority concerned should submit any request to attend an on-site inspection to ESMA in writing as soon as is practicable. Where a person opposes an on-site inspection, the competent authority concerned should afford officials of and other persons authorized by ESMA the necessary assistance. This should include requesting, where appropriate, the assistance of the police or of an equivalent enforcement authority, so as to enable ESMA to conduct its on-site inspection. In case of cooperation by way of assistance provided by a competent authority, ESMA will provide the core resourcing, while competent authorities to facilitate the execution of tasks.

ARTICLE 44

EXCHANGE OF INFORMATION

Andrea Miglionico

ESMA and the competent authorities shall, without undue delay, provide each other with the information required for carrying out their duties under this Regulation or their respective supervisory responsibility and mandates.

A. THE REGIME OF EXCHANGE OF INFORMATION

44.01 This article complements the provision of delegation of tasks between authorities by providing the obligation to exchange information required for undertaking the supervisory duties. This duty responds to the principle of correct and fair cooperation between ESMA and NCAs which should not delay the performance of respective supervisory responsibility and mandates.[1] The cooperation obligation and the information to be exchanged among competent authorities should be of a sufficient scope and nature to allow them to effectively discharge their supervisory, investigatory and sanctioning duties. The article intends to ensure that information supplied should be used solely for the purposes of delegated tasks. Requests to ESMA for information should be sent to the competent unit. NCAs should notify ESMA's contact point to which the EU authority should submit any requests for information. It is essential that, subject to national and Union law governing the protection of confidentiality of information and the processing of personal data, competent

1 ESMA, 'Guidelines on cooperation arrangements and information exchange between competent authorities and between competent authorities and ESMA' (27 March 2014), ESMA/2014/298, https://www.esma.europa.eu/document/guidelines-cooperation-arrangements-and-information-exchange-between-competent-authorities.

authorities are able to cooperate and exchange information throughout the entire process of their activities. This should include the exchange of relevant reports and specific information on the respective supervised entities, as well as information on on-going inspections or investigations and the imposition of sanctions.[2]

Similar to credit ratings, requests for information should, to the extent possible, specify: a precise description of their scope; the purpose for which the information is sought and why it will be of assistance; if the request results from investigations of violations of any laws or regulations, a short description of the relevant provisions that may have been violated and, if known, a list of the persons or institutions believed to possess the information sought; an indication of the sensitivity of the information contained in the request and whether the identity of the requester can be disclosed to persons who may need to be approached for information; whether the requester is or has been in contact with any other authority or law enforcement agency in the relevant Member State in relation to the subject matter of the request; any other authority which has an active interest in the subject matter of the request; places where the information may be obtained and; an indication of the urgency of the request, or the desired time period for the reply. Recipients of requests should: take all reasonable steps to obtain and provide the information sought within any time period indicated, to the extent permitted by law; use the relevant means at its disposal for the execution of the request, consulting and agreeing with the requester on the types of enquiry that may be necessary for the execution of a request. To the extent permitted by law, the requester should provide the recipient of the request with such further assistance as may reasonably be required for the efficient execution of the request including the provision of further information as to the circumstances surrounding the request, staff or other resources. ESMA, competent authorities, and all persons who work or who have worked for ESMA, for the competent authorities or for any other person to whom ESMA has delegated tasks, including auditors and experts contracted by ESMA are subject to the obligation of professional secrecy. **44.02**

It is worth noting that the ESMA has published the text of a new multilateral memorandum of understanding (MMoU) between EEA national competent authorities, and between national competent authorities and ESMA which **44.03**

2 ESMA, 'Final report on draft technical standards on cooperation, exchange of information and notification between competent authorities and ESMA, the EBA and EIOPA under the Securitisation Regulation' (8 January 2019), ESMA33-128-557, https://www.esma.europa.eu/document/final-report-draft-technical-standards-cooperation-exchange-information-and-notification.

entered into force on 29 May 2014.[3] The Agreement created a clear framework for exchanging information between the ESMA and NCAs while enhancing the effectiveness of their supervisory practices.[4] It has been signed by 33 authorities in the securities and markets area. The new MMoU was agreed in view of the increasing internationalization, harmonization and interdependence of financial services and markets in the European Union. It is designed to facilitate cooperation arrangements and the exchange of information between national competent authorities, and between national competent authorities and ESMA, in the application of their responsibilities under Union law relating to the securities and markets area. It also updates and replaces a previous agreement on the Exchange of Information and Surveillance of Securities Activities agreed by the members of the Committee of European Securities Regulators (formerly the Forum of European Securities Commissions) entered into by those members on 26 January 1999. The MMoU provides a set of guidelines where cooperation and exchange of information between competent authorities and the ESMA is needed. It serves to provide a coordinated and cohesive approach between the ESMA and competent authorities in the exchange of information and when cooperating for the purpose of oversight activities to ensure efficiency and consistency as well as to avoid duplication. Further, it aims to foster a common approach to the rules of procedure and timelines that apply in relation to cooperation and information exchange, including roles and responsibilities and means for cooperation and information exchange. The cooperation and information exchange should take into account a preventive and risk-based approach which should lead to a balanced allocation of tasks and responsibilities between the ESMA and competent authorities and should make the best use of the human resources and technical expertise available in each of the ESMA and competent authorities.

44.04 The article highlights the need of consistent, efficient and effective practices on the oversight cooperation and information exchange between ESMA and competent authorities. The practical details of the cooperation and information sharing between ESMA and competent authorities may be subject to various

3 ESMA, 'Multilateral Memorandum of Understanding on Cooperation Arrangements and Exchange of Information' ESMA/2014/608, https://www.esma.europa.eu/document/mmou-cooperation-arrangements-and-exchange-information.

4 This regulatory framework is part of the EU legislator's wider efforts to enhance the cooperation and information exchange between supervisors through a clear legal mandate. To fulfil this mandate, the ESMA together with the NCAs, have developed this Multilateral Agreement, which contains provisions on the type of information and underlying process for exchanging it; confidentiality and data protection provisions; situations where the request for information can be refused; means of communication and language used in the information exchange; the signing process; and the settlement of disputes procedures.

target operating models. Competent authorities shall closely coordinate their supervision in order to identify and remedy infringements of this Regulation, develop and promote best practices, facilitate collaboration, foster consistency of interpretation and provide cross-jurisdictional assessments in the event of any disagreements.

ARTICLE 45

NOTIFICATIONS AND SUSPENSION REQUESTS BY THE COMPETENT AUTHORITIES

Andrea Miglionico

1. **A competent authority of a Member State that finds that acts infringing this Regulation are being, or have been, carried out by an ESG rating provider on the territory of its own or of another Member State shall inform ESMA thereof. Where a competent authority considers it appropriate for investigatory purposes, that competent authority may suggest to ESMA that it assess the need to use the powers under Article 32 in relation to the ESG rating provider involved in those acts.**
2. **ESMA shall take appropriate action. ESMA shall inform the notifying competent authority of the outcome and, as far as possible, of any significant interim developments.**
3. **A notifying competent authority of a Member State that considers that an ESG rating provider listed in the register referred to in Article 14 whose ESG ratings are used within the territory of that Member State has infringed this Regulation in such a way that the protection of investors or the stability of the financial system in that Member State is significantly impacted, may request ESMA to suspend the provision of ESG ratings by the ESG rating provider concerned. The notifying competent authority shall provide ESMA with full reasons for its request.**
4. **Where ESMA considers that the request referred to in paragraph 3 is not justified, it shall inform the notifying competent authority thereof in writing, setting out the reasons for its opinion. Where ESMA considers that the request is justified, it shall take appropriate measures to resolve the issue and it shall inform the notifying competent authority thereof in writing.**

A. INTRODUCTION

45.01 The article establishes the regime of notifications between ESMA and NCAs in case of infringement by an ESG rating provider of the requirements set in this Regulation. The provision articulates the procedural matters in case NCAs considers appropriate to impose a sanction and takes enforcement action. The article states that ESMA retains the power to assess whether the findings of NCAs result into an infringement and if it is appropriate to proceed with an outcome of investigation. It is evident that the provision empowers ESMA to monitor the whole process in view to issue an agreed decision; however, in case the infringement can significantly impact the stability and integrity of financial system, and the protection of investors the NCA may request the suspension of ESG ratings by the ESG rating provider involved. In this context, the role of ESMA is to evaluate the emergency of measure and the reasons for request in order to resolve the issue. The exchange of information, opinions, findings, evidence must be in writing and detailed on the reasons to proceed with investigatory and enforcement powers. The provision responds to the principle of transparency in the cooperation between ESMA and the competent authorities which is fundamental for correct application of the procedure. The regime of notification is part of the surveillance and monitoring system of ESG ratings and complements supervisory measures and penalties. Similar scope is found in Article 31 of the CRAR ('Notifications and suspension requests by competent authorities'). In the course of notification and suspension requests, ESMA is responsible only for the accurate reproduction of the content of the notifications received from the relevant competent authorities. Further, ESMA is not able to provide any representation or warranty that the content of the notification is complete, accurate or up to date. The responsibility for the completeness and accuracy of the content of the notifications lies with the national competent authority mentioned in the request. In case of contested opinions about the findings of investigation, the final decision will be taken by ESMA according to the supervisory powers attributed by this Regulation. ESMA can issue guidelines to promote coordinated action between supervisory authorities; specifically to support NCAs for supervising complaint-handling by firms in their jurisdiction and improve harmonization on the findings of investigations which can vary according to the local laws and regulations as there is no uniformity across Member States on the decisions to suspend or remove a registered ESG rating provider.[1]

B. THE NOTIFICATION AND SUSPENSION REGIME

45.02 The article aims to afford investors across all Member States the same level of protection regardless of where they rely on ESG rating information. The competent authority is obliged to inform the competent authority of each other Member State: however, there is no obligation on the other competent authorities to follow its decision. The competent authority must immediately make its decision public and inform ESMA and all other competent authorities. All other competent authorities are obliged to take similar action, unless it would be likely to cause significant damage to the interests of the investors or the orderly functioning of the financial markets. The intended scope of this article is the facilitation of the task of supervision of rating providers through promotion of effective communication between competent authorities and ESMA. They should establish adequate processes and be aware of them in order to build and ensure effective communication; also they should contribute to developing a mutual understanding of their respective roles and responsibilities. In this way, ESMA fulfils its mission to enhance investor protection and promote stable and orderly financial markets by facilitating access to relevant investigatory documents for market participants, regulators and the general public.[2]

45.03 The investigatory and enforcement powers mandated to NCAs reflect a partial delegation of authority from ESMA in cases where the expertise and technical guidance of local authorities can address timely the infringement. These powers mainly apply only in specific, exceptional or emergency scenarios which are not intended to alter or affect the supervisory powers of ESMA which displays the ultimate control over the findings presented by the authorities. However, this powerful role to retain the final decision over the investigation and suspension requests advanced by NCAs 'appear to offer the ESAs the ability to interfere in Member State sovereignty, and in particular the activities of

1 Hans Christoph Grigoleit, 'Sanctions and Degree of Harmonization' in Rüdiger Veil (ed), *Regulating EU Capital Markets Union: Volume I: Fundamentals of a European Code* (Oxford: Oxford University Press 2024) 89–90.

2 Andreas Witte, 'Standing and Judicial Review in the New EU Financial Markets Architecture' (2015) 1(2) *Journal of Financial Regulation* 226.

NCAs, in significant ways.'[3] The Regulation centralizes to ESMA all supervisory and enforcement powers raising doubts on the arbitrary discretion in taking actions over the ESG ratings. What is missing is a balanced regime of the discharge of duties between the authorities involved in the procedure. It seems that limited powers are attributed to NCAs while they are recognized as strategic players in detecting infringements of ratings providers operating in the Member State. ESMA guidelines or consultation papers would likely to clarify the position of NCAs in case of urgent investigatory process which lead to sanctions in the local jurisdictions.

3 Jennifer Payne, 'The institutional design of financial supervision and financial stability' in Fabian Amtenbrink, Christoph Herrmann and René Repasi (eds), *The EU Law of Economic and Monetary Union* (Oxford: Oxford University Press 2020) 582.

ARTICLE 46

PROFESSIONAL SECRECY

Andrea Miglionico

1. **The obligation of professional secrecy shall apply to ESMA, the competent authorities and all persons who work or who have worked for ESMA, for the competent authorities or for any other person to whom ESMA has delegated tasks, including auditors and experts contracted by ESMA. Information covered by professional secrecy shall not be disclosed to any other person or authority except by virtue of Union or national law.**
2. **All information exchanged under this Regulation between ESMA, the competent authorities, EBA, EIOPA, and the European Systemic Risk Board established by Regulation (EU) No 1092/2010 of the European Parliament and of the Council,[1] that concerns business or operational conditions or other economic or personal affairs shall be considered confidential, except where:**
   - **(a) ESMA or the competent authority or another authority or body concerned states at the time of communication that such information can be disclosed;**
   - **(b) disclosure of such information is necessary for legal proceedings;**
   - **(c) the information disclosed is used in a summary or in an aggregate form in which individual financial market participants cannot be identified.**

1 Regulation (EU) No 1092/2010 of the European Parliament and of the Council of 24 November 2010 on European Union macro-prudential oversight of the financial system and establishing a European Systemic Risk Board (OJ L 331, 15.12.2010, p. 1).

A. INTRODUCTION

The article establishes the confidentiality regime in the exchange of information between ESMA and NCAs which extends to all parties involved e.g. persons to whom ESMA has delegated tasks or contracted persons such as auditors and experts. The provision regulates the framework of information disclosure which concerns business or operational conditions or other economic or personal affairs.[2] The article makes clear that information covered by professional secrecy shall not be disclosed to any other person or authority unless the Union or national law require to disclose.[3] Paragraph 2 of the article provides a few exceptions to this mandatory rule when disclosure is allowed by the ESMA or the competent authority or another authority or body concerned, in case it is necessary for legal proceedings for the adoption of decisions and for circumstances where the information disclosed is used as an excerpt which cannot be identified.[4] Similar scope is found in Article 32 of the CRAR ('Professional secrecy'). **46.01**

B. OBLIGATION OF PROFESSIONAL SECRECY

The article states that ESMA, competent authorities, and all persons who work or who have worked for ESMA, for the competent authorities or for any other person to whom ESMA has delegated tasks, including auditors and experts contracted by ESMA are subject to the obligation of professional secrecy. It is implicit that all non-staff involved in the Authority's activities should abide by the duty of professional secrecy, which entails the obligation not to disclose information received in this official capacity, unless it is explicitly permitted.[5] Preserving high standards of professional secrecy with respect to all non-staff involved in the Authority's activities is crucial for the Authority's credibility and reputation. Anyone attending their meetings should respect their **46.02**

---

2 René Smits and Nikolai Badenhoop, 'Towards a Single Standard of Professional Secrecy for Financial Sector Supervisory Authorities: A Reform Proposal' (2019) 44(3) *European Law Review* 295.

3 Emilia Korkea-aho and Päivi Leino, 'Who owns the information held by EU agencies? Weed killers, commercially sensitive information and transparent and participatory governance' (2017) 54(4) *Common Market Law Review* 1059.

4 Catherine Malecki, 'The EU proposal for a Regulation on the transparency and integrity of ESG rating activities on 13 June 2023: the missing piece of sustainable finance regulation' (2023) 17(2) *Law and Financial Markets Review* 156.

5 ESMA, 'Adopting Rules of Procedure on Professional Secrecy for Non-Staff, and repealing Management Board Decision on Professional Secrecy of 11 January 2011 (ESMA/2011/MB/4)' (25 January 2017), ESMA40-1432018523-304.

confidentiality and comply with the rules of procedure of the Authority as regards the obligation of professional secrecy. Similarly, persons appointed by the members of the Board of Supervisors to ESMA groups should also respect the confidentiality of the documents and information they have been granted access to.[6] If the obligation of professional secrecy is breached by a person who is involved in the process, the Authority should be able to take proportionate action in order to minimize the possibility that such a breach occurs again. However, the Authority is not in a position to take any direct action against a staff member of national competent authority. The Authority is only empowered to recommend action against those individuals in so far as they participate in an ESMA group as members or are advisers to the members and observers of the Board of Supervisors and the Management Board. Parties indicated in this Article whilst performing their duties must observe absolute confidentiality concerning ESMA's affairs, other than as required to perform their usual duties; keep information confidential, even if it is favourable and not adverse to the financial market participant concerned; take particular care in casual, social or other contact with journalists, financial market participants and individuals and other people operating in the financial markets; and seek guidance if they are at all uncertain as to whether confidential information can be disclosed. All other persons carrying out tasks for ESMA on a contractual basis are subject to the requirements of professional secrecy according to Article 339 of the TFEU and the relevant provisions in Union legislation, in particular Union legislation within ESMA's scope of action.

C. DISCLOSURE OF CONFIDENTIAL INFORMATION

46.03 All the information that is acquired by or exchanged between ESMA, the competent authorities, the sectoral competent authorities or other authorities and bodies referred to this article of the Regulation shall be considered confidential. Exceptions apply where ESMA or the competent authority or other authority or body concerned states at the time of communication that such information may be disclosed or where such disclosure is necessary for legal proceedings (e.g. enforcement of the delegated act). With prior consent of ESMA, competent authorities are permitted to use the services of third parties where they deem it appropriate for performing delegated tasks and may

6 In the event a member to an ESMA group fails to comply with this duty, the replacement should be made in reasonable time.

only disclose confidential information to such third parties, if the third party in question is subject to professional secrecy. Recipients of information should obtain the prior consent of the authority which provided the information if they propose to use it for any other purpose. The provision states that information can be used or disclosed where such use or disclosure is required in order to comply with the obligations under the Regulation or other legislation.

TITLE IV

DELEGATED AND IMPLEMENTING ACTS

ARTICLE 47

EXERCISE AND REVOCATION OF THE DELEGATION AND OBJECTIONS TO DELEGATED ACTS

Andrea Miglionico

1. The power to adopt delegated acts is conferred on the Commission subject to the conditions laid down in this Article.
2. The power to adopt delegated acts referred to in Article 10(3), Article 39(9) and Article 42(2) shall be conferred on the Commission for a period of five years from 1 January 2025. The Commission shall draw up a report in respect of the delegation of power not later than nine months before the end of that five-year period. The delegation of power shall be tacitly extended for periods of an identical duration, unless the European Parliament or the Council opposes such extension not later than three months before the end of each period.
3. The delegation of power referred to in Article 10(3), Article 39(9) and Article 42(2) may be revoked at any time by the European Parliament or by the Council. A decision to revoke shall put an end to the delegation of the power specified in that decision. It shall take effect the day following the publication of the decision in the Official Journal of the European Union or at a later date specified therein. It shall not affect the validity of any delegated acts already in force.
4. Before adopting a delegated act, the Commission shall consult experts designated by each Member State in accordance with the principles laid down in the Interinstitutional Agreement of 13 April 2016 on Better Law-Making.
5. As soon as it adopts a delegated act, the Commission shall notify it simultaneously to the European Parliament and to the Council.
6. A delegated act adopted pursuant to Article 10(3), Article 39(9) and Article 42(2) shall enter into force only if no objection has been expressed either by the European Parliament or by the Council within a period of three months of notification of that act to the European Parliament

and the Council or if, before the expiry of that period, the European Parliament and the Council have both informed the Commission that they will not object. That period shall be extended by three months at the initiative of the European Parliament or of the Council.

7. **If, on expiry of the period referred to in paragraph 6, neither the European Parliament nor the Council has objected to the delegated act, it shall be published in the Official Journal of the European Union and shall enter into force on the date stated therein. The delegated act may be published in the Official Journal of the European Union and enter into force before the expiry of that period if the European Parliament and the Council have both informed the Commission of their intention not to raise objections.**
8. **If either the European Parliament or the Council objects to the delegated act within the period referred to in paragraph 1, it shall not enter into force. In accordance with Article 296 TFEU, the institution which objects shall state the reasons for objecting to the delegated act.**

A. INTRODUCTION

47.01 The article empowers the EU Commission to adopt delegated acts for the period of five years according to the requirements set in this Regulation: to issue an equivalence decision for compliance of registered ESG rating providers in a third country, to impose fines or periodic penalty payments, and to determine the amount of an individual fee proportionate to the annual net turnover of the ESG rating provider concerned. The provision establishes a delegation of power from ESMA to the Commission in certain areas where it is needed a cooperation between EU institutions to facilitate simplification of procedural matters in line with the principles of Better Regulation[1] and Better

1 Better regulation regards the process of law-making and refers to the substance, implementation and enforcement of EU laws. Laws need to be targeted, proportionate, predictable and clear – as does their enforcement and implementation. See Zach Meyers, 'Better regulation in Europe. An action plan for the next Commission' (March 2024), https://www.cer.eu/publications/archive/policy-brief/2024/better-regulation-europe-action-plan.

Law-Making.[2] The Commission can conduct consultation of Member States' experts, as well as public consultations prior to the adoption of delegated acts.[3] However, this power is subject to the control of European Parliament and Council which can revoke the mandate at any time and have the authority to approve or object the delegated acts. The Commission has obligations to inform timely the Parliament and Council about the adoption of a delegated act.

B. THE DELEGATION OF POWERS TO THE EU COMMISSION

The article regulates the Commission's rule-making power to adopt delegated **47.02** or implementing acts according to the EU Better Regulation agenda.[4] It is a relevant provision that highlights the institutional role of the Parliament and Council in supervising the technical tasks attributed to Commission. The transfer of delegated authority responds to the simplification of the existing system of Commission rule-making. As noted, 'the procedures for the adoption of delegated and implementing acts remained the subject of interinstitutional bargaining' in which the EU Institutions allocate diverse negotiating interests.[5] The Commission prepares and adopts delegated acts after consulting expert groups, composed of representatives from each EU country, which

2 Interinstitutional Agreement between the European Parliament, the Council of the European Union and the European Commission on Better Law-Making (OJ L 123, 2016). It aims to improve the way the EU makes laws by ensuring that the European Parliament, the Council and the European Commission are committed to sincere and transparent cooperation throughout the entire legislative cycle. The agreement aims to ensure that EU policies and laws achieve their objectives at minimum cost and administrative burden.

3 The Agreement provides that Parliament and the Council have equal access to information regarding such expert consultations and systematic access to the meetings of such expert groups. See Laura Tilindyte, 'Interinstitutional Agreement on Better Law-Making' (3 March 2016), European Parliamentary Research Service, PE 579.06, https://www.europarl.europa.eu/RegData/etudes/ATAG/2016/579061/EPRS_ATA(2016)579061_EN.pdf.

4 Delegated acts are defined by the Treaties as non-legislative acts of general application. They can only be adopted if there is a delegation of powers contained in a legislative act. A delegated act is a non-legislative act adopted by the Commission to supplement or amend certain non-essential elements of a legislative act. This allows the Commission to react quickly and flexibly, for instance, to regulatory requirements using its technical knowledge. Implementing acts are not defined as to their legal nature, but to their purpose - where uniform conditions for implementing legally binding Union acts are needed. Under no circumstances may an implementing act modify anything in the basic act. See Micaela Del Monte and Rafał Mańko, 'Understanding delegated and implementing acts' (July 2021), European Parliamentary Research Service, PE 690.709, https://www.europarl.europa.eu/RegData/etudes/BRIE/2021/690709/EPRS_BRI(2021)690709_EN.pdf.

5 Eljalill Tauschinsky and Wolfgang Weiß (eds), *The Legislative Choice Between Delegated and Implementing Acts in EU Law* (Edward Elgar 2018) 9–10.

meet on a regular or occasional basis.[6] The committee enables EU countries to oversee the Commissions work as it adopts an implementing act – a procedure referred to 'comitology.'[7] As part of the Commission's better regulation agenda, citizens and other stakeholders can provide feedback on the draft text of an implementing act for four weeks before the relevant committee votes to accept or reject it. The Commission adopts delegated acts on the basis of a delegation granted in the text of an EU law.[8] The Commission's power to adopt delegated acts is limited to certain requirements: the delegated act cannot change the essential elements of the law; the legislative act must define the objectives, content, scope and duration of the delegation of power; Parliament and Council may revoke the delegation or express objections to the delegated act.[9] Once the Commission has adopted the act, Parliament and Council have a period of three months to formulate any objections. If they do not, the delegated act enters into force. Adopted acts contain an 'explanatory memorandum' summarizing the feedback received and how it was used. Delegated acts differ from implementing acts with regard to the procedural aspects of their adoption (after consulting Member States' experts, but their view is not binding). The implementing acts differ in the comitology procedure, where experts designated by the Member States, sitting on specialized committees, can object to a draft implementing act. In the case of delegated acts, however, the Parliament and Council can introduce, in the delegation itself, a right to object to a draft act or even to revoke the delegation altogether. Delegated and implementing acts are subject to judicial review by the Court of Justice of the EU which controls their conformity with the basic act.

C. THE PRINCIPLE OF BETTER LAW-MAKING

47.03 The principle of Better Law-Making established in the Interinstitutional Agreement on Better Regulation between the EU institutions is designed to make cooperation between them smoother and clearer.[10] The Agreement

6 European Commission, 'Implementing and delegated acts,' https://commission.europa.eu/law/law-making-process/adopting-eu-law/implementing-and-delegated-acts_en.

7 Comitology refers to a set of procedures that enable EU countries, via special committees, to oversee how the European Commission adopts implementing acts.

8 For a commentary see François Lafarge, 'The impact of the Better Regulation policy on EU delegated and implementing acts rule-making' in Eljalill Tauschinsky and Wolfgang Weiβ (eds), *The Legislative Choice Between Delegated and Implementing Acts in EU Law* (Edward Elgar 2018) 65–66.

9 Giulia Gallinella and Thomas Christiansen, 'Delegated Rule-making in Times of Crisis: New Challenges for Democratic Scrutiny?' (2024) 15(4) *European Journal of Risk Regulation* 812.

10 It has been adopted in the framework of the Better Regulation Agenda and has replaced the 2003 Interinstitutional agreement on better law-making. The Agreement underlines the contribution of better

sets rules to clarify and facilitate the use of delegated and implementing acts according to Articles 290 and 291 of the TFEU and contains an annex with standard clauses to this effect.[11] Specifically, it was agreed that the Commission consults EU countries' experts in the preparation of delegated acts, and Parliament and Council experts have equal access to all related meetings and documents; there is a prompt alignment of all pre-Lisbon Treaty files, a further negotiation takes place to specify non-binding delineation criteria for delegated and implementing acts, and a public register for delegated acts is set up (the Interinstitutional Register of Delegated Acts, which gives access to the various steps in the preparation, adoption, scrutiny and publication of delegated acts, as well as to the planning, adoption and publication of implementing acts).[12] The better law-making agreement aims to improve the way the EU legislates and to ensure that the legislation better serves citizens and businesses.[13] It should make the legislative process more transparent open to stakeholder input (e.g. consultation process, guidelines, opinions) and easier to follow. It also helps assess the impact of EU law for small and medium-sized enterprises, local industry and ordinary citizens. It is a regulatory tool of collaboration and cooperation between the EU institutions. One of the main aims of the better law-making agreement, or 'better regulation' or 'smart regulation' is to ensure that EU policies and laws achieve their objectives at minimum cost and administrative burden.[14] It is a way of working to ensure that political decisions are prepared in an open, transparent manner, informed by the best available evidence and backed by the comprehensive involvement of stakeholders. Better regulation covers the whole policy cycle – policy design and preparation, adoption, implementation, application, evaluation and revision. For each phase of this cycle, there are specific principles, objectives, tools and procedures to make sure that the EU has the best regulation possible.

---

regulation tools to the better quality of legislation, including ex-ante impact assessment, stakeholder consultation and ex-post evaluation of legislation.

11 María José Martínez Iglesias, 'Better law-making and the interinstitutional (dis)agreements: Some comments' (2020) 26 (1-2) *European Law Journal* 108–109.

12 See https://webgate.ec.europa.eu/regdel/#/home. A new Interinstitutional Register of Delegated Acts was launched in December 2017. It provides a complete view of the lifecycle of delegated acts and allows users to subscribe in order to receive notifications about the files of their interest.

13 European Council, 'Better law-making agreement,' https://www.consilium.europa.eu/en/policies/better-regulation/#:~:text=The%20better%20law-making%20agreement%20aims%20to%20improve%20the,open%20to%20stakeholder%20input%20and%20easier%20to%20follow.

14 Mark Dawson, 'Better regulation and the future of EU regulatory law and politics' (2016) 53(5) *Common Market Law Review* 1209.

ARTICLE 48

COMMITTEE PROCEDURE

Andrea Miglionico

1. The Commission shall be assisted by the European Securities Committee established by Commission Decision 2001/528/EC.[1] That committee shall be a committee within the meaning of Regulation (EU) No 182/2011 of the European Parliament and of the Council.[2]

2. Where reference is made to this paragraph, Article 5 of Regulation (EU) No 182/2011 shall apply.

A. PROCEDURAL MATTERS

48.01 The article defines the procedure of Commission's rule-making decision to adopt delegated or implement acts by providing the assistance of the European Securities Committee (ESC). It mandates the ESC to be regulated under the rules governing mechanisms for control by Member States of the Commission's exercise of implementing powers. This control takes place in line with the 'comitology' system,[3] which refers to the ESC that the Commission consults

1 Commission Decision 2001/528/EC of 6 June 2001 establishing the European Securities Committee (OJ L 191, 13.7.2001, p. 45).

2 Regulation (EU) No 182/2011 of the European Parliament and of the Council of 16 February 2011 laying down the rules and general principles concerning mechanisms for control by Member States of the Commission's exercise of implementing powers (OJ L 55, 28.2.2011, p. 13).

3 Comitology committees are set up by the legislator (Council and European Parliament or Council alone). They include one representative from every EU country and are chaired by a Commission official. Each committee decides its operating procedures, based on standard committee rules of procedure. Commission departments submit draft implementing acts to the responsible committees for an opinion. Before each meeting, the Commission sends national authorities the invitation, agenda and draft implementing act. After the meeting, the Commission publishes the voting results and the summary record of the meeting

on draft implementing acts.[4] Specifically, the provision refers to the examination procedure by which the ESC provides its opinion for acts to be adopted on a proposal from the Commission. Where the committee delivers a positive opinion, the Commission shall adopt the draft implementing act but needs conduct consultations with the Member States. The examination procedure is mainly used for implementing acts of general scope and implementing acts with a potentially significant impact or referring to certain policy fields (e.g. agriculture, fisheries, environment, health, common commercial policy and taxation).[5] The whole procedure refers to Article 291 of the TFEU, which allows the Commission to adopt implementing measures for a legal act when uniform conditions of implementation are necessary.[6] The basic legal act must explicitly confer on the Commission the power to adopt implementing acts. Similar provision for credit ratings is found in Article 38 of the CRAR ('Committee procedure').

B. THE EXAMINATION PROCEDURE

In the examination procedure, the committee delivers its opinion by qualified majority (i.e. 55% of EU countries representing at least 65% of the total EU population). If the committee's opinion is positive, the Commission adopts the act; in case of negative opinion the Commission does not adopt the implementing act. Whether the ESC does not provide an opinion, the Commission may adopt the draft implementing act with the exception of the cases specified in the comitology regulation. In the event of a negative ESC opinion or in the absence of a committee opinion preventing the adoption of the implementing act, the Commission has either one month to submit the draft measure to the appeal committee, also made up of Member States' representatives, or two months to submit an amended version of the draft implementing act to **48.02**

in the comitology register. The Commission publishes an annual report on the work of the comitology committees, which details their activities in each policy sector.

4 In 2017 the European Commission adopted a proposal amending the 'Comitology Regulation' in order to increase the transparency and accountability of the decision-making process leading to the adoption of implementing acts. See Rafał Mańko, 'Reform of the Comitology Regulation' (March 2021), European Parliamentary Research Service, PE 689.360, https://www.europarl.europa.eu/RegData/etudes/BRIE/2021/689360/EPRS_BRI(2021)689360_EN.pdf.

5 See 'Mechanisms for control of the European Commission's exercise of implementing powers,' https://eur-lex.europa.eu/EN/legal-content/summary/mechanisms-for-control-of-the-european-commission-s-exercise-of-implementing-powers.html.

6 Gijs Jan Brandsma, 'Delegated and implementing acts: rule-making by the Commission' in Gijs J. Brandsma (ed), *Handbook on European Union Public Administration* (Edward Elgar 2024) 253–254.

the same committee.[7] The Commission can only adopt an implementing act supported by a qualified majority of the committee. If the committee opposes an implementing act or if it does not adopt an opinion, the Commission may only adopt the implementing act under specific conditions; there are several possibilities, including an appeal committee. Member States have the possibility to impede, as a first step, the Commission from adopting an implementing act. The examination procedure should be used in particular if it concerns an implementing act of general scope, or relates to programmes with substantial implications.[8] If the Commission is prevented from adopting a proposed implementing act (particularly where the comitology committee voted against it), it can refer the case to the appeal committee. The appeal committee functions in a similar way to the other comitology committees: it is made up of EU countries' representatives but at a higher level of representation. It is chaired by the Commission and follows the same voting rules. It gives EU countries the opportunity to have a second discussion; if the appeal committee rules against the Commission's proposed implementing act, the Commission must abide by its decision. In addition to EU member countries through the comitology committees, the Commission's implementing powers are also subject to supplementary checks by the European Parliament and EU Council, which have a right of information (all proposed Commission actions discussed in the committees are simultaneously disclosed to Parliament and Council), and a right of scrutiny (where Commission actions relate to a legislative act passed by the ordinary legislative procedure, Parliament and Council can object to the proposed implementing act if it exceeds the Commission's powers defined in the initial act). The Commission is then obliged to review its proposed act in the light of this input and decide whether to maintain, amend or withdraw it.[9]

C. THE EUROPEAN SECURITIES COMMITTEE

48.03 The establishment of the supervisory and regulatory committees was designed to facilitate the achievement of a single market in financial services according

7 European Council, 'Implementing and delegated acts,' https://www.consilium.europa.eu/en/council-eu/decision-making/implementing-and-delegated-acts/.

8 European Parliament, 'Handbook on delegated and implementing acts' (February 2013), https://www.aaronmcloughlin.com/wp-content/uploads/2018/04/EP-Handbook-on-Delegated-and-Implementing-Acts.pdf.

9 European Commission, 'Comitology,' https://commission.europa.eu/law/law-making-process/adopting-eu-law/implementing-and-delegated-acts/comitology_en.

to the regulatory framework set in the Financial Services Action Plan.[10] The committees' law-making role reflects the practice of delegated legislation adopted by the executive and having the same legal force as parliamentary legislation. The ESC fulfils both comitology and advisory functions; it assists the Commission in adopting implementing measures for EU Directives and provides advice on policy issues in the securities field. The ESC responds to the need to support the European Commission in regulating and supervising of financial services and securities markets. Its creation meets the needs of the four-level regulatory framework advocated in the report by the Committee of Wise Men, the Lamfalussy report in 2001.[11] The ESC is a body for consultation and reflection and it is responsible for advising the Commission on policy issues and draft proposals which it could adopt in the field of securities.[12] As an advisory body, it participates in preparing and applying the measures for implementing the framework principles laid down in the relevant directives and regulations. As it oversees developments on securities markets, this advisory committee participates in drawing up the implementing measures for the framework principles. It is also responsible for assessing risks which represent a major factor in financial stability.

10 Commission Communication of 11 May 1999 entitled 'Implementing the framework for financial markets: action plan' COM(1999) 232 final.

11 Alexandre Lamfalussy, 'Reflections on the Regulation of European Securities Markets' (2001) SUERF Studies, No. 14, https://www.econstor.eu/bitstream/10419/163446/1/suerf-study-14.pdf.

12 The ESC is composed of high-level representatives of Member States and is chaired by a representative of the Commission. Observers from the European Central Bank, the Committee of European Securities Regulators, the EFTA countries and the candidate countries are also invited to attend. The ESC is run by the European Commission and generally meets once a month. See 'Securities markets: Advisory, regulatory and supervisory committee,' https://eur-lex.europa.eu/EN/legal-content/summary/securities-markets-advisory-regulatory-and-supervisory-committee.html#:~:text=The%20ESC%20was%20set%20up%20in%202001%20to,of%20Wise%20Men%2C%20the%20Lamfalussy%20report%20in%202001.

ARTICLE 49

AMENDMENT TO REGULATION (EU) 2019/2088

Andrea Miglionico

In Article 13 of Regulation (EU) 2019/2088, the following paragraph is added:

3. Where a financial market participant or a financial adviser issues and discloses to third parties an ESG rating, as defined in Article 3, point (1), of Regulation (EU) 2024/3005 of the European Parliament and of the Council,[1] as part of its marketing communications, it shall include on its website the same information as that required by point 1 of Annex III to that Regulation and it shall disclose in those marketing communications a link to those website disclosures.

The ESAs shall, through the Joint Committee, develop draft regulatory technical standards to specify the information referred to in the first subparagraph of this paragraph, taking into account the information already disclosed pursuant to Article 10 of this Regulation.

The ESAs shall submit the draft regulatory technical standards referred to in the second subparagraph to the Commission.

Power is delegated to the Commission to supplement this Regulation by adopting the regulatory technical standards referred to in the second subparagraph of this paragraph, in accordance with Articles 10 to 14 of Regulations (EU) No 1093/2010, (EU) No 1094/2010 and (EU) No 1095/2010.

1 Regulation (EU) 2024/3005 of the European Parliament and of the Council of 27 November 2024 on the transparency and integrity of Environmental, Social and Governance (ESG) rating activities, and amending Regulations (EU) 2019/2088 and (EU) No 2023/2859 (OJ L, 2024/3005, 12.12.2024, ELI: http://data.europa.eu/eli/reg/2024/3005/oj).

A. SUSTAINABILITY DISCLOSURES

The article amends Regulation (EU) 2019/2088 on sustainability-related disclosures in the financial services sector (SFDR), by adding a provision to Article 13 of the SFDR.[2] Specifically, the provision requires financial intermediaries to disclose all information about an ESG rating issued in their marketing communications and website as prescribed by point 1 of Annex III to the Regulation (EU) 2024/3005.[3] Regarding the disclosure of information, the European Supervisory Authorities (ESAs) are mandated to draft regulatory technical standards in order to indicate the characteristics of ESG ratings which needs to be submitted to the Commission for integration and approval. The intended purpose of the article is to integrate the transparency framework of the EU SFDR with the disclosure regime of ESG ratings providers. The revision of sustainability-related disclosures has relevant effect on Article 13 of the SFDR which requires financial market players to display the information indicated in point 1 of Annex III on their websites if they reveal an ESG rating to third parties as part of their marketing activities. Examples of the information that is required by such players to be displayed on their websites are the methodologies used, the relevant industry classification, data sources and processes, the limitations of methodologies and data sources, objective of rating and the scope of rating (E, S, or G factors; if all, then also including the weighting of each factor). In order to avoid any duplication of disclosures, those issuers which publish the required information pursuant to this new Article 13(3) of the SFDR are not required to do the exercise again for the purpose of the same obligation under the Regulation. The amendment to the SFDR responds to the need to harmonize transparency rules for financial market participants and financial advisers on how they integrate ESG factors into their investment decisions and financial advice and on their overall and product-related sustainability strategy.[4] 49.01

2 The SFDR harmonizes ESG disclosure standards, requiring financial market participants to integrate sustainability risk in the investment process and to report on such integration at both the entity and product level. The SFDR is designed to help investors assess how sustainability risks are integrated into the business decision process, thereby contributing to one of the EU's objectives of attracting private funding to boost the shift to a net-zero economy.

3 The marketing communications in question, whether a website page, article, presentation slide deck or other, will need to include a link to those website disclosures.

4 Financial market participants and financial advisers must publish on their websites information on how they consider the negative externalities of their business models, namely the principal adverse impacts

B. THE ROLE OF ESAS

49.02 The ESAs and the Commission work together to develop regulatory technical standards to specify the details of the presentation and content of the information to be disclosed according to the requirements set in the ESG ratings Regulation. Technical standards are binding standards adopted by the Commission, usually in the form of a regulation, intended to supplement or implement EU legislation and to address issues that are highly technical in nature. Technical standards are usually based on draft standards produced by the ESAs.[5] They will take into account the need to avoid duplication with information already published in accordance with applicable regulatory requirements, including SFDR.[6] The ESAs through the Joint Committee draft the necessary regulatory technical standards on the content, methodology and presentation of the relevant information and submit these to the Commission.[7] They draft the implementing technical standards to determine the standard presentation of information on the issuance of ESG ratings, and report on best practices and make recommendations on voluntary reporting standards

---

of investment decisions or financial advice on ESG sustainability; or information explaining why they consider there to be no such negative impact. The websites of financial market participants and financial advisers must also include information on how they integrate sustainability risks into their investment decision-making process and financial advice; their remuneration policies are consistent with integrating sustainability risks.

5 Technical standards are legally binding and are directly applicable in all Member States. This means that, on the date of their entry into force, they become part of the national law of the Member States. They will apply directly from that date or from the date of application (where a separate date of application is specified in the regulation containing a set of technical standards). The development of technical standards forms a key part of the EU's work towards creating a single rulebook for financial services, which is intended to be a harmonized core set of standards applied throughout the EU by all competent authorities. If neither the Council nor the Parliament has objected to the regulatory technical standards they will be published in the Official Journal as a Delegated Regulation or a Delegated Decision.

6 For example, an asset manager can be subject to the new rules either as a provider of the ESG rating to a regulated financial undertaking in the EU which discloses the ESG Rating to its investors in its marketing communications (in which case, the Asset Manager would need to collate and provide the disclosable information to that party); or as the person disclosing the ESG rating to third parties in its marketing communications (in which case, the asset manager would need to procure the relevant information from the provider and publish this on its website with a link to such web page in its marketing communications). See 'ESG rating regulation in Europe: Key takeaways for asset managers' (March 2024), https://www.herbertsmithfreehills.com/notes/esg/2024-03/esg-rating-regulation-in-europe-key-takeaways-for-asset-managers.

7 In June 2024, the ESAs issued an Opinion on the assessment of the SFDR recommending the introduction of a categorization system and/or a sustainability indicator for financial products to enhance transparency and empower retail investors to better understand the sustainability profile of these products. See 'Joint ESAs Opinion On the assessment of the Sustainable Finance Disclosure Regulation (SFDR),' (18 June 2024), JC 2024 06, https://www.esma.europa.eu/sites/default/files/2024-06/JC_2024_06_Joint_ESAs_Opinion_on_SFDR.pdf.

to the Commission.[8] These standards aim to strengthen protection for end-investors; improve the disclosures to investors from a broad range of financial market participants and financial advisers; and improve the disclosures to investors regarding financial products. The amendments to the EU SFDR ensure that if financial undertakings develop and disclose their own ESG ratings they disclose the same information as specialized ESG rating providers. The Commission will also provide practical guidance to market players and seek to address gaps, usability concerns and uncertainties, with specific focus on integrating the EU Taxonomy, and the Platform on Sustainable Finance into the investment strategies of financial firms. The role of ESAs in drafting regulatory technical standards to address potential issues in the disclosure framework of ESG ratings providers reflects the objective to ensure consistency in the supervisory and enforcement regimes for sustainability matters.

8 The report is made public and forwarded to the European Parliament and the Council. The EU Member States ensure the relevant authorities monitor compliance with the legislation may apply the regulation to manufacturers of pension products operating national social security schemes and to microinsurance intermediaries and investment firms.

ARTICLE 50

AMENDMENT TO REGULATION (EU) 2023/2859

Andrea Miglionico

In Part A of the Annex to Regulation (EU) 2023/2859, the following entry is added:

> **20. Regulation (EU) 2024/3005 of the European Parliament and of the Council of 27 November 2024 on the transparency and integrity of Environmental, Social and Governance (ESG) rating activities, and amending Regulations (EU) 2019/2088 and (EU) No 2023/2859. (OJ L, 2024/3005, 12.12.2024, ELI: http://data.europa.eu/eli/reg/2024/3005/oj)**

A. INTRODUCTION

50.01 The article provides an amendment to Part A of the Annex A to ESAP Regulation by adding the reference to the legislative act of ESG ratings. It is a provision which integrates the text of ESAP legislation recognising that ESMA is responsible for centralized electronic access to the information on ESG ratings providers. Specifically, Part A of the Annex A to ESAP Regulation refers to Article 1, paragraph 1 of this act that requires to make public information about entities and their products which is of relevance to financial services, capital markets, sustainability and diversity. This would help investors, organizations, and financial intermediaries identify and prioritize impacts and risks throughout the investment decision-making process.[1] These

1 Menghan Li and Qi Chen, 'ESG Rating Disagreement and the Quality of Analysts' Forecasts: Information or Noise' (2024) *International Journal of Finance & Economics*, https://doi.org/10.1002/ijfe.3089.

rules aim at maintaining consistent, transparent methods and ensuring an appropriate level of independence among providers.[2] The intended scope of this article is to update the ESAP data space that companies and investors use to disclose and report regularly. ESAP is expected to give stakeholders in ESG ratings and it will serve as a source of input data for ESG rating providers, reducing estimations and contributing to strengthen the integrity and comparability of ESG ratings.[3] This centralized platform facilitates structured access to reported or disclosed financial and non-financial related company information.[4] The ESAP will improve the accuracy of ESG ratings and address information asymmetries which affect investors and users.[5] Collecting sustainability-related data on a single platform will foster investments in sustainable projects: market participants have access to reliable data to assess their own and other entities' ESG risks, dependencies, opportunities, and impacts with a view to simplify ESG due diligence.[6] The ESAP will thus facilitate the consultation and comparison of public data by any investor as it has been designed to cover sustainability data and will likely to reduce subjectivity inherent in ESG ratings.[7] The regulatory regime will mitigate dependency on data and metrics produced by ESG ratings providers from investors in order to improve their responsible investment approaches, such as integrating ESG factors within the investment process.

2 Lucy Fisher and Kenza Bryan, 'UK set to unveil regulatory regime for ESG ratings industry' *Financial Times* (8 November 2023), https://www.ft.com/content/61a61fc5-fedd-4c01-bb24-99c1606d446d.

3 The information should be easily accessible, storable (download) and machine-readable as far as possible.

4 Klaus Rainer Kirchhoff, Sönke Niefünd and Julian von Pressentin, *ESG: Sustainability as a Strategic Success Factor* (Springer 2024) 86–87.

5 European Council, 'Easy access to corporate information for investors: Council agrees its position on the European Single Access Point (ESAP)' (29 June 2022), https://www.consilium.europa.eu/en/press/press-releases/2022/06/29/easier-access-to-corporate-information-for-investors-council-agrees-its-position-on-a-single-access-platform/.

6 Mahir Alman and Julia Weippert, 'European Single Access Point (ESAP): How does it impact financial firms' data availability?' (10 September 2024), CAPCO, https://www.capco.com/intelligence/capco-intelligence/european-single-access-point.

7 Verena Ross, 'The role of ESG in building an effective Capital Markets Union,' Keynote speech, HCMC public conference, Athens, 29 May 2024, ESMA24-671865080-1303.

TITLE V

TRANSITIONAL AND FINAL PROVISIONS

ARTICLE 51

TRANSITIONAL PROVISIONS

Andrea Miglionico

1. ESG rating providers which operated in the Union at the date of entry into force of this Regulation shall notify ESMA by 2 August 2026 if they wish to continue operating in the Union and apply for authorisation or recognition in accordance with Title II. In that case, they shall apply for authorisation or recognition within four months of 2 July 2026. In the absence of such an application to ESMA within that four-month period, they shall cease their activities.

2. After notifying ESMA pursuant to paragraph 1, the ESG rating provider shall be temporarily listed in the register referred to in Article 14 and be permitted, until its application has been approved or denied, to continue operating in the Union, and may endorse an ESG rating provided by an ESG rating provider established outside the Union and belonging to the same group under Article 11.

3. By way of derogation from paragraph 1 of this Article, ESG rating providers categorised as small ESG rating providers, within the meaning of Article 5(1), which operated in the Union at the date of entry into force of this Regulation shall notify ESMA in accordance with Article 5 no later than 2 November 2026 if they wish to continue operating in the Union. In the absence of such notification by that date, they shall cease their activities.

A. INTRODUCTION

51.01 The article delineates the transitional and final provisions of the Regulation. It provides a timeline of the operational function of ESG rating providers according to the requirements and procedural matters set in this Regulation. Specifically, the recognition and authorization regime follows the application process required by ESMA within four months of the date of entry into force of this Regulation otherwise, they must discontinue operations. Paragraph 1 of the article states that ESG rating providers which operate in the Union at time of on the this Regulation's entry into force (2 January, 2025) must notify ESMA by 2 August, 2026, if they desire to continue functioning and apply for the related authorization or recognition. Paragraph 2 of the provision affirms that after notification to ESMA, ESG rating providers are allowed to be temporarily listed in the register and be permitted, until its application has been approved or denied, to continue operating in the Union, and may endorse an ESG rating provided by an ESG rating provider established outside the Union. The intended scope of the article is to permit providers to operate in the interim phase of approval decision by ESMA: the temporary recognition regime for ESG ratings aims to enable firms and users to access valuable sources of information for making their investment analysis. Paragraph 3 of the article states that after notification to ESMA, ESG rating providers classified as 'small ESG rating providers' that operated in the Union at the date of entry into force of this Regulation must notify ESMA no later than 2 November 2026 if they wish to continue operating in the Union otherwise they must terminate their activities.[1]

B. TIMELINE FOR RATING PROVIDERS

51.02 The Regulation entered into force on 2 January 2025 and applies from 2 July 2026. By 2 August 2026 ESG rating providers (other than small or medium sized undertakings) that were providing their services on 2 January 2025 need to notify ESMA if they want to continue offering their services. By 2 November 2026 ESG rating providers (other than small or medium sized

1 Dori Felber, 'ESG Ratings Get a Makeover: What the New EU Regulation Means for the Future of Sustainability!' (20 January 2024), https://ecamaastricht.org/blueandyellow-zoomingin/esg-ratings-get-a-makeover-what-the-new-eu-regulation-means-for-the-future-of-sustainability.

undertakings) that were providing their services on 2 January 2025 need to apply for authorization or recognition. This deadline also applies for ESG rating providers that are than small or medium sized undertakings that were providing their services on 2 January 2025 which need to notify ESMA if they want to continue offering their services.

ARTICLE 52

REVIEW

Andrea Miglionico

1. The Commission shall evaluate the application of this Regulation by 2 January 2029.

2. The Commission shall present a report on the main findings of the evaluation to the European Parliament and the Council. In carrying out the evaluation, the Commission shall take into account market developments and the relevant evidence at its disposal. The report shall in particular assess the following:

(a) the impact of this Regulation on the transition to a sustainable economy, on the gap of investments needed to meet the Union climate targets as set out in Regulation (EU) 2021/1119, and on redirecting private capital flows towards sustainable investments;

(b) the impact of this Regulation on the market structure, including the evolution of the number and diversity of ESG rating providers;

(c) whether the scope of this Regulation is appropriate to achieve its objectives in accordance with Article 1, including whether providers of data products on environmental, social and human rights, and governance factors should be included in the scope of this Regulation;

(d) the adequacy of the requirements for ESG rating providers established outside the Union to operate in the Union;

(e) the functioning of the market of ESG rating providers in the Union, including potential conflicts of interest, and its supervision by ESMA;

(f) whether this Regulation, including the non-interference principle referred to in Article 28, have contributed to improving the quality and reliability of ESG ratings and reduced the use of misleading ESG ratings.

3. Where the Commission finds it appropriate, the report shall be accompanied by a legislative proposal for amendment of the relevant provisions of this Regulation.

A. THE REVIEW PROCESS	52.01

A. THE REVIEW PROCESS

The article mandates the Commission to carry out an assessment of the application of this legislative act. The Commission's review process reflects the evaluation or fitness check of an EU action which is regulated in the better regulation agenda.[1] The Commission is responsible for making sure that all EU countries properly apply EU law and it is referred to as the 'guardian of the treaties.'[2] The Commission takes steps if an EU country does not fully incorporate a directive into its national law by the set deadline might not have applied EU law correctly.[3] The impact assessments look at the problems to be tackled, the objectives to be achieved, the trade-offs to consider, options for action and their potential impacts.[4] An impact assessment is forward-looking, it is an exercise to gather and analyze evidence to support policy or law making. It involves: verifying the existence of a problem; identifying its underlying causes; assessing whether EU action is needed; and analyzing the advantages and disadvantages of available solutions. The role of Commission is to evaluate if specific laws, policies and spending activities are fit for purpose and have delivered, at minimum cost, the desired changes to European businesses and citizens. The evaluation findings support the Commission decision-making process whether EU actions should be continued or changed. On ex-post evaluation, the Commission remains committed to the 'evaluate 52.01

1 Better Regulation ensures that EU policies and laws are prepared in an open, transparent manner, informed by the best available evidence and backed by comprehensive stakeholder involvement so that they achieve their objectives at minimum cost. In line with the 'evaluate first' principle, evaluation precedes work on the revision of an existing policy or law and provides evidence to the problem definition. Commission evaluations and fitness checks analyze the performance of existing policies, programmes and legislation. Based on evidence, evaluations assess how an existing policy or legislation is effective, relevant, coherent and has an EU added value. These evaluations then inform preparation of reviews or new initiatives. Impact assessments examine whether there is a need for EU action, analyze the possible impacts of available solutions and guide Commission choice and preparation of the proposal. This analysis is carried out during the preparation phase, before the Commission finalizes a proposal for a new or revised law. See European Commission, 'Better Regulation,' https://commission.europa.eu/law/law-making-process/better-regulation_en.

2 The Commission systematically evaluates whether existing EU laws, policies and spending activities are fit for purpose and have delivered, at minimum cost, the desired changes to EU businesses and citizens.

3 The 2016 communication EU law: better results through better application explains how the Commission ensures the application, implementation and enforcement of EU law for the benefit of all citizens, consumers and businesses. It sets out a strategic approach and priorities for the Commission's enforcement action. See European Commission, 'Implementing EU law,' https://commission.europa.eu/law/application-eu-law/implementing-eu-law_en.

4 Felice Simonelli and Nadina Iacob, 'Can We Better the European Union Better Regulation Agenda?' (2021) 12(4) *European Journal of Risk Regulation*, 851–852.

first' principle in the policy revision context.[5] As part of the regulatory fitness and performance (REFIT) programme, evaluations seek to identify potential for simplification and burden reduction.[6] REFIT initiatives evaluate whether existing EU legislation is still fit for purpose. Identified burdens will be looked at through the lens of regulatory offsetting; evaluations need to check the initially estimated costs and benefits against actual outcomes.[7] An evaluation report assesses a specific impact of EU law, policy or funding programme in terms of effectiveness (whether the EU action reached its objectives); efficiency (what are the costs and benefits); relevance (whether it responds to stakeholders' needs); coherence (how well it works with other actions); and EU added value (what are the benefits of acting at EU level).[8] The Commission needs to present a report on the main findings of the evaluation to the European Parliament and the Council that consider the elements assessed and, where appropriate, the legislative proposal for amendment of the relevant provisions of this Regulation.[9] The report shall focus on the measures Member States have taken to implement and apply the Regulation. It assesses whether Member States implemented the Regulation within the specified timeframe, and whether national legislation and practice achieve the objectives and fulfil the requirements of the Regulation. The description and analysis contained in this report should evaluate the impact of the legislative act on the transition to a sustainable economy and climate neutrality (the targets set in the European Climate Law);[10] on the market structure and evolution of ESG ratings indus-

5 The Commission intends to make more use of fitness checks a means to maintain the coherence and relevance of the body of EU legislation. See Stefano Vettorazzi and Irmgard Anglmayer, 'What is new in the Commission's 2021 Better Regulation Guidelines?' (February 2022), European Parliamentary Research Service, PE 699.463, https://www.europarl.europa.eu/RegData/etudes/BRIE/2022/699463/EPRS_BRI(2022)699463_EN.pdf.

6 European Commission, 'REFIT – making EU law simpler, more efficient and future-proof,' https://commission.europa.eu/law/law-making-process/evaluating-and-improving-existing-laws/refit-making-eu-law-simpler-more-efficient-and-future-proof_en.

7 Siôn Jones, Greta Dohler and Luke Pate, 'Better regulation in the EU' (October 2023), PE 737.058, https://www.europarl.europa.eu/RegData/etudes/STUD/2023/737058/IPOL_STU(2023)737058_EN.pdf.

8 European Commission, 'Evaluating laws, policies and funding programmes,' https://commission.europa.eu/law/law-making-process/evaluating-and-improving-existing-laws/evaluating-laws_en#:~:text=The%20Commission%20evaluates%20if%20specific%20laws%2C%20policies%20and,whether%20EU%20actions%20should%20be%20continued%20or%20changed.

9 The joint collaboration between EU institutions and Member States responds to the objective of Improving EU law-making. The European Parliament shares with the Council and Commission the determination to and responsibility for improving the quality of legislation applicable throughout the Union. An impact assessment is a tool to aid decision and policy-making in the three institutions. It is not a substitute for political decisions within the democratic decision-making process.

10 European Commission, 'European Climate Law,' https://climate.ec.europa.eu/eu-action/european-climate-law_en.

try; the operation of rating providers in the Union under the supervision of ESMA and the improvement of the quality and reliability of information. The report shall put forward the Commission's position on the main conclusions and recommendations about the Regulation's provisions. The results of the evaluation help the Commission decide whether to amend or reform the Regulation.

ARTICLE 53

ENTRY INTO FORCE AND APPLICATION

Andrea Miglionico

This Regulation shall enter into force on the twentieth day following that of its publication in the *Official Journal of the European Union*.

It shall apply from 2 July 2026.

This Regulation shall be binding in its entirety and directly applicable in all Member States.

A. APPLICABILITY OF THE REGULATION

53.01 The article provides a closure provision stating that the Regulation enters into force 20 days after the publication in the EU's Official Journal.[1] The Regulation has completed its progress through the ordinary legislative procedure and it was published in the Official Journal on 12 December 2024. However, the application of legislative act starts applying 18 months after its entry into force which provides time for ESG rating providers to comply with the new requirements set in the Regulation. EU regulations will have the force of law on the date on which they enter into force. The entry into force represents the point when the measure has legal existence in the EU legal order and in the national legal order of each Member State. If no date is specified in the

1 Once an EU law has completed its adoption procedure, it is published in the Official Journal of the European Union. The way that an EU law takes effect and becomes binding and applicable depends on the nature of the legislative act. All EU legal acts will have the force of law once their date of entry into force has passed, but their provisions may not apply and be binding yet. EU Regulations become binding on individuals and enforceable in national courts once their dates of application has passed. The legal effect also depends on whether the dates of entry into force, application and transposition have passed.

act, the act will enter into force 20 days after publication in the Official Journal of the European Union. EU legislation can only become legally binding once it has been published in the Official Journal which is the official publication of record for the European Union. The date of application is the point at which a regulation is fully enforceable and its legal rights and obligations can be effectively exercised. In certain cases, the application date is the same as the date of entry into force. However, a measure can also apply (exceptionally) retrospectively or (more commonly) from a later date or have staggered application (with several application dates for different parts of the measure). The binding effect and directly applicability to this Regulation means the ability of a piece of EU legislation to become part of a Member State's national law without the need for any domestic implementing legislation.[2] It refers to Article 288 of the TFEU which states that EU regulations are directly applicable: they come into force and are legally binding without any action on the part of Member States. Direct applicability of Regulation is related to, but different from, the concept of direct effect.[3]

2 Tarjei Bekkedal, 'Understanding the nature of the EEA Agreement: On the direct applicability of regulations' (2020) 57(3) *Common Market Law Review* 773. See also J. A. Winter, 'Direct applicability and direct effect; two distinct and different concepts in Community Law' (1972) 9(4) *Common Market Law Review* 425.

3 The ability of a piece of European Union (EU) legislation to be enforced by an individual in a court of a Member State. A provision of EU law may be capable of direct effect if it is clear and precise, unconditional and does not give the Member States substantial discretion in its application.

INDEX